CONSTRUCTIVIST APPROACHES AND RESEARCH METHODS

SAGE was founded in 1965 by Sara Miller McCune to support the dissemination of usable knowledge by publishing innovative and high-quality research and teaching content. Today, we publish over 900 journals, including those of more than 400 learned societies, more than 800 new books per year, and a growing range of library products including archives, data, case studies, reports, and video. SAGE remains majority-owned by our founder, and after Sara's lifetime will become owned by a charitable trust that secures our continued independence.

Los Angeles | London | New Delhi | Singapore | Washington DC | Melbourne

CONSTRUCTIVIST APPROACHES AND RESEARCH METHODS

A PRACTICAL GUIDE TO EXPLORING PERSONAL MEANINGS

PAM DENICOLO
TREVOR LONG
KIM BRADLEY-COLE

$SAGE

Los Angeles | London | New Delhi
Singapore | Washington DC | Melbourne

⑤SAGE

Los Angeles | London | New Delhi
Singapore | Washington DC | Melbourne

SAGE Publications Ltd
1 Oliver's Yard
55 City Road
London EC1Y 1SP

SAGE Publications Inc.
2455 Teller Road
Thousand Oaks, California 91320

SAGE Publications India Pvt Ltd
B 1/I 1 Mohan Cooperative Industrial Area
Mathura Road
New Delhi 110 044

SAGE Publications Asia-Pacific Pte Ltd
3 Church Street
#10-04 Samsung Hub
Singapore 049483

Editor: Jai Seaman
Editorial assistant: Alysha Owen
Production editor: Tom Bedford
Copyeditor: Richard Leigh
Marketing manager: Sally Ransom
Cover design: Shaun Mercier
Typeset by: C&M Digitals (P) Ltd, Chennai, India
Printed and bound by CPI Group (UK) Ltd,
Croydon, CR0 4YY

Library of Congress Control Number: 2016933337

British Library Cataloguing in Publication data

A catalogue record for this book is available from
the British Library

ISBN 978-1-4739-3029-2
ISBN 978-1-4739-3030-8 (pbk)

At SAGE we take sustainability seriously. Most of our products are printed in the UK using FSC papers and boards. When we
print overseas we ensure sustainable papers are used as measured by the PREPS grading system.
We undertake an annual audit to monitor our sustainability.

We would like to dedicate this book to our families, particularly to our partners Vincent, Nikki and Todd, who not only tolerated that our time and energies over the last year have been devoted to the construing of others but also provided the succour needed to maintain our stamina through the process.

Contents

List of figures and boxes

Figures

Further Explanations

Activities

Procedural Examples

About the authors

Pam Denicolo, now professor emerita at the University of Reading and consultant/ visiting professor at the University of Surrey and other universities worldwide, was a founder member and long-term Guidance Panel member of the European Personal Construct Association (EPCA).

Her academic and organisational research has included developing the research skills of her 60-plus successful doctoral researchers, their colleagues in the graduate school she developed and led, and their subsequent students and colleagues. She continues to provide workshops for researchers, while the focus of her consultancy is on improving doctoral education and training, working with students, supervisors, examiners and senior staff in higher education. With colleagues she organises the Postgraduate Interest Network of the Society for Research into Higher Education and was a long-serving member of the executive of the UK Council for Graduate Education.

Using constructivist techniques, she contributed to the research base and co-authored the Research Councils UK Researcher Development Framework. She is a prolific author of guidance texts for researchers in the SAGE series *Success in Research*, contributes chapters on constructivist techniques to other books, and co-edits and contributes to the Sense series *Critical Issues in the Future of Learning and Teaching*.

Trevor Long has 30 years' experience in education and consultancy in the UK and in many countries around the world. He is on the associate faculty with several leading UK business schools, designing, facilitating and supervising research and consultancy projects on MBA, MSc and executive education programmes. His areas of interest include strategy, leadership, organisational and personal development with a particular focus on psychological dynamics, and areas that are especially open for constructivist exploration.

Trevor's doctoral research employed personal construct psychology (PCP) techniques in a work setting to investigate the inner experience of meaningfulness and personal engagement. He is passionate about the use of constructivist techniques and continues to develop models and educational offerings to demonstrate the power of PCP for both academic and in-company research and application in practice.

He has balanced his academic activities with consultancy projects in a wide range of service and manufacturing organisations primarily focused on the impact of change on people, and the introduction of new processes. These have often involved the development and implementation of complete projects which, in a practical setting, have required pragmatic interventions whilst being based on rigorous underpinning theory.

Kim Bradley-Cole is a Chartered Psychologist and an Associate Fellow of the British Psychological Society. She has a PhD in Leadership and Organisational Behaviour from the University of Reading, and an MSc in Occupational and Organisational Psychology from the University of Surrey. Kim retrained as a psychologist after a successful career in fast-moving consumer goods marketing and innovations, working on developing some of Britain's best-loved brands, including Heinz, Bisto, Mr Kipling and Twinings. She has held marketing and human resources roles in large organisations, as well as working agency-side in market research and as a freelance work psychologist and coach. She actively uses constructivist methods in both academic and practitioner contexts and has taught MSc and PhD students how to effectively develop, apply and analyse different tools in their own research. Her award-winning PhD was funded by the Economic and Social Research Council (ESRC) and used constructivist techniques to bring greater clarity and depth to an important, but contested, theoretical field by exploring managers' implicit beliefs concerning authentic leadership. Kim currently works as a coaching psychologist and is a Teaching Fellow at the University of Surrey and principally teaches in the fields of work psychology, organisational behaviour and qualitative research methods at both undergraduate and postgraduate levels.

Acknowledgements

We would like first to express our appreciation for all fellow constructivists who have stimulated our thinking and added to our understanding over the years. We hope we have done you justice in this book.

Importantly, we would like to offer particular thanks to the following who have made specific contributions to the book:

Matthew Bradley-Cole, for his patience and dedicated effort in re-creating some of our drawings and figures so that we could 'show' as well as 'tell' the story of constructivist research.

The international contributors of a the range of stimulating cases, who condensed their work to fit our rubric: Britt-Marie Apelgren; Elvira Apraiz; Kim Bradley-Cole; Dorota Bourne; Pam Burnard; Sarah Dentry-Travis; Bethan Douglas; Michael Dunn; Gulden Ilin, Trevor Long and Stephen Javes; Julia Osgerby, Pru Marriot and Maria Gee; Marie-Louise Österlind; Nicola Simmons; Jamie Sutcliffe, Viv Burr and Nigel King.

Professor Emerita Maureen Pope, whose chapter about how PCP wove an important thread through her life is inspirational, as was her support to generations of constructivist researchers.

Brian Gaines, who has provided in Appendix B an update of internet resources and sources of support and who, with his wife Mildred Shaw, has made a significant contribution in many ways to the global PCP community.

PART I

Making decisions based on philosophy, theory and project purpose

Introduction and orientation to constructivist research

Preamble

We will start with a conundrum: this book was prepared to provide advice and guidance to a diverse audience and yet it is written to meet specific needs of individual researchers, like you. The solution to this puzzle is in the following four sections of this Introduction: 'What this book is about', 'Who should read this book, 'How this book can help you' and 'How to use this book'. The first section summarises the scope and focus of this book, outlining the nature of constructivism as a perspective through which we may explore how people see their world and how their personal perspectives influence their behaviour. The next two sections introduce the purpose of the book, its style and scope and the techniques we employ throughout the book to alert you to possibilities, to intrigue, challenge and stimulate you. They will help you to make decisions about, and perhaps then engage with, a particularly productive form of research, one that many proponents recognise as both complementing and enriching their life views or personal philosophies (an evocative, lived example is provided in Chapter Twelve). The final section provides guidance on how to make the best use of the book depending on your background, circumstances and needs, and it summarises the different parts that make up the book to give you an overview of your potential journey.

What this book is about

This book is about the research process, explaining from inception to completion how to conduct interpretive, **constructivist research**. Building on George Kelly's

(1955a, 1955b, 1991a, 1991b)[1] personal construct psychology (PCP) approach to understanding people's perspectives and interactions with the world, it demonstrates the potential power and versatility of this approach and its wide variety of methods while alerting the reader both to practical considerations and caveats about its use. Throughout this book you will meet some of our colleague constructivists, academics and practitioners in a wide variety of professions when we provide examples of how various approaches and techniques/methods from within the field of constructivism have been used. In particular, you will see in Chapter Eleven several case studies drawn from a variety of disciplines and geographical contexts which illustrate both the wide range of applications within which constructivism can be applied and the range of techniques available.

We intend to introduce you to the many ways in which you could go about collecting and analysing data, including processes, activities, methods, tools and techniques, using approaches that are rooted in constructivism. Constructivism is a particular way of discovering how people understand their worlds, or their **paradigm**. This implies that several paradigms are possible. We explore constructivism in contrast to some other key research paradigms in Chapters Two and Three. For now we simply recognise that constructivism is one of a number of distinct paradigms, but we also argue that constructivism provides a general approach which elicits particularly rich and deep insights into people's inner experience. By distinguishing 'approaches' from 'research methods' we also wish to establish our clear position about research. Whilst a method or technique may be used in a variety of different research projects, it is important that all research should be clearly underpinned by a particular philosophical perspective and, further, the whole research **methodology** should be congruent to that underpinning philosophy.

Constructivism, as an underpinning philosophy, points to methods or techniques that most effectively elicit data which represent a person's constructed sense of reality. Thus the main focus of this book is research practice, getting into the field and trying to find out what is going on. We discuss some aspects of theory, but only to the degree that this serves our primary aim of helping you, the reader, to understand how to do constructivist research most effectively. We intend that you use this book as a guide. Consistent with the nature of constructivism itself, we recognise that there is no single best way to do constructivist research, no formula or rigidly defined process. As such, whilst practical, and whilst based on a solid consistent philosophy, this is not so much a 'how to' manual, as a presentation of possibilities, offering you options about what you could do. In order to make good,

---

[1]Kelly's original 1955 two-volume publication is no longer readily available. The first three chapters of volume 1 were published in a book entitled 'A Theory of Personality' in 1963. The whole of volume 1 was published by Routledge in 1991. The 1963 and 1991 publications are currently in print. In this book, page numbers for quotations from Kelly's two volume publication refer to the 1991, not the 1955, publication.

relevant choices, you will need to understand key aspects of the underpinning philosophy and theory as well as alternatives you might apply, and we cover both of these in different parts of the book.

A key feature of this book and of constructivist research is 'exploration'. Constructivists start with the view that they do not know, and do not make assumptions about, what might be. Rather, they seek to put to one side (or 'bracket') personal views, beliefs or bias, and remain open-minded to wide-ranging possibilities from the research. With this in mind, constructivists seek to understand a person's internal experiences from that person's personal perspective, not the researcher's own perspective. This does raise paradoxical possibilities based on the ubiquitous research need to interpret data since this interpretation will inevitably be subject to the researcher's inner experiences, and we discuss this in early chapters. However, for now, we raise this complexity simply to underpin the proposition that constructivists do not seek to define, confirm, formulate or find 'truth' or 'facts', but rather to move around in the territory in search of insights into personal meanings. A constructivist's task is to seek understanding about how people make their own sense of their personal world. Two people may be in the same event at the same time and yet make sense of it, or experience it, entirely differently. This emphasis on research participants' personal meanings is central to the constructivist's philosophy and practice. Understanding people's personal meanings about their world creates possibilities unlike any other research perspective because it gets to the heart not just of what people do nor even how, but of *why*. This, in turn, creates profound possibilities for maintaining, reinforcing or changing perspectives (in other words, learning) to develop or improve personal experience and outcomes.

In summary, this book presents choices and opportunities that may be used to build insights, and understand implications, about how and why people construct their worlds as they do, how these constructions have developed or might develop over time and how they influence behaviour.

Who should read this book

Projects that might benefit from a constructivist approach are those that seek to understand individuals' internal processes: attitudes, interests, beliefs, values, different perspectives and identities as they interact and influence behaviour in personal, work or social settings.

To give you a sense of the versatility of constructivist approaches and methods we will refer throughout the book to examples from different disciplines and professional areas, as well as presenting case studies in Chapter Eleven. For now, though, you might like to have an indication of its range. This list is neither exclusive nor exhaustive, but we have collaborated with, met or read of people who have worked within this philosophy on issues arising in:

- Every sector of education from pre-school to continuing professional training;
- The field of health, considering the viewpoints of patients, carers, and all kinds of professionals in the field;
- Management, business and marketing activities, covering a range of roles and contexts;
- A wide range of disciplines, such as: philosophy; psychology (all branches); sociology; arts, literature and languages;
- Numerous professional and other areas of work, including: law; architecture and the built environment; youth work, careers work and counselling; the social and emergency services; factory, farm and circus workers; civil service activities; the armed services and the police.

Saúl et al. (2012) provide a bibliometric review of recent relevant publications which indicates an even wider range of interests met by constructivist research. Participants whose perspectives are explored in such research range from very young children through to professional and older people, from people challenged by circumstances such as physical and cognitive disabilities or lack of resources and/or education, to the very articulate. You may be surprised by the richness of the data that can be elicited from all of these groups; we provide several caveats about the potential danger of being overwhelmed by both the quality and quantity of data that can be obtained using constructivist techniques. Fear not, though, for all our caveats will be accompanied by advice on potential ways of dealing with the challenges within them.

Equally diverse are the kinds of issues and **research questions** that can be explored using constructivism as a framework. The most frequent articulation of research topic expressed generically is 'an exploration of individual or group perspectives/viewpoints/beliefs about, or experiences of, particular objects, events, or people'. Such studies may be focused on understanding situations as they exist currently or are changed by some happening such as a particular intervention. Constructivist approaches and methods answer *why* and *how* questions about people's attitudes, beliefs and behaviour. You will encounter examples of these and other fascinating topics as you read on. You will also be introduced to the work of George Kelly who devised and explicated the foundations of personal construct psychology. PCP is one of several orientations to research subsumed within the family of constructivist approaches. How it is related to other constructivist approaches is outlined in Chapter Three, where links can be found to similar theoretical frameworks that emerged with or from Kelly's original work (Kelly, 1955/1991).

Before we explore the many possibilities that constructivist research encompasses, let us emphasise from the outset that conducting such research, exploring personal meanings and perspectives, is not without constraints and limitations. While we will suggest that it can reach rich, in-depth, authentic data that are normally and generally inaccessible through other approaches, this can only be achieved by:

- Understanding the philosophical underpinnings and main tenets of the approach;
- Developing expertise in the use of techniques;
- Articulating well a refined research question;
- Carefully designing the project, including the data analysis;
- Recognising that there are likely to be several interpretations of circumstances and data;
- Devoting time and energy to planning, executing and delivering the project.

We will, during the course of this book, provide you with detailed guidance on all of these challenges. If you are committed to getting to grips with how others see their world, what particular things mean to them and how that influences their behaviour, then we invite you to join us in an exploration of how this approach and its plethora of techniques might help you to do so.

How this book can help you

This book is intended as a guide, a road-map if you like, rather than as a completely comprehensive and detailed manual of how to do your particular research project. We will indicate points of interest and alternative routes along the way, but cannot venture into descriptions of every town and village you might tarry in on your own journey. However, as you delve into this book we will introduce you to key ideas and fellow researchers and writers in the field, with references to detailed accounts of their work. This will inevitably involve you in learning the jargon that pervades the literature, enabling you to understand their discussions as well as enabling you to argue your research case with such experts. All professional areas and groups develop such terminology to provide for succinct discussion between themselves and some-times to differentiate their field from that of others. To help you overcome that linguistic barrier we introduce through the chapters key words and concepts with explanations, and the first appendix is a glossary of words and key concepts used in constructivist research. Words in the glossary are bolded on first presentation.

For now though, let us start with the notion that by constructivist research we mean an exploration of the meaning attributed to aspects of the world as individual people experience it. We will explore this more deeply in Part I of this book, which will help you further in deciding whether or not this approach is suitable for an impending or future research project. Should you then decide against it, you will have gleaned enough knowledge to justify its rejection and hence your selection of an alternative approach or paradigm. You will also have in your mental research toolbox some ideas that might be explored further in subsequent research on other topics.

To orientate you, each chapter begins with a list of key points covered, while summaries and checklists will be interspersed in the text to remind you of particular learning points. This is a complex topic that becomes more accessible with the application of ideas and practice of techniques, so we have laced chapters with opportunities for you to engage with the material more thoroughly than simply absorbing words on the page. These opportunities take the form of thought experiments, exercises and activities that you can try out for yourself, alone or with others. Our advice is not to skip these, because we have devised them to be revelatory as well as illustrative and, sometimes, entertaining. We have also used boxes to highlight such things as important tips or guidance notes to help you easily find them again, perhaps when you are beyond the theoretical stage and actively engaged in your project. Hopefully the index at the end of the book will serve a similar purpose of helping you find particular references or sections. The reference list at the end of the book includes all of the authors and works mentioned in the text.

We also include at the end of some chapters an indicative reading list of particular relevance to the ideas explained in it. It is worth noting that, by and large, these will address research conducted within an interpretivist framework along with prominent theorists engaged with research in general or constructivism in particular. Some of the latter may be clinicians rather than researchers: they have been selected for particular insights they bring to the way people think and act or may contribute to the development of incisive techniques that may be used in research. However, our focus here is firmly on research, not therapy, and we urge you to take care in applying PCP and using its very sharp instruments. We elaborate on this in Chapter Six, which deals with the special relationship between constructivist researcher and research participants, which we urge everyone to read, no matter how extensive their previous research experience.

It is also useful to reveal something of the style of writing. Each of us contributing to the book have different histories and experiences, in general and with constructivist research and PCP, and thus we bring different voices to bear as we weave the story for you. Our various experiences provide different perspectives on what might be useful for readers at different stages in research careers. Nevertheless, our long-term relationships with each other allow us to reflect and comment on each other's ideas and writing such that we hope we have produced a coherent and rigorous tale. However, you will inevitably hear our different accents as the tale is told, and we hope that this will serve to add zest and interest.

The examples and the metaphors we use to illustrate concepts also tend to have personal relevance. They are intended to make the account lively and relevant, whilst we also need to use them to convey ideas that are abstract and intangible. The literature about constructivism itself is replete with metaphors, as is any explanation of psychological inner workings, and the founder of PCP, George Kelly, was particularly adept at using metaphors and similes to convey his meanings. On the first page of Chapter One of the first volume of his two-volume opus (Kelly, 1991a: 3), he prefaces his perspective on understanding human beings thus:

> Nor has the stream of the individual man's [sic] life escaped the attention of curious students. The highly articulate William James was fascinated by the currents and eddies in the stream of consciousness. ... The sensitive Sigmund Freud waded into the headwaters of the stream in search for the underground springs which fed it. And the impulsive Henri Bergson jumped from the bank into the current ...

Throughout this book we will use such quotations to provide insight into his, at that time, revolutionary ideas. (Find out more about Kelly in Fransella, 1995.) These will be interlaced with those from others who have worked with and developed his theory in different ways, all the while embedding these in our own interpretations of how this multiplicity of ideas can be used in revelatory ways in research. This is, if you like, a taster menu which we hope will stimulate your hunger to learn more by seeking out Kelly's original work and reading more recent literature, savouring ideas having gained some insights from this introductory overview of research based on constructivist or constructionist approaches.

To clarify, the terms 'constructivism' and 'constructionism' (see the section on ontology in Chapter Three for elaboration of the differences between the two) are derived from words used in building processes, implying that we actively build our perspectives on the world. The units of our perspectives are called **constructs**, the means by which we make meaning of our worlds. We will also introduce the term **construct systems**, proposing that meaning-making is accomplished by the application of organised networks of constructs which all eventually join together in a system to make up each person's approach to the world.

There will be much more later in this book about the nature of constructs as this term is used in PCP, particularly in Chapter Four where the formal theory is explained as a prelude to exploring methods of applying it to practice, but, for now, recognise that it derives from the general dictionary use of the word, defined as an idea or a theory rather than a tangible entity. In both cases, in normal discourse and in PCP, ideas, theories, and constructs, are human inventions concocted to explain what is happening in the world and are thus susceptible to change or evolution under certain circumstances, for instance as we test them in practice or find better tools to investigate them. But before we go further down that path, let us return to immediate practicalities, in particular how you might engage with this book to suit your personal needs.

How to use this book

We have attempted to compile as comprehensive and accessible an account as is possible in book form of a holistic, integrated research approach. We have incorporated practical guidance on how to apply a range of its techniques within a design structure that aims to produce meticulous, rigorous and ethical research that illuminates a particular human **phenomenon.** This is arranged into three main parts which could be followed as a step-by-step guide for novice researchers. Thus Part I, which focuses on the philosophical and theoretical foundations of constructivist research, contains a rationale for choosing this particular research approach, so that its particular philosophy matches your research question and aim. This is followed by explanation of the central tenets of constructivist theories, particularly PCP, and then consideration of their application to the reader's own experience and understanding of it.

Part II focuses on the practicalities of engaging with this research paradigm with important considerations about: how to get ready for and implement the basic techniques, including ethics, health warnings and practical tips; a range of techniques that serve different purposes and suit diverse participants; how these methods and tools can be most effectively combined into a research design that meets the aims of the project; the practicalities of managing the fieldwork and the data derived from it. Particular consideration is accorded to analysis methods for different data sets and to the interpretation of data, recognising that language is but a poor representation of the complexity of human thoughts and so needs judicious and sensitive consideration.

The purpose of Part III is to provide readers with a wealth of examples of how the approach, and its variants, have been employed to solve a range of questions and further the progress of a research career involving the complex, vulnerable, exciting and awe-inspiring world of others' meanings, understandings, beliefs and values, hopes and fears, concerns and joys.

Of course, for many of you who are new to research it might well be helpful to read and participate in the chapters in a linear fashion, though some might like early on to dip into the case studies in Chapter Eleven to gain an impression about the potential variety of topics and fieldwork designs that the approach affords. In so doing you could encounter something akin to your own research purpose that will help you to concentrate particularly on specific designs/techniques or to consider alternative interpretations of the research problem. To those of you who have not previously given much thought to paradigms and their implications, the early chapters could seem rather challenging, but it is worth persisting with those chapters to ensure that you are comfortable with the worldview presented and that its **epistemology** is consonant with yours.

For more experienced researchers, who are familiar with the paradigm debate and can argue well their selection, a rapid review of Chapters Two and Three may suffice, though we would urge a more careful reading if you are at all unsure about the obligations/responsibilities inherent in assuming a constructivist identity and applying its methods as they are explicated in practical situations in later chapters.

Those who are already familiar with aspects of PCP but seek to extend their repertoire of techniques might concentrate on Chapters Seven to Ten. Indeed, Chapter Seven might well provide even very experienced researchers with food for thought or an introduction to some new or novel research practice and data analysis ideas. We have tried both to incorporate sufficient repetition to enable you to select the most relevant chapters for your current requirements and to include signposts to where in this book or in the literature topics are explained in more depth, should you need further information.

We hope that you will find all the following chapters stimulating in terms of providing you with insight into some perceptive research into intriguing problems as well as raising your awareness of the seductive and productive nature of constructivist research.

Suggested further reading

Fransella, F. (1995) *George Kelly*. London: SAGE.

Fransella provides a unique introduction to Kelly, demonstrating how his experiences influenced his thinking and theory development, acknowledges and responds to criticisms of the theory and demonstrates its validity by noting its pervasive usefulness.

Kelly, G.A. (1955) *The Psychology of Personal Constructs*, Vols 1 and 2. New York: Norton. Republished in 1991, London: Routledge.

Although Volume 1 will be of most relevance to researchers, Volume 2 is intriguing for its insights into the human condition.

Understanding the nature of constructivist approaches

Key Points

- Different interpretations
- The psychological bases of constructivist approaches
- Alternative realities
- Questions of how, what and why
- Focus on your interests
- How PCP can illuminate situations

Introduction

A friend was giving advice over the telephone to his father, who had asked how to open an icon on his computer screen. 'Place the cursor over the icon and click twice with the mouse's left button,' the friend said. 'Nothing's happening,' was the response. 'You need to click the mouse button twice quickly.' ... 'Still nothing.' ... 'Are you sure you have the cursor right over the icon?' ... 'Yes.' ... 'Try clicking again, two clicks, in quick succession.' Still nothing. My friend's confusion gave way to frustration on what was, after all, the simplest of computer tasks. Just as a tourist will use varied intonations and volumes, but still the same words when trying to communicate in a different language, the friend repeated the guidance. Still nothing. A step-by-step approach was needed. 'Let's start again. Make sure the cursor is over the icon.' 'OK,' his father said, 'it's over the icon, but just how close above the icon does it need to be?!'

This true story illustrates a key message of this chapter. People see things in different ways. No two people's sense of reality is exactly the same. In this example, the friend used established terminology for computer users, but his father's understanding of computing was limited and his perception of the guidance was based on the more general idea that something over something else meant vertically on top of, not in front of. Neither of them was wrong, but they each had a sense of reality that differed, in this case simply, but it fundamentally undermined their ability to communicate and understand. Likewise, everyone's sense of reality varies. Often this variation is subtle, but is still different and personal to each of us individually. This variation occurs because each person's sense of reality is constructed. This construction builds from innumerable personal experiences over a lifetime, and it then underpins each person's perception and understanding of an event or behaviour. Since we all have different experiences, each one in turn interpreted through the results of previous ones, we each construct different realities. We elaborate on this principle in what follows.

So, what do we do when we wish to understand others, when we wish to carry out research into attitudes, thoughts, feelings, perceptions and meanings? We can never get inside another person's mind to explore their reality, and we cannot directly measure this inner experience. However, we can indirectly access these phenomena, gaining insights into people's sense of reality, or their 'lifeworld' (Alvesson and Sköldberg, 2009: 76), through 'constructivist' approaches, and, in particular, through the approaches and methods of personal construct psychology (PCP).

This chapter explores how individuals perceive, or **construe**, their own realities and argues why a constructivist (particularly a PCP) approach and methods are an appropriate, if not the most appropriate way to study situations involving human interactions. We will show how PCP helps us to answer 'why' type research questions, as well as 'how' and 'what' type questions, providing insight into underlying dynamics that explain meanings and behaviours. Drawing on the original theoretical principles of PCP, and later developments, we will demonstrate how it fits with a particular realm of research interest as well as explaining the means by which it may facilitate research in powerful ways often neglected in more common approaches. Through this exploration, the reader will gain sufficient orientation into the approach to decide its appropriateness both for the nature of a particular project, and for the researcher him or herself.

A constructed reality

Empirical research into the way people experience reality is a relatively recent endeavour, though even pre-Socratic philosophy sought to understand the nature of reality, knowledge and meaning from mythological and cosmological perspectives. The rise of classical Greek philosophical thought through Socrates, Pluto and Aristotle established principles of understanding through logical argument and exploration of the 'soul', but it was not until the late nineteenth century that the **scientific method** was applied through experimental psychology to seek understanding of mental processes. ('Scientific method' is a general term referring to systematic observation, measurement, experimentation and analysis.)

The roots of different schools of thought within psychology can be seen in the interests and propositions of its early exponents. Wundt (1832–1920), through laboratory experiments, founded the structuralist school, which argued that the mind could be understood by analysing individual fundamental units, which integrate to form more complex constructed inner experiences. Titchener (1867–1927), a student of Wundt, suggested that there are three main types of units – sensations (or perceptions), images (or ideas) and affections (or emotions) – and each could be assessed in terms of such criteria as clearness or intensity. James (1842–1910), however, in contrast to Wundt and Titchener, explored the mind from a functionalist perspective, arguing that it can most effectively be understood as comprising utilities, or functionalities, that have an effect through behavioural outputs. Functionalism emphasised the *processes* of the mind, structuralism the units of the mind, and these preceded such schools as behaviourism. Watson (1878–1958) rejected structuralism and emphasised behavioural dynamics based on reactions to situations, and Skinner (1904–1990) argued the possibility of behavioural reinforcement through operant conditioning. Operant conditioning is the process of learning through rewards and punishments. Freud (1856–1939), on the other hand, aligned with the methods of structuralism, in particular introspection as a means of accessing inner, often subconscious mechanisms, to analyse the psyche, and Jung (1875–1961), a close colleague of Freud until their beliefs about underpinning drives diverged, emphasised individuation – the process by which a person becomes a unique individual through the integration of inner experiences – as the key driver in the development of the self.

Whilst the seminal evolution of psychological thought through the nineteenth and early twentieth centuries varied in perspective and emphasis, it was united through the methods of enquiry, underpinned by natural science investigation. And it was into this tradition, in the mid-twentieth century, that the radical new school of thought that was PCP emerged through the work of the former physicist, later clinical psychologist and educationist, George Kelly (1905–1967). Similar to all of the key thinkers noted above, Kelly's formal education and early career focused on natural science and mathematics. However, he objected fundamentally to both behaviourism and the psychodynamic approaches of Freud and Jung, because they implied that people have little active choice over their development: for the behaviourist, the self developed primarily from external forces, while from a psychodynamic perspective, the self developed principally through subconscious drivers. Rather, Kelly believed that: people are active players in their development rather than passive responders; each one has a unique journey through life; this uniqueness confers particular inner experiences; and these experiences construct the reality that he or she inhabits. As a clinician he recognised that the patient's condition would be interpreted through the theoretical framework of the particular clinician involved (the behaviourist would speculate about the conditioning that the patient was exposed to; the Freudian psychotherapists would call into play early childhood traumas). Instead Kelly sought the perspective of his patients, as experts on their own experiences.

Whilst Kelly rejected much established psychology, he did not reject the scientific perspective that underpinned psychology at this time. But he turned it on its head.

He argued that it is not for the expert 'scientist' to look on and assess a 'human subject's behaviours', or analyse that person's mind to determine his/her state. It was the persons themselves who were best equipped to describe their own state – to explore, question, challenge, analyse and communicate. In this sense, we are all scientists. This is a cornerstone of constructivism, and PCP in particular: every person constructs their own reality, each person's reality is unique, understanding that reality provides unique insights into why a person thinks and behaves as they do, and we can understand that reality most effectively through the person him- or herself, not through observation of behaviours or analysis of subconscious dynamics.

The following scenario illustrates how this works. From our earliest experiences, perceptions are internalised to progressively form our sense of who we are. Significant others and events have the greatest influence. Contextual factors, including family and culture, create a deep underpinning about the way things are. These integrate internally to form our sense of reality. This internalising and integration is a continuous process of negotiation and assimilation of new experiences with the existing sense of self. The self is therefore constructed, and this construction is dynamically changing and adapting. Butt (2013: 28) described the self thus:

> From a constructivist perspective, there is no central command mechanism providing integrity to the person. Instead, the sense of self is distributed but co-ordinated according to **core** role construing, leading to self as a community as a better metaphor.

Butt's emphasis on self as a community highlights a further foundation of constructivism, and one that is especially important as we consider it underpinning research. That is that self is a complex integration of those characteristics that are often termed traits, preferences, needs, interests, motivations, and other dynamics. Human experience is therefore not reducible to these constituent parts (Raskin, 2012) and any research that seeks to focus only on one such part as a means of exploring what it is to be human is impoverished as a result.

To explore the idea of construction in more depth, we recognise that the reality of this constructed sense of self is a representation. When a person important to us acts in a significant way, it is not the act itself that is internalised, but rather our interpretation of the act. We would expect that particular discrete events, such as a traumatic accident, might influence us profoundly. Underlying cultural or family **norms** and **mores** would be more subtle, but nevertheless have an enhanced foundational impact on our sense of reality. Our interpretation is influenced by existing patterns or beliefs. These patterns or beliefs are termed 'constructs'. Constructs are the units that make up the sense of self and are used to judge the efficacy of a new experience. We 'construe' a new experience because we interpret it on the basis of our existing constructed sense of self. This means that each person, as a closed system and active meaning-maker, is unique (Raskin, 2011). For the same external event, what is real to one person may be very different from what is real to another. This is why different reports of the same incident can vary widely. We have *represented* the incident, as it appears to us. You could try out Activity 2.1 now.

Activity 2.1

Different realities

Imagine that you and a number of others witness a car accident. Think about the different perspectives that are possible, for example: who is to blame; what was the cause; who might be hurt; what will the cost be; it could have been me, or my loved one, etc. Think about how each lens might influence the way in which the event is viewed by different witnesses and participants: the driver, passenger, perhaps the car owner if s/he is not the driver.

We use constructs to help us navigate our life journey. For example, when we start a new job, joining a new organisation, we take with us an existing view, or construction, about the way things work in organisations. This construction has developed over our experience of organisational work settings and our place in them, and this would already have been modified by the research we have carried out about the new organisation we are about to enter. For example, we have constructs about how to behave in meetings. We try out certain constructs such as how formal we should be, the use of humour and who we defer to, and our interpretation of responses to these 'experiments' modifies these constructs. We can therefore think of constructs as 'hypotheses' about the way things are, which we try out in different contexts.

We develop this understanding of our social world by building up cross-references between constructs and people, each helping to explain the other, so that people themselves, along with perceptual attributions of their behaviour and attitudes, are all 'a matter of construction' (Kelly, 1991a: 215). To illustrate this point, Kelly used the example of how a child develops an initial construal of 'mother' from his or her own mother's behaviours and then, through comparisons of constructs of his or her own mother, to other women, through accommodation and assimilation, develops the wider construct of 'motherliness'.

We act, construe and modify continuously so that our construction system is most effective for that context. Of course, whilst the process of construing is fluid and evolving, deep-seated or fundamental beliefs about how things should be, or about who I am, will not be as fluid and subject to change as those that are less deeply held, and we dance with the continuous negotiation of experimenting, construing reactions, accommodation, assimilation and willingness to change.

How does this fit with your worldview?

We will explore these notions in greater depth later in this chapter and later chapters. However, for now we wish to build a picture of constructivism and PCP in sufficient detail to allow you, the reader, to begin to make a judgement about whether this is the most appropriate **theoretical underpinning** and approach for your research interest, and for you personally.

So far we have discussed some fundamentals: that external reality is construed through the senses, mediated and filtered through prior experience, and each person's unique constructed reality adapts continuously. As you read this, you will begin to recognise that this perspective is especially appropriate for particular research endeavours. We do not argue that PCP is the only approach that should be used when researching people but we do argue that it has particular benefits in many different applications. You may find it useful at this stage to scan the case studies in Chapter Eleven to see how your research interests compare.

As you start to think about your research project, questions that come into your mind may include 'interviews or questionnaires?', 'qualitative versus quantitative data?', 'target population', 'how many respondents?', 'internet or face-to-face interventions?', and so on. Practicalities will influence your decision but, as we note in the next chapter when we discuss in much greater detail the philosophical and methodological issues that you need to explore in formulating your research design, these should be decided critically on the basis of your research question and the nature of the **phenomena** you wish to investigate. For now, we continue our discussion with general guidance about criteria that will inform your overarching research design decisions and the appropriateness of PCP for you. First we provide a summary of some frequently used contrasting approaches. This is not a comprehensive discussion. There are many publications that present methodological alternatives (we recommend some at the end of this and the following chapter). Those specific to constructivism are discussed in detail later in this book. The following is intended just to help you initially consider whether constructivist and PCP approaches might work well for you.

Let us first consider more traditional research techniques. If you are interested in what people do, how they behave or actions they take in certain circumstances then you may wish to observe them. Observation can be more effective than simply asking people what they do because you will gain first-hand insights rather than their (inevitably expurgated, consciously or not) reports. You can classify behaviours you observe and this may enable you to develop a taxonomy for use in categorising behaviours. Belbin (2013), for example, used this approach when exploring team roles. Observation can be costly in terms of resources and time, restricting the number of respondents you can include. Thus, observation is unlikely to be appropriate if you need to investigate a large number of respondents. It also only tells you what people do but not why they do it. In this case a questionnaire survey might be effective, and the disadvantages associated with not being able to observe directly might be outweighed by the benefits of a larger amount of data in a consistent survey format. Internet or postal surveys can elicit quantitative or qualitative data which may then be analysed statistically or thematically to develop or test theoretical models in particular contexts. This will provide breadth of data, and may include behaviours, attitudes or emotional criteria that are assessed using different response formats from **Likert scales** to open comments.

However, if you need to explore phenomena in depth, then observation or questionnaires will not be ideal, and interviews may be more effective. Structured interviews are means of carrying out surveys directly with respondents. Semi-structured interviews provide a more flexible framework to allow depth of exploration of issues as they arise. Whilst interviews allow depth and flexibility, they again are not normally a viable method for a large number of respondents, and they also, like questionnaires, have the disadvantages of 'researcher bias' (following up the researcher's ideas about what is going on) and the aforementioned tendency of participants to provide socially acceptable responses. Mixed methods may be helpful in providing some balance, for example where an initial questionnaire survey is used to elicit key themes that are then explored in depth in subsequent interviews (see our later discussion on research design in Chapter Eight), but still have some disadvantages.

Typically, the approach used within these methods allows the researcher to investigate *what* is happening, and possibly *how* things unfold, by exploring dependencies and relationships between factors. So, for example, the researcher who investigates the impact of leadership communications on team morale might use questionnaires or interviews to elicit data that indicate what types of communications seem to be the most influential and in what ways this affects levels of morale. However, critically, these methods as described are not ideal for exploring *why* particular communications influence morale in the way noted. To explore 'why' type questions, approaches that allow access to inner meanings are required. PCP techniques allow just such access. The PCP methodology may be incorporated into an interview design and, to some degree, questionnaire surveys. However, without an approach such as this, in-depth insights into meanings will most often be missed.

Why are 'why' questions important? They are important because they help us get below the surface of behaviours, to reveal fundamental attitudes, which in turn allow us to make better choices. For example, continuing the leadership example, if we consider only leadership behaviours that affect morale, without insights into deeper meanings, we run the risk of being prescriptive. We might suggest that morale is improved with increased individual autonomy – which is generally supported by literature (for example, Pink, 2011) – but if this is applied in practice with little or no consideration for why this might increase morale we will have little insight into when it actually might not do so (for example, when a person is already overstretched).

At this point you might like to try thinking like a constructivist in an everyday situation: try Activity 2.2.

Activity 2.2

An everyday adventure into construing

Find yourself a public place in which you can hang around for a few minutes observing others (without getting arrested!) - near a shop doorway as if waiting for a friend usually works well, as does the entrance to a work's canteen or a waiting room of some sort.

Observe – that is watch and think about – how different people present themselves when in a public arena. Why are some dressed smartly and others in working clothes, or are their smart clothes their working clothes? Why are some sporting a fashionable hairstyle, expensive jewellery, tattoos and piercings, a tidy or scruffy appearance? What are they trying to tell the world and why? What does that tell you about how they view this public place and why they are there, doing what they are doing?

Now think about this. What are you telling the world through your appearance? What views about the world and this public place in particular are you revealing, the tip of your iceberg of constructs?

If you are very brave and becoming more interested in the people around you, you might try smiling as people pass by. Do they smile back, or scowl, or look away? It is likely that you will find a variety of responses.

What might their views of the world be that they respond in those particular ways?

If a stranger smiles at you do you respond in a friendly way or with suspicion or embarrassment? Why?

If these questions seem intriguing then you are well on the way to thinking like a constructivist.

If you wish to explore what people do and possibly how attitudinal and behavioural factors relate at a general level then established research approaches could be adequate. If, however, you wish to explore *why* people behave as they do then PCP could be the most appropriate approach for you, and you should read on.

In the next section, we build on the discussion about constructed reality by explaining in more detail the components of PCP and how they operate to allow access to people's individual meanings.

Personal construct psychology

In 1955 George Kelly wrote two volumes, the culmination of 20 years' work, about the development and application of PCP. These are now available free of charge as pdf files, and if you plan to apply PCP as the central underpinning theory in your research you might like to obtain these (Kelly, 1955/1991). However, they are very detailed and much of Volume 1 and all of Volume 2 concentrate on clinical and therapeutic applications. If you use PCP at all, then you should at least read the first three chapters of Volume 1, which have also been published separately as a book (Kelly, 1963), summarising the background to and central theory of PCP, and the nature of personal constructs. We will discuss these ideas in detail in the next two chapters. Meanwhile, in this section, we summarise the key components of PCP from a research perspective, so that you can more thoroughly consider its application in your research project. (PCP is placed in a broader philosophical perspective in Chapter Three.)

Let us explore a little further the sort of explanations that PCP can help with. We have noted the existence of internal constructs that form each person's individual sense of self and reality, and which are used, or 'tried out', as patterns or templates in life's experiences. They help us to explain and manage our life journey and to predict how a future experience involving our self might play out. We construe the world using constructs. When a construct appears to us to fit our world well, it is reinforced. Where it does not fit well we either deny the efficacy of the event we experience, and so keep our construct intact, or we have to adapt our construct. For example, continuing the leadership scenario, our leader trying to improve morale might believe, or have a construct representing, a reality that close communication has a positive effect. Trying this out on his or her team might, however, be met with (construed as) accusations of micro-management. The leader can then either maintain his or her belief about the value of close communication, keeping the construct intact, or adapt his or her construct to more effectively fit the new reality experienced. The wise leader would consider the latter rather than simply thinking that his or her team have misunderstood him or her. The wise researcher, having observed the interactions, might find it useful, therefore, to find out why the leader and the team react in the ways they do.

To help explanation we have used the notation of, and examples relating to, single constructs. However, constructs form complex interconnected and integrated 'construct systems', which are continuously subject to degrees of reinforcement and adaptation in a sort of real-time negotiated dance. Within any particular construct system, constructs form a hierarchy of importance, from **subordinate** to **superordinate constructs**, within what we might describe as an array of construct subsystems. In our example, a leader will have a broad sense, or superordinate construct system, of what it is to be a leader, involving general ideas of, for example, style, behaviours, relationships and power. The belief that close communication is important is a subordinate construct within this system. As a subordinate construct, when it is challenged, the leader may find it relatively easy to accept that it does not fit well and adapt it, because even in doing so, he or she maintains the overall integrity and security of the superordinate system. If, however, the leader's superordinate system about the nature of being a leader is challenged, that is, his or her deep-seated beliefs, then the ability to adapt might be very much more difficult. A leader may reject the adaption of a subordinate construct, or the adoption of a new subordinate construct, if it in some way offends the superstructure. For example, an established leader who is faced with the prospect of one of his or her team taking a leading role in a project may find that prospect so radical that he or she rejects the idea out of hand. Thus knowing something about how the leader's constructs are linked together helps a researcher to understand the scenario even better than discovering the nature only of the constructs applied in it.

Researchers could be challenged to understand behaviours in any number of professional or life situations. Similar examples to that above could be drawn from teaching, with teachers wedded to particular pedagogical frameworks having as subordinate constructs how lessons should be conducted. For instance, a teacher with a teacher-centred approach may adapt how computers are used in a classroom to fit in with his or her superordinate construct, which will be different from the style of computer interaction used by a student-centred teacher. You can probably think of other examples, for instance how different patient care regimes might be adopted or adapted by nurses or doctors with alternative perspectives on their professional roles, or how characters in a play might be understood and presented differently by actors from different schools of thought, or how bad behaviour might be interpreted and responded to by people with a retributive rather than a restorative mind-set, and so on.

Earlier in this chapter we discussed the notion that different people interpret, or construe, the same objective situation in unique ways, due to their unique constructed reality. Another interesting aspect of construct systems is that one person when experiencing the same objective event at different times can try out, or apply, different constructs. This emphasises the argument made earlier that people have choices about how they respond to a particular situation and may not be constrained by circumstances or personal history. For example, when leading a team project which has fallen behind schedule, a leader could apply egalitarian, person-centred constructs, or, alternatively, directive, function-focused constructs. Each could fit the event but are likely to have very different consequences. The notion that the world may be construed by the same person in various ways is what Kelly termed **constructive alternativism**. Some alternative constructs might fit an event equally well, such as those based on different but equally valid values, but some may be less helpful than others, based on the accuracy with which each predicts the nature of the event. An experienced leader, or teacher, or doctor would be expected to have developed construct systems that more effectively predict future outcomes than those with less experience, and be able to apply constructs that most helpfully fit the circumstances. A very skilled professional might have developed a portfolio of choices, or alternative construct systems, with insights into how each might play out if applied to a particular situation.

As researchers we too can stick to familiar approaches and methods and/or our constructions of what might be appropriate ways of conducting research. On the other hand, we could consider alternative ways of conducting research so that we can make more effective choices about which approaches to apply in responding to diverse research questions. Further, we consider alternative methods and techniques embodying a PCP philosophy in later chapters, providing another layer of choice. It is such an adventure that we invite you to share here.

Summary

It is time to draw this chapter to a close because we have covered sufficient ground to help you consider if a constructivist approach, and PCP in particular, might fit with any of your potential research topics and be right for you. We have touched on the nature of constructivism, recognising that every person dynamically develops their unique view of their world and that this fundamentally affects the behaviours they employ. We began this exploration by considering the nature of reality and self. This may have seemed somewhat philosophical for a book claiming to assist with practical aspects of research. However, we argue that all research activities are underpinned by particular beliefs about the nature of the phenomena we seek to investigate, and that all aspects of a particular investigation should be consistent with those beliefs. With that in mind, we move on to Chapter Three with the aim of developing deeper philosophical and theoretical insights into constructivism as an underpinning paradigm for research into personal meanings, as a prelude to Chapter Four which considers in more detail the formal principles and main assumptions of the theory.

Suggested further reading

Bryman, A. (2008) *Social Research Methods*. Oxford: Oxford University Press.

Linking approaches and methods, Bryman shows how to assess the contexts within which different research methods may be used, and how they should be implemented.

Crotty, M. (1998) *The Foundations of Social Research: Meaning and Perspective in the Research Process*. London: SAGE.

Researchers are aided to navigate the maze of the philosophical origins and implications of different schools of enquiry so to choose the most appropriate methodology for their task.

Linking philosophy and theory to research purpose

Introduction

In a book such as this, where we seek to offer the reader practical guidance on approaches to research, it may seem somewhat out of place to start a chapter with a fundamental philosophical question: 'What is the nature of reality?' And yet, in order to establish a clear foundation for your research, such questions require attention. However, we are on safe ground because we are not asking you to produce, and we certainly do not intend to produce, a definitive answer. Let us explain.

'What is the nature of reality?' is actually an unanswerable question for constructivists because it implies that there is a single reality and that it is possible to define that reality. Constructivists do not believe that there is a single reality, rather we believe in multiple realities. It seems perfectly reasonable to claim that there might be a reality of objective things 'out there' but there are also individual realities. This is simply because we cannot access the 'out there' except through senses, which are limited and tuned in our own peculiar human way, and we then interpret as we internalise and integrate with our existing frame of reference. For example, the reality of the sights, smells and sounds that surround you at this moment depends on your visual, olfactory and auditory sensitivity, which will differ in often subtle ways from other people, relating to age and many other factors, and this reality is further influenced by our experience of sights, smells and sounds. As we have argued in the previous chapters, each person constructs their own sense of reality, and so there are as many realities as people. We discuss this further in the section on **ontology**, below.

So why do questions such as these require attention? Precisely because there *are* multiple realities. In research, we need to be very clear about the nature of the reality, or phenomena, we seek to investigate. This will reward us with two important benefits. First, we will be ideally placed to ensure that we use the most appropriate tools and techniques. Second, we can be confident that all aspects of our research, from the research question, to methodology, analysis and implications, form a congruent and cohesive process.

In this chapter we invite you to explore with us the nature of the phenomena you seek to research, how it links with your own experience of reality, and to develop clear arguments for the approach you take. We will do this systematically. Working from perspectives on the nature of reality (ontology) we refine our understanding to address the nature of knowledge and how we experience it (epistemology) and develop insights into congruent methodology, so that by the time we close this chapter, you will have assessed the value of constructivism from fundamental perspectives for your research and developed a complete and robust research paradigm.

The nature of phenomena

As we begin a research project we need to define quickly the territory of our research, with perhaps a broad question, aim or scope of exploration, and we need to define clearly the phenomena at the heart of our endeavour. This goes far beyond questions such as what the symptoms or underpinning causes or behaviours or motives or cultures or foundational value systems might be, which demand clarity as we decide on the purpose of our research. No, the phenomena at the heart of our research are buried within its focus and purpose and are to do with the substantial essence of the things or experiences we seek to explore. What it actually is, rather than what it does.

Let us make sense of this argument using an example. We are in a factory setting in which components are assembled to make desktop printers. Productivity has been falling and we have been asked to research ways in which improvements might be made. The technology is operating effectively. If we decided that low productivity is a symptom of the way the work is designed (the cause), the phenomenon we might explore would be the behavioural response of people to different work designs. We could, for example, organise the work in different ways and measure output against each. This could elicit some useful data but, being based on the assumption that we know the cause, researching this phenomenon might not get to the root of the issue. Whilst it might tell us something about what is happening, it will give us little data to explain why. Taking a different approach, avoiding leaping in with assumptions, instead seeking richer data to gain insights into both what is really happening and why, could lead us to focus on entirely different phenomena. For example, having established that the technology is sound, and recognising that productivity is something to do with the people involved, we could take an exploratory approach, being open to any possible explanation. In this case we might wish to explore motivational phenomena, seeking insights into what drives or what diminishes certain behaviours. Before we can explore these phenomena, we need to have a clear understanding about their nature. That is, we need to answer the question about what motivation is before we can then establish ways of accessing this phenomenon and eliciting data that are useful for explaining behaviours.

So this example illustrates what we mean by the notion of phenomena and the importance of clarifying both which phenomenon we should focus on and the nature of that phenomenon. The example also begins to explain one of the key benefits of a constructivist approach to researching people's meanings: it explicitly avoids imposing terms, constructs or ideas from the researcher, in favour of open elicitation of constructs from participants. We develop this theme later in this chapter.

Having established what the real analytical focus of our research is, we can then define our research paradigm, beginning with the underlying philosophy and approach that would be most effective for our investigation. As we do this we are able to determine how closely we align with the constructivist paradigm, or indeed any other one.

Research philosophy and paradigm

We began this chapter with a question about the nature of reality. As we have discussed the need for clarity about the phenomena we research, we have started to unravel the philosophical position of the constructivist. We have argued that constructivism recognises many realities because reality for an individual is personally constructed, albeit in a social context. We now explore the constructivist paradigm in greater detail. Each aspect of the paradigm we adopt will be considered in contrast to alternatives. Working through each step of this process will help you to explore your own position and how this aligns with the phenomena you wish to investigate.

We start by considering in more depth these broad philosophical questions about the nature of reality, or 'ontology'. Having recognised that there is no single perspective on reality, in this section we note possible alternative views.

Ontology

Objective and subjective

Subscribers to *objective* reality suggest that things actually exist, and that it is possible to define them independently of each other (Bryman, 2008). If we wish to research things, as objective phenomena, we can do so using tools and techniques of the natural sciences. We can quantify and describe physical properties like size, weight, colour and location, providing common understanding, and can control these attributes as we research cause and effect or correlation. In our example above, researching the effect of technology on production output could be carried out using objective measurements and then applying statistical tests of probability that they occurred by chance or because of our experimental interventions, for instance.

However, in this example, we began to explore the limitations of an objective paradigm when we wish to understand people and their role in a system. A *subjective* paradigm recognises that reality is created experientially (Alvesson and Deetz, 2000). When we explore subjective realities we develop richer insights into people's meanings, which are not accessible through manipulation of objective phenomena. Philosophical idealism is a more extreme view, suggesting that reality consists only of ideas in the mind (Crotty, 1998), or at least that reality is fundamentally grounded in an internal mind or spirit.

As constructivists, we reject the notion of idealism in favour of the belief that things might well really exist independently, even though our interest is primarily in subjective phenomena. This is illustrated in Figure 3.1, which locates a constructivist position on the continuum between subjective and objective. Here it is located closer to the subjective than objective position, but constructivists vary in the degree to which they emphasise objective and subjective realities in relation to the other.

Objective and subjective as ontological perspectives should not be confused with **objectivism** and **subjectivism** as epistemological positions. This is explained in a later section.

Realism and relativism

The ontological perspective of **realism** asserts that reality exists externally, independent of human activity and people's consciousness of it. It aligns with the objective perspective and suggests that things as phenomena are out there waiting to be discovered (Gill and Johnson, 2010). Things as entities and their interaction can, again, be measured and described and are often understood as 'facts' that behave in accordance with natural laws. Notwithstanding variations attributed

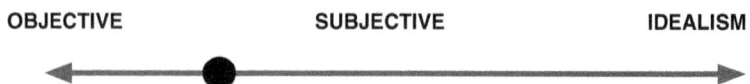

OBJECTIVE   SUBJECTIVE   IDEALISM

Figure 3.1 The constructivist's position: objective versus subjective

more recently to quantum theory, realists align to natural science theory and the possibility of accurately predicting future behaviour of phenomena.

The perspective of critical realism claims that reality exists externally, but recognises social dynamics, and therefore socially constructed realities, as integral to objective reality. A key difference therefore is that whilst realism aligns to the view that 'normal' cause and effect relationships of events can be established, social interactions bring into play a more dynamic mechanism that undermines the possibility of prediction.

As we have already argued, whereas constructivists would not adopt a realist perspective, we recognise the impact of constructed realities, and in this sense at least, we align with aspects of critical realist views. However, critical realism does not go far enough for the constructivist, whose interest is not in a particular (social) mechanism, but rather in internal realities which have been constructed through the dynamic interaction of many factors and experiences, of which social is just one, to create infinite internal possibilities.

We distinguish constructivism from constructionism because whereas constructivism recognises the internal development of self from a wide range of dynamics, social constructionism gives primacy to relational, linguistic and social factors in the development of the individual person (Gergen, 1999; Raskin, 2002). But they are related. Social constructionists believe that social experience both shapes and limits the self, and that, within this social process, people adopt 'roles' within groups and then enact those roles fluidly 'in the light of [their] understanding of the attitudes of [their] associates' (Kelly, 1991a: 68). Much of what follows in this book about methods and techniques, ethics and analysis, applies equally well in constructionist and constructivist research, with the difference in perspective being manifest mainly in the emphasis placed on the individual or social context in the interpretation phase.

Constructivists align with a relativist ontological perspective. **Relativism** claims that because reality is uniquely individual, a person's 'truth' is individually defined (Easterby-Smith et al., 2002). A relativist perspective is appropriate for researchers who seek to explore individual meanings. By falling squarely on individuality, constructivists are not impeded by particular theories, beliefs, mind-sets or preconceived ideas (such as social mechanisms) but remain open-minded and focused on realities experienced, and defined, by individuals themselves. Figure 3.2 therefore places the constructivist at the relativist end of the continuum.

PCP can be argued to be a relativist theory because Kelly regarded the universe as integral, with reality only distinguishable at the level of the individual and built up of experiential and perceptual contrasts rather than absolutes (Jankowicz, 2004). Relativism has also been presented as a humanistic theory, because of its optimistic

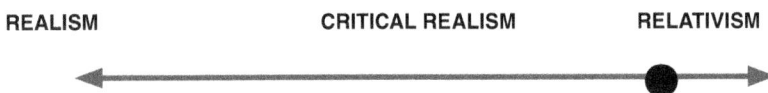

REALISM   CRITICAL REALISM   RELATIVISM

Figure 3.2   The constructivist's position: realism versus relativism

view that man can improve himself. Having said this, Kelly himself defied people to constrict his work within categories, because he saw his work as an alternative to extant theories rather than a replacement for them. He presented PCP as a 'bridge' between realism and relativism and also contended that the theory rendered onto-logical assumptions irrelevant because it is a theory of 'knowing' rather than a theory of reality and can therefore be applied regardless of one's philosophical view of the world (Bannister and Fransella, 1986).

This emphasis on knowledge takes us to the next philosophical consideration, epistemology. However, before we do so, this is a good point for you, the reader, to reflect on your own ontological position. You may never have actively reflected on your philosophical perspective about reality before. It is likely that most of us have not needed to do that. However, take a few minutes for Activity 3.1 because this will help you to establish your own perspective on the nature of reality.

Activity 3.1

Consider your own ontology

Put this book down. You might like to close your eyes.
   Imagine yourself at each position on the continua of the two ontology diagrams in the section. Be aware of your internal response, ease or discomfort, at each position.
   What does this tell you about your personal ontological perspective?
   What are the implications of this personal position for your research project?

Epistemology

Whilst ontology is the philosophical study of reality, or being or existence, episte-mology is the philosophical study of the nature of knowledge. It is the branch of thinking that addresses such questions as: 'what is knowledge?'; 'what do I know?'; 'how do I know what I know?' It is important for the researcher to consider differ-ent epistemological perspectives because, first, such reflection recognises various ways by which reality might be known; second, it furnishes the researcher with a language with which to categorise these perspectives on knowledge; and third, it helps the researcher to ensure that the paradigm they apply in their research is con-gruent and consistently applied. These assertions will become clearer as we progress with our discussion about philosophy and research purpose.

Objectivism and subjectivism

Objectivism is the view that meaning resides in things themselves (Crotty, 1998). For example, the identity of a tree, and all that being a tree means, is exter-nal and implicit in the tree itself, independent of any perceptual or conceptual

OBJECTIVISM   **SUBJECTIVISM**

Figure 3.3 The constructivist's position: objectivism versus subjectivism

processes of an observer. The essence of a thing exists, or categories of things exist, independently, out there. This suggests that because people can only experience external phenomena through sensory and perceptual processes, they can only ever experience an approximation of the thing itself. The more people experience the thing, and the more they are able to revise their constructs of it through experimentation, the more accurate, or helpful, their perspective becomes.

As discussed, constructivists therefore align with the belief that both external objective reality and internal subjective realities may well exist, but the latter is more difficult to access through the instruments we have, our senses. However, they are interested in the diversity of internal subjective phenomena and as such they align closer to a *subjectivist*, and not an *objectivist*, epistemological perspective. This is illustrated in Figure 3.3. Objectivism aligns with realism, and subjectivism with relativism.

Subjectivism assumes that 'the knower imposes meaning on the known' (deMarrais and Lapan, 2004: 175). It is the individual's subjective experience of the tree, not the tree itself or increasing precision in understanding what the tree itself is all about, that is of interest to the constructivist. Further consideration of the notion that meaning is imposed on the known is helpful. The human brain is predisposed to make sense of sensory inputs. As people perceive an external reality, they seek to give it meaning. All of us do this, but researchers are particularly driven to do so. As we have discussed, the meaning that each person gives to a thing or situation stems from their own existing construct system and will be uniquely individual. Meaning-making is not, therefore, a passive process but rather is an active process of continuous negotiation between existing constructs and new sensory inputs. You might like to try Activity 3.2 now to explore your own meaning-making through reflection.

Activity 3.2

What is a tree, or a chunk of stone?

You first need to find or bring to mind a particular tree! What does it mean to you? Do you know its variety, or is it simply a tree? Is it something to make an area pretty, or is it useful in blocking an unpleasant view? Does it clean the air or litter the place with falling leaves? Is it one that was planted by a loved one or neglected by a neighbour? Is it a source of current delight, or chagrin, or future delight as wood for a fire or planks for a floor or a beautifully carved object?

You could do the same with a chunk of stone – surely something quite 'real' in your environment. How did it get there? What is it made of? What is its purpose now, and what alternative purposes could it have? Would someone building a pathway or a sculptor or landscape gardener view it differently?

How do the meanings these objects are imbued with change with these perspectives?

Positivism, interpretivism and phenomenology

Positivism is a research paradigm that asserts that those things that exist can be described factually. It therefore aligns with objectivism and realism. A positivist approach, including the extreme of logical positivism, which emphasises empiricism in all research (Crotty, 1998), and post-positivism, or neo-positivism, which recognises limitations in objectivism and aligns with critical realism, follows natural scientific principles and involves a researcher who (attempts to) take a disinterested, value-neutral role (Denzin and Lincoln, 2005). Post-positivism has dominated as a means of establishing theories, rules, laws and proof. Since the industrial revolution, work and organisations have been designed primarily on post-positivist principles with emphasis on efficiency, prediction, planning and control. Whilst scientific post-positivist principles remain dominant, recent decades have seen the emergence of non-positivist approaches to situations involving humans, for instance management in organisations, recognising uncertainty and non-factual probabilistic dynamics, and the crucial importance of empowering and engaging people as unique producers of value towards organisational success and individual well-being. Similarly, in health sciences the role of the patient's view, and those of significant others, on the illness and medicine regime is considered alongside randomised controlled trial data. In contrast, the recent past in education research has been dominated by projects seeking the views and perspectives of those engaged in it, teachers and those who are taught, whereas funding councils and government bodies seek quantitative data from neo-positivist research because those various stakeholders hold different views about what kind of data or information will be useful to them.

You will recognise that constructivists do not align with positivism because their interest lies in phenomena that cannot be reduced to scientific elements that can be objectively described, manipulated and controlled. A constructivist would also recognise that he or she can never be value-neutral and that the phenomena that are explored are always subject to interpretation. Constructivists recognise that a researcher is an integral player in the research: not a distant, isolated observer, but part of the system being studied.

Constructivists would therefore align with **interpretivism**, the approach to research that seeks understanding of people's meanings at an individual level (Crotty, 1998), but recognises that this understanding is always subject to interpretation. Nevertheless, the constructivist strongly aligns with the imperative of seeking to understand how a person experiences their sense of the world from their own perspective. This is the theory of **phenomenology** (Bryman, 2008). Understanding a person's reality and meanings from their own perspective is a fundamental principle of constructivism and, as we will discuss in later chapters, all methodologies in constructivist research are designed to allow and encourage respondents to communicate their own meanings in their own way. The constructivist position is illustrated in Figure 3.4.

Now that we have considered some philosophical aspects of research, from the perspective of both the nature of existence and reality, ontology, and the nature of

POSITIVISM   INTERPRETIVISM PHENOMENOLOGY

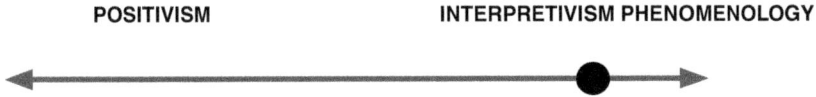

Figure 3.4   The constructivist's position: positivism, interpretivism and phenomenology

knowledge, epistemology, it is time for you to reflect again about your own research investigation. Take a few minutes on the reflective Activity 3.3 before moving on to the next section.

Activity 3.3

Where does your research fit?

Remind yourself about the purpose and focus of your current or prospective research. Remember the importance of clarity about the nature of the phenomena you are exploring.

With your knowledge now about the philosophical aspects that we have discussed, consider the degree to which a constructivist paradigm would work for you.

We now turn away from philosophical issues and consider methodology, although we keep in mind our journey so far as we endeavour to develop a congruent holistic approach to our research. The methodology which we adopt, which is orientated by our philosophy, will in turn lead to methods, tools and techniques. These are the subject of later chapters.

Methodology

Deduction, induction and grounded theory

As we have noted, the approach we take in our research project depends critically on the nature of the phenomenon and the research question or issues we wish to address. Constructivism may be applied to various perspectives, and this section will summarise some of the main approaches that the researcher can take, concluding with a discussion of issues that we need to consider to ensure that our research is carried out to the highest levels of quality.

One of the first questions a researcher should ask once he or she has decided to explore a particular topic is: 'Is this research about exploring the application of an existing theory or model in a particular context, or is it about developing insights into a situation through data collected without guidance from an existing theory or model?' The first is **deductive research**; the second, **inductive research**. Deductive research tests existing concepts and theory through empirical investigation (Gill and Johnson, 2010: 46). Inductive research develops explanations, concepts and theories from empirical data (Gill and Johnson, 2010: 56).

In many areas of research, the researcher will develop insights into what is currently understood about the topic before they embark on their project. Often this is most effective through a review of appropriate literature. Appropriate literature is often that which reports rigorous, peer-reviewed studies, but practitioner literature can often help to place this in a practical context. From this exploration, the researcher may identify a theoretical model that has previously been found to explain the phenomena that he or she wishes to investigate, in certain contexts, and so decide to apply this in his or her own research focus. This is deductive research, and it has the advantage of using an existing validated model.

Constructivist techniques can, for example, be used to elicit from respondents their own inner construction of different components of the model. Continuing the example about factory work, introduced earlier, the researcher may wish to investigate motivational phenomena by applying an existing established theoretical model, 'the job characteristics model' (Hackman and Oldham, 1980). This model has several factors and components that purport to influence motivational drives and behaviours. Participants' inner experiences of these factors and elements could be explored using constructivist techniques, and this would enable the researcher to say something about the relationship between the way the work is designed and responses of job-holders. Similarly, in relation to health, a person's perspective on an illness may well influence how they cope with it and use their medicines. This is a topic worth exploring after the usual drug safety procedures have been undertaken, because randomised controlled trials do not take into account medicine use in the normal world in which people are not being monitored as part of a trial.

However, the researcher may not have a theoretical model that they wish to test. They may find that the literature does not address their primary interest and so the research project needs to fill this gap. In this case an inductive research project would be appropriate, requiring the researcher to collect, analyse and elicit meaning from data to develop insights, patterns and ideas that may not have been illuminated in the literature. Constructivist techniques are especially helpful in inductive research because, implicit within constructivism, as discussed, is the openness to elicit meanings from respondents' perspectives and in their own terms. Continuing the work design example, the researcher might wish to explore motivational dynamics for leaders of virtual teams, but there is little in the literature to illuminate this. Here, the researcher might use constructivist techniques to explore rich meanings and inner motivational dynamics of virtual team members and leaders, without resorting to any existing insights, or factors or drivers that dominate motivational dynamics in non-virtual contexts. Similarly, in the medical example, a researcher might want to explore the patient's perspectives that influence their medicine use, and the faith they have in it.

An extreme form of inductive research is **grounded theory**. Grounded theory, discussed in detail in Chapter 10, is the development of concepts or theories that are rooted entirely, or essentially, in empirical data (Seale et al., 2004). One advantage advocated by grounded theorists is that the researcher comes to the research issue with few or no preconceived ideas about it and so is open-minded about the factors that might be involved. A researcher seeking to carry out a grounded theory investigation would not normally seek initially to explore current thinking through literature or any other form, and might avoid all existing insights into the research topic. On the other hand, constructivists will recognise that the possibility of coming to a research topic, especially one relating to personal meanings, with nothing or very little by way of existing understanding or beliefs, is very remote indeed. However, constructivism can play a part in grounded theory research which seeks to understand people's meanings, because it aligns closely to the philosophical principles of phenomenology, interpretivism, subjectivism and relativism. But it remains as important in this research approach as it is in the previous two, that the researcher recognises and declares any potential influence that their own values and beliefs bring to the research, the lenses through which they view that aspect of the world. Alternative tools and techniques that may be used in different research perspectives are discussed in Chapter Seven, with their respective analysis modes described in Chapter Ten.

Quantitative and qualitative data

The researcher may then address the question of what type of data s/he should collect. This should be based, again, on research purpose and focus. There are essentially two types of data, quantitative and qualitative. Quantitative and qualitative are terms that are often used to refer to types of research, although this is inappropriate. These are terms that refer to types of data, not types of research, since some research projects require more than one type of data. Quantitative data are, literally, metrics – numbers of one kind or another. Qualitative data are the words used to describe ideas, thoughts or feelings associated with and evaluative of your target phenomena. You need to consider which data type will be most appropriate for your purposes.

Quantitative data have the advantage of being available for statistical manipulation, for descriptions, graphical representations, comparisons, and assessing relationships between factors. Quantification is often associated with rating scales and survey responses, and these techniques can have the advantage of readily collecting information from or about a large number of participants. Continuing the example, it may be possible to calculate that 65 per cent of employees indicate that they are motivated at work. However, quantifying phenomena that cannot naturally be quantified and attributing meaning via statistics can be misleading. For example, how motivated is 'motivated' for each individual respondent, and does 65 per cent indicate continuous motivation of the same proportion or a varied proportion at any one time?

Where richer meaning is required to address the research topic, qualitative data can be especially helpful. Exploring constructs and eliciting deep inner meanings is not possible through quantitative data collection alone, so qualitative data are required in these cases. However, it is normally not practical to collect rich, qualitative data from a large number of respondents; such study takes time and resources that are seldom available to researchers. In practice the number of people providing qualitative data in research projects is often much lower compared to those providing quantitative data. Quantitative data allow us to measure/quantify phenomena; however, this is not the case with qualitative data. Qualitative data are used for identifying and assessing or evaluating or giving meaning to phenomena.

Because constructivist research seeks to understand inner meanings, it is often most helpful in such research to elicit qualitative rather than quantitative data. However, greatest value might be gained through mixed methods, involving different paradigms or at least mixed techniques, using triangulation. For example, you might carry out a research stage consisting of surveys and statistical analyses with a large number of respondents, followed by an in-depth qualitative data research stage with fewer respondents in which issues identified through surveys may be explored in depth. Or, indeed, in-depth studies can provide the language and concepts used by people in a situation which can then be used with a greater number as part of a well-designed survey that has relevance to the participants and which asks questions they can understand and relate to. This is explored further in Chapter Eight on research design and is illustrated by exemplar case studies in Part III.

Ensuring quality in research

The need for high-quality design, administration and analysis is fundamental in research. This is not a question of choice over the level of quality that may be adequate considering the cost or resources that we may expend, like buying a carpet or choosing a holiday, although, of course, there are always limited resources in research. Rather, whilst a low-quality carpet might wear more quickly, or a low-quality hotel be less comfortable than expected, they do not undermine their essential purpose and will more or less do the job. Low-quality research, on the other hand, can fundamentally undermine its value and application, and can even be misleading. Moreover, verifying quality in interpretivist research can be more difficult than in positivist research because the latter involves data from some standard measuring instrument used under particular conditions. It is important, therefore, that we give particular attention to key factors that must be considered to ensure that constructivist research is carried out to the highest standard in order to demonstrate the quality of its product.

The criteria used to assess quality in interpretivist research are different from those applied in positivist forms of research. These are summarised in Figure 3.5, and the contrast is discussed below to show which criteria are applied, and why, to ensure quality in constructivist research.

Any reader of your research will want to know that it is sound and authoritative. As previously noted this can be straightforward in positivist research, partly by demonstrating objectivity, through eliciting 'factual' data, and partly by showing that

POSITIVIST RESEARCH		INTERPRETIVIST RESEARCH
Validity	*Measuring what is purported*	
	Appropriateness of research design	Credibility
Objectivity	*'Factual' data*	
	Support by other researchers	Confirmability
Reliability	*Consistency and accuracy of measurement*	
	Trustworthiness	Dependability
Generalisability	*Reproducibility across settings*	
	Application to other settings	Transferability

Figure 3.5   Quality measures in different paradigms

the research is valid, that is, that the research measured those phenomena that it claims to have measured using arguably appropriate instruments. It is not possible to 'validate' constructivist research, as such. Sound and authoritative constructivist research is demonstrated by showing that its design is robustly appropriate for the phenomena and research purpose and that the techniques used facilitate access to the meaning provided by participants, that is, it is credible to the data providers and those who view it, rather than valid. Thus its authenticity may be supportively confirmed by the participants, and recognised by other researchers as being elicited well and appropriately. In essence, showing that your research conforms to rigorous principles, such as those discussed in this book, and that other established researchers affirm your approach by endorsing or replicating it, is a strong indication of well-founded, persuasive and credible research.

In positivist research, if validity is about measuring the correct phenomena, then reliability is about measuring the phenomena correctly. High-quality positivist research will be demonstrated where the means by which phenomena are measured are accurate and produce consistent results. As we have discussed, constructivist research cannot be assessed using these criteria because it does not measure at all, and constructivists do not align with the notion of accuracy because this alludes to the possibility of identifying distinctly independent criteria. Further, a large part of their research and approaches involves themselves and their participants, whose views can change simply because they have been asked about them and given them additional thought – or possibly thought about them for the first time. Constructivist research recognises influences of contextual and temporal dynamics. Constructivists should seek therefore to ensure that their research is dependable, rather than 'reliable', and this is demonstrated through employing a trustworthy approach, that is, a methodology delivered with integrity and transparency.

Finally, quality in constructivist research is demonstrated by the degree to which it is transferable to other settings. This is distinct from positivist research which, because it works with objective data, may be generalisable across or within settings and possibly underpin theory, models or laws that describe behaviours or phenomena in a range of contexts. Constructivists cannot claim such consistency in findings, nor would they wish to. As constructivism recognises individuality in constructions and meanings, it would never be appropriate to claim any degree of reproducibility of research findings. However, the degree to which the research design, methodology, tools and techniques may be transferred to other settings is an indication of the quality of the research, as are the clues or insights that the findings may provide to help others explore and understand similar situations.

The notion of quality in research, and the distinguishing characteristics of different paradigms discussed throughout this chapter, may raise a question in your mind around which approach is better. The answer, we are bound to say, is that it all depends. And this response returns us to the beginning of the chapter in which we argued that the approach you take depends critically on the nature of the phenomena you wish to explore and the focus and purpose of your research. But we would like to develop this a little further here as we conclude this chapter. Suffice to say for now that post-positivist research has received such a strong grounding through the scientific movement, from pre-industrialisation through to all that has built from scientific management of production and organisations, that a post-positivist paradigm has been given the status of being superior to other less tangible or less objective paradigms in many disciplinary arenas. However, as we shall continue to argue, for certain phenomena and research terrains, an interpretivist paradigm in general, and constructivism in particular, is neither second best nor neutral against the dominance of positivism; in many circumstances it is superior and the only paradigm that will do the job. We hope that you will read on to discover why.

Suggested further reading

Denzin, N.K. and Lincoln, Y.S. (2005) *The Handbook of Qualitative Research*. London: SAGE.
This huge anthology of expert digests on the paradigms, strategies and techniques of research seeking qualitative data is a vast reference resource.

Seale, C., Gobo, G., Gubrium, J.F. and Silverman, D. (2004) *Qualitative Research Practice*. London: SAGE.
Again a compendium of perspectives, the focus of this book is on the debates and practice of research in the qualitative field.

4

Constructing personal realities

Key Points

- Social and cultural influences on individual construing
- Main tenets of PCP in relation to research
- The experience of construing

Introduction

In the preceding chapters we have emphasised and provided some illustrations of how particular individuals might view things differently under different circumstances and of how different individuals might view things differently under similar or the same circumstances. These ideas lie at the foundation of PCP theory, as we briefly indicated in Chapter Two where we discussed the evolution of psychological thinking, because it was a reflection on how different therapists understood the source of a patient's problem and then derived approaches to solving it that stimulated George Kelly to theorise a different way of responding to and addressing his patients' problems. We will now explore Kelly's ideas further beginning by reviewing how his ideas developed as a clinician and then going into more detail about aspects of his full theory that provide researchers with a coherent structure and set of instruments with which to explore the life-worlds of all kinds of people in a plethora of situations.

Origins and orientations

To summarise, we can consider the views of therapists working in different paradigms. For instance, a behaviourist would suspect that various external reinforcing mechanisms had impacted on the patient and thus would devise other external reinforcements to change the exhibited behaviour that was considered problematic. In contrast, a Freudian psychoanalyst would surmise the source of the same problem to be internal, unconscious forces, probably unresolved from early childhood, and suggest a suite of in-depth analysis encounters to probe the source and confront/ resolve the issue. Each of these therapists is orientated by the ideas and tools from their own branch of scientific psychology, their professional culture, in exploring and responding to the issue. If the patient is neither a behaviourist nor of a psycho-analytic persuasion, then s/he will likely have a different set of explanations, derived from experience and influenced by culture. Therefore Kelly suggested that it would be more helpful to ask the patient, exploring his/her ideas, and supporting revision or restructuring or reconstruing of these ideas. He translated that notion into his role of professor, telling his research students that they:

> should not overlook what their subjects [sic] have to contribute, for psychological research, as I see it, is a co-operative enterprise in which the subject joins the psy-chologist in making an enquiry. I am very sceptical of any piece of human research in which the subject's questions and contributions have not been elicited or have been ignored in the final analysis of results. (Kelly, 1969: 132)

As a researcher, then, Kelly proposed that his theory and its methods could help resolve some of the puzzles about why people do what they do, especially by focus-ing on how they understand or interpret the world they inhabit. In Activity 4.1 we invite you to begin to explore the world you inhabit.

Activity 4.1

Influences on personal construing

Consider how your personal, professional or disciplinary background influences how you respond to situations.

To help you begin to do this, we suggest that you consider *where* you are reading this. How would you describe it, and how might it appear, say, to a person interested in conditions conducive to study or to another interested in ambient light or to one concerned with access to educational resources? How might it seem to a person from another country – or another planet?

Each will have views influenced by a combination of personal experience/culture and pro-fessional experience/culture, and some perspectives might surprise you. Your own view of this location is influenced by your familiarity with it. You could be reading this in your own home, in which case a multitude of aspects surrounding you will have special significance; or you could be reading in a train travelling to or from work/study. If this is a regular commuter journey then you may well have become immune to the shakes and rattles and smells and noise around you that irritate or frighten or annoy an infrequent traveller.

Such considerations are important because how we view the world is reflected in how we act in it, and vice versa, while what response we get when we act in it in that way impacts on how we continue to act in it.

Now that you have responded to where you are reading, we can now consider that how you respond to *what* you are reading will be influenced by your previous research experience, your previous education and your professional/disciplinary background. One of us had a doctoral student who eventually shared how disorientating he found the first few months attending a research methods course. He had come from a background that combined both a strongly religious and a 'scientific' orientation that focused on seeking truth to add to the nuggets of truth already collected by researchers – an accumulative fragmentalist (Kelly, 1955a/1991); Harrison and Leitch, 1996). He found the talk, and the general acceptance of, a relativist interpretivist philosophy a challenge to his entire worldview. He expressed it thus: 'It was as if everything that I thought was real was being challenged; at first I just couldn't take the insecurity of everything being ambiguous.' Fortunately, he became used to our strange ways and enjoyed the challenge of learning alternative perspectives, changing and extending his hypotheses about the world alongside us and providing us with new perspectives too.

As we have noted, as a clinician and as a researcher Kelly saw value in considering people as personal scientists, continuously in the process of formulating hypotheses and testing them out for utility in their lives. He called these hypotheses 'constructs' and went on to formulate a comprehensive theory about the nature of these constructs, how they relate to each other, and how they can be explored and then perhaps challenged and changed. In his various roles as clinician, researcher and educator he elaborated his theory, and encouraged others to do so, challenging many of the traditions and tenets of the dominant schools of thought at that time. His theory can be seen as an optimistic approach to human construing, one that values individual dignity yet endows people with potential to learn throughout life:

> the successive revelation of events invites the person to place new constructions upon them whenever something unexpected happens. ... The constructions one places on events are working hypotheses, which are about to be put to the test of experience. As one's anticipations are successively revised in the unfolding sequence of events, the construction system undergoes a progressive evolution. (Kelly, 1991a: 50-1)

Interpretivist approaches are now mainstream, whereas they were new and therefore required considerable defence as a paradigm in Kelly's time. Similarly, we have now imbibed so much of the interpretivist-constructivist philosophy that no proponent would use the term 'subject' to describe those people whom we now consider as 'participants' in our research. The degree of 'participation' may range from being a co-researcher, in action research for instance, to one who is prepared to share some constructs with us so that we might better understand his/her perspective on a topic. Even in the latter case, though, the resultant data – the constructs and any links we perceive between them – belong to the participant, not to the researcher who has to seek permission to use them in documents about the research. You may sense a shift in power here compared to the post-positivist approach, discussed in Chapter Three.

Further, in keeping with his personal philosophy, Kelly put forward his theory, and all its ramifications into practice, as tentative hypotheses – inviting us to try them out as if they could be useful ways of exploring human life. We hope that we are following that tradition here, introducing you to his and others' ideas and research in an invitational mode – suggesting they might be useful for you to experiment with in your research practice. The formal tenets of PCP and our interpretations, presented next, pave the way to an explanation of the first steps in eliciting constructs (attitudes, values, beliefs, ways of approaching and dealing with their world) of your research participants.

Formal tenets and our interpretations in the field of research

Kelly wrote in the formal academic terminology of his times, initially for fellow psychologists, despite radically reinterpreting the traditional terms of that cultural group. As such, a first encounter with his theoretical position can be daunting to those new to PCP. We have therefore included his original main proposition (which he called the **fundamental postulate**) and the eleven main consequences and ramifications of this proposition (which he termed **corollaries**) as Appendix A for you to refer to in future when you have gained confidence in understanding the jargon of psychology from the 1950s. To support your growing confidence, we will describe the essence of those entities in this chapter, focusing on those most relevant to research activities and using our own words to convey what they mean to us as researchers. First, though, let us explore further some key terms that we will be using.

In Chapter Two we introduced the idea that human experience is irreducible to constituent parts (Raskin, 2012). One of Kelly's challenges to the status quo was therefore to formulate a more holistic notion about how people interact with their worlds, rejecting separation of cognition, emotion and action by combining them all into one term: 'construing'. Thus, construing means 'placing an interpretation on' something by combinations of thinking, feeling and reacting. The process of construing includes the generation, reinforcement, modification or dismissal of constructs. Constructs are personal creations which allow individuals to interpret or make discriminations between things. They allow similarities and differences between things to be recognised. We might recognise surfaces of some things as being smoother than others, for instance. So our construct of smoothness may allow us to differentiate surfaces along a dimension from 'very smooth indeed' to very 'not smooth' or 'rough'. Indeed, we cannot understand or recognise smoothness without being alert to 'what is not smooth', just as we cannot appreciate warmth without experiencing coldness and so on. With this understanding that the way we distinguish a characteristic or idea requires a reference point, a construct therefore has two facets. One facet is the primary focus of the construct, for example its smoothness. The other facet gives this primary focus a context, in this example, what not being smooth is like. A construct therefore a dimension with two poles – it is **bipolar**. Formally, the two poles are described as the **emergent pole** (the primary focus), and the **contrast pole** (the context).

The emergent pole (sometimes referred to as the **elicited pole** in research contexts) is simply the one that first comes to mind when considering an array of items.

The contrast pole is often implicit and may even be submerged or not simple to articulate. It is, according to Kelly, nevertheless there somewhere though it may not have been translated into words. We may describe our journey to work as 'difficult' (emergent pole), by which we mean that it contrasts with journeys that we experience as, to some degree, 'relaxing'. When we describe data as 'rich' (emergent pole) we are making a comparison to data that are 'superficial' (contrast pole). Because constructs are bipolar dimensions we can judge various journeys in terms of how difficult or relaxing there are, while data we encounter can be considered in terms of their degree of richness or superficiality. The journeys or data can be organised along the appropriate dimensions bounded by poles. We cannot, Kelly and common sense suggest, really understand the meaning of one **construct pole** without experience of the other. Further Explanation 4.1 elaborates on the use of verbal labels for our complex responses.

Further Explanation 4.1

Constructs and pole labels

A quick reminder with an important point – like all involved in psychology, we are trying to make sense of the complex and intangible 'goings-on' inside humans using our only means of communicating at a distance – language. Language has its limitations, a theme we will return to later, but it is the best tool available in this situation. Thus we are not suggesting that constructs are actual entities, but we are using them as a way of describing what seems to be happening during these 'goings-on'. Similarly, when we use verbal labels for the poles to describe/delineate these dimensions we must remember that these words are merely symbols, and are only the best attempt in the circumstances to describe reactions that are often hard to describe. Imagine you are late for a special event and someone just pips you to the only convenient parking spot, or the bus/train just pulls away before you can board it. That feeling is not an easy one to put into words and each of us might describe it differently – perhaps using our favoured expletive. The **contrast pole**, the feeling when we grab the last parking spot or leap on the public transport at the last second, is perhaps even harder to describe. Further, describing these reactions is not something we regularly or frequently do, during the business of our daily lives when we are just getting on with things, so we generally need help and guidance with the process of noting and articulating them. This is where the researcher, or in other circumstances a counsellor or clinician, comes in. If asked to do so, you might, for our example, use the words 'frustration versus relief', but those words are poor representations of the actual responses described above.

Thus, we construe things, events or people through a process of discrimination. We discriminate using constructs perceived as relevant in that situation and in relation to where we experience those phenomena as fitting on the dimensions between the poles of the constructs. Fransella and Bannister (1977: 5) provided a captivating example to explain this:

> When we say that Bill Bloggs is honest, we are not saying he is honest, he is not a chrysanthemum or a battleship or the square root of minus one. We are saying that Bill Bloggs is honest, he is not a crook.

Here the emergent pole is 'honest', while the contrast pole is 'a crook'. Bill Bloggs fits near the honest end of the dimension, while it may be that Jake Jepp fits nearer the crook pole. The description used in the contrast tells us more about what the label of the emergent pole really means to the construer. Another person might use the adjective 'honest' to describe a colleague but the contrast for that person might be 'beats about the bush', while for another it might be 'tries to wrap things up in kind words' or, worse, 'fiddles his data'. Each of these contrasts reveals something extra about the meaning of 'honest' for each person and the kinds of experiences that they have had. In fact, without the contrast pole, it would be extremely difficult to understand what the meaning is of a single idea, such as honesty. Try the following activity with friends, family or colleagues to get a sense of how exploring contrast poles can be illuminating.

Activity 4.2

Exploring contrast poles

Select a fairly innocuous topic (for us, the contrast to innocuous is 'tendentious' and we do not want to stimulate angry arguments!) and then devise a list of about five words to describe it. For example, you might choose a particular food dish and describe it as: pricey, good for you, readily available, like it a lot, easy to eat.

Then compile a list of the contrasts from your perspective of those descriptions. For our example, this might be: cheap as chips, junk food, hard to find, can't stand it, fussy to eat. (Note that our constructs - like our prior experience of food items - are probably not the same as yours!)

Then ask your chosen participants for each of your descriptors: 'If describing [food item] what would be a contrasting or opposite description to --?'

Consider the alternative meanings, subtle though they may be, that they demonstrate for words you have used. Beware if you ask teenagers for contrasts to words like 'yummy', because their alternative descriptions can be quite graphic!

In the chapter that follows we will examine how we can explore personal meanings in greater depth, so keep the results of your Activity 4.2 to hand to use later, after we have got to grips with some more precepts and assumptions embedded in PCP.

Our discussion here illustrates an important precept, which we have already touched on: that people are not merely driven by instinct, nor are they at the mercy of whatever external stimuli they encounter, rather they use a representational model of the world, constructed through their experience of it, to predict future experiences. That is, they form hypotheses (constructs) about what is going on or what things are like and act in relation to those hypotheses in ways that they have previously found to be appropriate, or at least has got them through the encounter. (We know what food to buy or choose from a menu, for instance.)

Further, as we noted in Chapter Two, life is a continuous process of hypothesising and reacting – it is as if we are forever 'in motion', mentally if not always obviously physically. We are testing out our hypotheses or constructs, predicting what will happen next, and sometimes we may find that our hypothesis/construct is challenged by unexpected reactions/happenings. (We might bite into a favoured food and find it tastes horrible.) If those challenges are small or few, we are likely to hang on to constructs that have been helpful in the past. (We put the bad taste experience down to the food being 'off'.) For constructs that are very important to us, such as seeing a close friend as trustworthy and ourselves as being a good judge of character, then it will take a lot of evidence to the contrary to make us revise our construct. Such resistant constructs, often ones that have helped us to survive for a long time, may become subconscious or implicit notions of the 'way things are' for us. These deep, resistant constructs form the **core of our construct system**. More loosely held, more readily changed constructs are said to be **peripheral** in the construct system. In many ways peripheral constructs are more experimental, ones that we are tentatively trying out based on little experience. An example of a core construct might be about whether different situations or people make you feel valued or loved, whereas a more peripheral construct example could concern whether your emails get noticed and responded to amidst the many others that people receive. Core constructs are the basis of who you are; they give some consistency to the way you are in the world. Peripheral constructs are more fluid and less central to our selves. They allow us to learn to be different without shattering the inner being completely.

In addition to being located at some point on the continuum between being core and being in a more peripheral part of a construct system, constructs form a hierarchical network. Any particular construct is likely to be **subordinate** or **superordinate** to other particular constructs, as we mentioned in Chapter Two. A construct about work colleagues held by person P could be 'dedicated to our project' in contrast to 'our project is not a main interest'. A superordinate construct that includes dedication to the project might be 'enjoy working with' (emergent pole) – 'feel distant from' (implicit pole). On the other hand, one particular very subordinate construct, probably one of several, might be 'responds quickly to my emails' as opposed to 'only responds when it suits'.

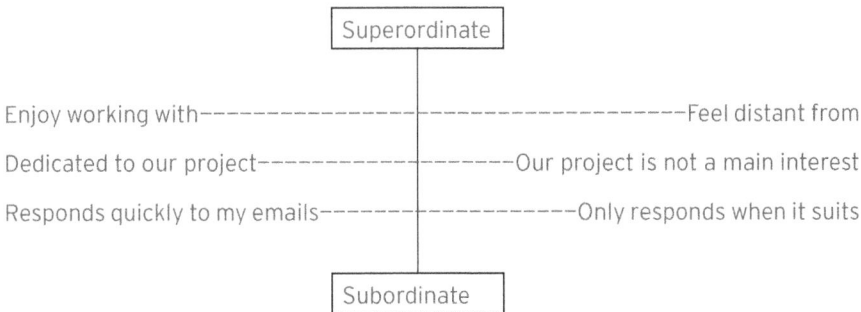

```
                        ┌─────────────────┐
                        │  Superordinate  │
                        └─────────────────┘
                                 │
Enjoy working with──────────────────┼─────────────────Feel distant from
                                 │
Dedicated to our project─────────────┼───────Our project is not a main interest
                                 │
Responds quickly to my emails──────┼───────────Only responds when it suits
                                 │
                        ┌─────────────────┐
                        │   Subordinate   │
                        └─────────────────┘
```

Remember that these are one person's perceptions or constructions of another within a particular situation. P may not apply these constructs to all people, only those she/he has worked with. You may not find these particular constructs relevant to your life, but you will have your own constructs about colleagues based on your own experiences. In the example above one particular colleague, C, might well also consider the joint project to be important but demonstrates this in ways other than answering emails speedily. Because our original construer, P, takes speed of replying to emails as an indicator of dedication to the project, s/he may misunderstand C's behaviour with emails, relate this to disinterest in the project and thus find C less enjoyable to work with. Being a construct close to the core for P, this is unlikely to change readily, but there may be some hope that C could join P's favoured colleagues group if the construct related to speed of response to emails is challenged and amended. For instance, P may learn that limited availability of a computer, or a phobia about emails, or even showing dedication by spending hours working on the project's statistics, restricts speed of email response from C. This could modify P's perception of C.

How easy it is for P to change that construct will also depend to some extent on the degree to which the team culture favours rapid responses to emails and how open P is to understanding the constructs of C (such as prioritising the statistics). On the other hand, C, who values P as a colleague, could discover from P's reactions and interactions that rapid email response is important to P and therefore make an effort to respond more quickly to P's emails, if not others. This is an example of one of the corollaries in PCP, which is the sociality **corollary** (see Further Explanation 4.2).

The tale above is also an illustration of the key concept of **constructive alternativism**, as described in Chapter Two, that there is always the potential to perceive or construe things in another way. This is in contrast to the philosophy of **accumulative fragmentalism**, that facts or truths are gradually gathered about the world as it is. Either or both of our friends P and C might change their worldviews about emails and the meaning of the speed of responses to them, about what actions demonstrate commitment to a project and/or about each other as colleagues or even friends.

Now we can get to grips with some of the other key tenets of this approach: see Further Explanation 4.2. In this box we have ordered the fundamental postulate of PCP and its corollaries so that those related to an individual's ways of perceiving or construing their world form the first part while the last two relate to how we interact with others. The first part of each explanation is our interpretation of Kelly's words which are presented in brackets.

◢ Further Explanation 4.2

Key PCP tenets translated

When George Kelly formalised his theory (Kelly 1955/1991) he postulated that we respond to situations (events, people, things) in our world in relation to the way they meet our expectations. (The **fundamental postulate**: 'A person's processes are psychologically channellized by the ways in which they anticipate events'.)

One consequence of this is that we build expectations or constructs by comparing particular situations to ones that we have experienced previously, responding in ways that were previously successful. We look for patterns in our experience and respond in ways that worked previously. (The *construction corollary*: 'A person anticipates events by construing their replication'.)

Constructs are related to each other in a hierarchical system. (The *organisation corollary*: 'Each person characteristically evolves, for their convenience in anticipating events, a construction system embracing ordinal relationships between constructs'.)

Each construct in the system has two contrasting poles that is, they are *bipolar*, much like the yin and yang of Chinese philosophy. (The *dichotomy corollary*: 'A person's construction system is composed of a finite number of dichotomous constructs'.)

When we recognise a situation as fitting one particular pole of a dichotomous construct (an elicited pole) it is likely to be the pole that gives us the best chance of confirming that construct and elaborating the construct system, helping us to understand, thus anticipate, the world more effectively, from our perspective. (The *choice corollary*: 'People choose for themselves that alternative in a dichotomised construct through which they anticipate the greater possibility for the elaboration of their system'.)

Constructs can change as we experience similar situations and responses to our actions in them. This is the fundament of learning – reconstrual and elaboration of constructs. (The *experience corollary*: 'A person's construct system varies as they successively construe the replication of events'.)

Constructs are each relevant to a particular set of situations and not to others. You may be interested in whether the people close to you, and who may share your bathroom, leave the lid on or off the toothpaste, but not interested in applying that construct to your bank manager or the bus driver – it only applies to a particular range of people. (The *range corollary*: 'A construct is convenient for the anticipation of a finite range of events only'.)

Some constructs, and construct systems, can be flexible enough to cover new situations or responses to them; others are more rigid. If you find yourself sharing a bathroom at a conference venue with a colleague, your toothpaste lid construct may be permeable enough to accommodate that person, if only temporarily, but it still will not apply to the bus driver. (The *modulation corollary*: 'The variation in a person's construction system is limited by the permeability of the constructs within whose **range of convenience** the variants lie'.)

Because the system is like a complex web with some sets of constructs being relevant only to particular circumstances, we can hold simultaneously constructs that are apparently contradictory. For instance, we may hold strong ideals about the freedom of individuals, which may well be contradicted by our parental values with regard to our young teenagers. (The *fragmentation corollary*: 'A person may successively employ a variety of construction systems which are inferentially incompatible with each other'.)

We each experience situations differently because we have had different opportunities to experience them previously and received different responses to our actions. You may not be or have been a teenager's parent, indeed you may even be a teenager, so may not appreciate the tension inherent in the example above. (The *individuality corollary*: 'People differ from each other in their construction of events'.)

When we respond in a similar way to another person in a particular situation it is likely that we share a similar way of construing it. So if you have been a teenager's parent, you may view the different aspects of individual freedom in a similar way to others like you. (The *commonality corollary*: 'To the extent that one person employs a construction of experience which is similar to that employed by another, their processes are psychologically similar to those of the other person'.)

If we can understand why someone responds in a certain way to a particular situation then we can interact with them in a beneficial way. Thus, if you can remember your own teenage years you may recognise and empathise with the contradictory constructs described previously. (The *sociality corollary*: 'To the extent that one person construes the construction process of another, they may play a role in a social process involving the other person'.)

Constructs have other facets that it is worth a researcher becoming familiar with. One particularly important one is that constructs are mental entities which only acquire verbal labels when we try to articulate them to ourselves or to others. Some may well have been formed before we could speak and may never have gained a verbal label – the feeling when cradled by a parent, for instance. We may recognise that feeling again later in life and just know that it feels safe, or right, or secure, with or without necessarily giving it a label. We might think of it as a 'gut response'. In construct theory these are known as 'pre-verbal constructs' – and are often hard to put into words even if we try. This has implications for our practice of eliciting constructs, which we discuss Chapter Five. Pre-verbal constructs are not only generated in our early years, since we can have 'gut reactions' to new things we encounter throughout our lives. We do not need to conjure up extraordinarily nasty or wonderful things to illustrate this – a simple consideration of, say, the skin on rice pudding or a plate of tripe may draw a construct from you which may be a positive response of lip-smacking or a negative exclamation like 'ugh!', or a simple turning up or twitching of your nose! (Remember that constructs can have different proportions of cognitive, emotional and physical reactions – described as cognitive, affective and conative in some of the literature.)

A related important point to remember is that even when we do articulate our constructs, give them verbal labels, these labels are only the best symbols within our repertoires to represent our meanings. Some of us have larger vocabularies than others, or a greater facility with words or even a greater motivation to convey things as accurately as possible at any particular time, under any particular circumstance. This too has ramifications both for how we conduct our research (see Chapters Five to Seven) and how we interpret our results (see Chapter Ten).

Another feature that is worth mentioning to researchers (there are several more that clinicians might encounter or you might be interested in as you become more adept at constructivist thinking) who may encounter it when exploring participants' worlds is the notion of loose and tight construing. A tight construct is unchanging, always leading to the same response, whereas loose construing can lead to varying responses as we experiment with how we might perceive the world. As we continue to test out the construct and find more about its applicability, we tighten it up. Loose constructs allow us to be creative, whereas tight constructs make us more predictable. Kelly proposed a creativity cycle in which we loosen some constructs, perhaps through imaginative play with ideas, and then tighten them again in a new form to allow for a more structured response. You might recognise that very rigid constructs might lead to stereotyping and prejudice, whereas too loose construing might make us difficult, capricious people to live with. Nevertheless, Kelly suggests that it can be useful to loosen a construct or two occasionally to aid creativity. He describes loose constructs thus:

> The loose construction is like a rough sketch which may be preliminary to a carefully crafted design. The sketch permits flexible interpretation. This or that feature is not precisely placed. (Kelly, 1991a: 357)

If your previous forays into research have been dominated by a neo-positivist paradigm (see Chapter Three) or a particular leaning towards another theory of human behaviour then, since you have reached this far into this book, you presumably have loosened somewhat your constructs about possible ways to conduct research. We hope that by the time you reach the end of the book and have had time to experiment with the approach and techniques, as we will urge you to do in the next and subsequent chapters, you will tighten them enough to include personal construct approaches within your repertoire of potential ways to address certain research questions.

It might help if you keep the key principles of the theory, summarised below, in mind as you read on:

- Constructivist researchers recognise that each person individually constructs a model of the world they inhabit.
- Researchers try to suspend ('bracket') their views on a topic sufficiently to allow and encourage others to describe a particular aspect of their world as they perceive it, without prompts or censure.
- Each person's model is based on their experience of results of their experiments using hypotheses about how things, events, people are.
- Researchers recognise that the template of constructs that their participants place on their worlds reflects their experience of it to date, and those experiences may be very different to their own.
- Schwandt (1994: 118) saw the essence of constructivist research as having 'the goal of understanding the complex world of lived experience from the point of view of those who live it ... as an abiding concern ... for the **emic** point of view, for understanding meaning, for grasping the actor's definition of a situation, for **Verstehen**'.
- The model can change and develop over time through further experimentation and experience, although some aspects in the core of the model are resilient to change since they have in the past been, for example, critical to survival.
- The researcher cannot assume that the construct system or particular constructs will remain constant beyond the point when they are elicited. The very act of elicitation can result in reflection and change, though some constructs may not change despite challenge.
- Lakatos (1970: 104) suggested that 'conceptual frameworks can be developed and also replaced by new, *better* ones; it is *we* who create our "prisons" and we can also critically demolish them'.
- This echoes Kelly (1991a: 11) who said: 'We assume that all of our present interpretations of the universe are subject to revision or replacement. This is a basic statement .... We take the stand that there are always some alternative constructions available to choose among in dealing with the world. No one needs to paint himself into a corner; no one needs to be completely hemmed in by circumstances; no one needs to be a victim of his biography. We call this philosophical position constructive alternativism.'
- The model can be described as a complex system of constructs, each of which is a bipolar dimension along which items can be arranged to differentiate them from each other.
- Researchers can better understand participants' constructs by having them try to articulate what the contrast is to the words used to describe something or someone (the emergent pole) and then consider how various examples fit along the dimension between the emergent and contrast poles.
- Constructs have differing proportions of thinking, feeling and doing components. They can differentiate few or a wide range of items and can be apparently contradictory when they are used in different contexts or at different times or applied to different sets of items.

- Researchers should recognise that constructs are not simply cognitive, thought-out responses but generally contain varying degrees of emotional and physical reaction. For example, dislike of something might be a conscious, rational evaluation of something, an emotional reaction to it, or a physical repulsion, or any combination of those three.
- Researchers can explore sections of the system in order to gain a better understanding of the way in which a person (alone or in a group) interacts with a specific aspect of their world (contextual in time and space).
- It is impossible to explore a person's whole construct system in all its complexity, not even our own, but small portions can be investigated using carefully selected tools as described in Chapters Five, Six and Seven.
- Researchers can seek out constructs and relationships between constructs in order to note individual differences and similarities between individuals (commonality) by trying to see the world through another's constructs (sociality).
- There is a range of analysis techniques that supports interpretation of others' worlds, and some of these are described in Chapter Ten.
- Researchers may find the way that others view the world quite challenging to their own view, so they have to loosen, temporarily at least, their constructs a little to understand that the reality for the other person is different to their own.
- Becoming a constructivist researcher can be challenging to the security of one's own beliefs and understandings about the world, each challenge to one's constructs potentially causing revision, otherwise known as learning.

Summary

We discussed the notion that perceptions of the world vary by individual and over time for the same individual. We then introduced Kelly's personal construct theory which provides a logical and integrated set of principles that explain how such perceptions or constructs influence the thinking, feeling and behaviour of individuals and groups of individuals. This theory and the methods derived from it provide a sound basis for exploring/researching one's own and others' worlds.

Suggested further reading

Dalton, P. and Dunnett, G. (1999) *A Psychology for Living: Personal Construct Theory for Professionals and Clients*. Farnborough: EPCA Publications. (Previously published in 1992 by Wiley.)

Chapters 1–4 explore the key aspects of PCP theory, relating it particularly to understanding oneself. It is a particularly accessible account with myriad examples carved into a structure based on the kinds of questions asked by students, colleagues and friends of the authors.

Fransella, F. (2005) *The Essential Practitioner's Handbook of Personal Construct Psychology.* Chichester: Wiley.

Although the major portion of the book is devoted to clinical aspects of PCP, the first three chapters provide a different articulation of some of the ideas presented in the foregoing chapter.

PART II

Practicalities of engaging in constructivist research

This part of the book contains details to enable researchers to plan and execute a research project that involves the exploration of people's meanings, including the analysis and interpretation of those meanings. Practical hints, tips and examples lace the discussion of essential components of project implementation.

5

Exploring personal realities

- Individual differences in participants which influence choice of elicitation technique
- Eliciting constructs in simple conversation
- Construct ownership
- Elaborating and exploring constructs
- The boundaries of the researcher's role

Introduction

In the preceding chapter we emphasised that each person lives within a uniquely constructed world. Part of that unique construction is the way in which they most readily access their ideas and share them with others. Constructivist approaches place an onus on researchers to strive hard to capture the personal meaning portrayed in the language of participants within their research. Therefore, when collecting research data, an interactive and more **idiographic** approach is taken in which control is shared between the researcher and participants. The researcher's aim is 'verstehen' – an understanding and illumination of the rich diversity of meanings participants have in relation to their lives. In order to help participants to illuminate and share their personal meanings in relation to the focus of the research, constructivist researchers try to provide opportunities for reflection and articulation that suit the style, experiences and preferences of their participants.

Those participants may have had from few to many, rich to impoverished, experiences, no matter what their age, and may have a poor or extended vocabulary in relation to the focal topic, no matter what their level of education and literacy.

Whatever their background or circumstances, some people are more comfortable with either words or images; they may love or hate numbers, and be readily able either to quantify or to judge the quality of particular entities. One of the joys of using a constructivist approach is that Kelly and others after him have devised numerous techniques covering a wide range of styles and processes so that it is possible to select one or more that will be suitable for specific participants in distinct circumstances, or, indeed, with skill and practice, to adapt techniques appropriately or invent new ones. In the next chapter we will explore a broad, but by no means exclusive, range of techniques that you might find useful in different contexts. We will indicate from our experience the circumstances and/or participant groups in which they have been found valuable. First, though, we will focus on the simplest technique of eliciting constructs during conversation. This will enable us to introduce further facets of constructs and some of the processes that will reappear when using other more elaborate techniques. In the process you will have the chance to explore some more of your own constructs before letting yourself loose on the wider public!

A conversational approach

In Chapter One we alluded to the possibility of incorporating PCP-type questions into interviews or even questionnaires. In this section we will explore what this type of questioning involves because it will form the basis of many different techniques for accessing the less publicly accessible inner worlds of others and, indeed, even our own inner worlds. A conversation is the normal, comfortable way in which we communicate with others and thus is a good starting point from which to begin to develop this form of questioning technique. Indeed, Potter and Edwards (1992) suggest that conversation is the root model for the analysis of social interactions.

In everyday conversations we usually adapt our language to the company in which we are engaged: the tendency is to use less formal, less technical, fewer-syllabled words in the home, with children and with friends than we do in professional circumstances. We unconsciously or subconsciously adjust our vocabulary to words we think the others will be familiar with, so we are sure that our partner or spouse will know just what we mean when we say 'pass the TV thingy' (remote control), just as we might say to our lab technician 'would you mind switching on the centrifuge?' or invite a visiting professor to 'join a colloquium on epistemology in research'. In those conversations we assume that the words we use and the concepts we discuss are mutually understood in similar ways, though we sometimes find ourselves confused to discover they are not – as was illustrated at the beginning of Chapter One in the discussion about opening an icon. Our task as researchers is to check out our assumptions and the assumptions of others, and to seek out the meanings they have attributed to words and concepts, in other words, to explore with them their constructs.

Let us start with an everyday example, discussing with a friend a recent holiday she took – see Activity 5.1.

Activity 5.1

Making assumptions

Your friend describes her foreign holiday thus: 'It was a total disaster. The weather was cold, the hotel full of old folk and the entertainment was naff.' Pause for a moment and conjure up a picture for yourself of what this holiday was like. What temperature do you think it was, how old were the 'old folk' and what sort of entertainment might it have been?

It is likely that your first thoughts will reflect your own ideas about what constitutes cold, old and naff.

Does your picture change if you think of your friend as being 60 years old, well travelled and of a lively disposition? What if she is 40 years old, has seldom left England and has difficulty walking? What if she is 19, has previously been on exotic holidays with her parents and loves to dance?

We will make different assumptions depending on how well we know the other person and what experiences we have had ourselves. Your authors have varied ages, predispositions and backgrounds, so the 'cold' could range from 12 to 20 degrees Celsius, 'old' from 50 to 85 years, and the naff entertainment from karaoke through hang-gliding to bingo.

We could, of course, explore our friend's constructs further in the course of normal conversation by asking what the daytime temperature was, how old, roughly, the other hotel guests were and what the entertainment was. That would give us some specifics, and show our personal interest in her experience, but we could explore further to elaborate our understanding of her experience, should our friend tolerate us going into researcher mode, by working with what we understand of constructs and construct systems. For instance, we could go on to investigate the range of temperature that would be comfortable for our friend: what would be too hot a temperature for you on holiday? We could find out what would constitute a young age for fellow guests. Even more interesting might be to explore what she means by the description 'naff'. She would have her own words to describe 'naff' and it would almost certainly bring us closer to a joint meaning. However, in order to gain deeper insights, and linking to our understanding of constructs being bipolar, discussed in Chapter Four, you might ask her what the contrast of naff is. If she said 'exciting' or 'meaningful' or 'stimulating', each of these would give you a much clearer understanding of what she means by naff. (What would it be for you? Stimulating or restful or challenging or energetic, or even 'being left alone to make my own entertainment'?)

Thus the cold, old and naff are what we have been labelling as elicited poles of constructs, while the contrast descriptions represent the contrast or **submerged poles**. However, they only represent the outer edges of the construct dimensions. We could go further to find out our friend's preferences in relation to those dimensions by simply asking what temperature, age group and type of entertainment she currently prefers while on holiday, which may be somewhere between the elicited and contrast poles. These latter points, holiday and now, are important because her ideas about temperature, companions and activities every day, or at work, or next year or when she was younger may be very different.

We have used the example of a conversation with a friend to illustrate that, as Kelly proposed, we are scientist-like in our commonplace encounters, curious about situations, events, people and things, but we are also, as are scientists, prone to make assumptions based on our own experience. We can, however, in informal or more formal ways gain more information by using some more probing questions. We must raise a caveat here. We mentioned above the notion of our friend tolerating us going into researcher mode as we probed further. If we had continued in this vein it could be that our friend would wonder about, and become annoyed by, the more interrogating turn of the conversation. They could see it as prying or snooping rather than understandable curiosity or empathy. It is very important that both parties in a dialogue understand and agree to the nature of that dialogue and acceptable procedures within it. This is most often, especially in a social setting, an unsaid understanding or agreement, established by years of experience, which might be modified in real time by nuances in the tone or non-verbal behaviours such as degree of head nodding to indicate understanding (relatively slow nods), simple agreement (slightly faster nods) or agreement with a desire to put own point of view (rapid nods). We will delve into this further in the next chapter, but keep this in mind as we investigate further modes of questioning.

As researchers working with participants (again, see the following chapter for ways of establishing an appropriate context and rapport for such situations), we can learn more using a procedural framework for asking exploratory questions that help us map out their constructs, than by informal unstructured conversation.

It is important at the outset to agree not only the purpose and context of the conversation but also the focus of the activity. Thus, both parties must recognise that the conversation is a form of research activity in which the researcher is using research skills to help the person identify his or her constructs in relation to a particular topic and to share them with the researcher. Although the researcher may, and would be advised to, adopt a friendly stance, this is not simply a friendly chat. Nor is it any form of counselling or therapy. Although these techniques are used in both counselling and therapy it is important that researchers do not stray into areas within which they have no expertise or which go beyond what has been agreed with the participant. We will also discuss this further in the next chapter, providing guidance on how to deal with ethics and potential ethical dilemmas.

Working through a flexible structure

Since working with constructivist approaches has the potential to delve deeply into a person's perspectives and feelings as well as actions, it is important that both researcher and participant agree the topic to be considered and why the researcher might want to know about it and is interested in the participant's views. Thus the research conversation (or interview) should begin with explicit attention to these points. The dialogue might go something like that described in Procedural Example 5.1a.

Procedural Example 5.1a

Initiating a research conversation

Researcher (R):	Thank you for agreeing to talk to me about your perspectives on your professional activity of [insert relevant topic] for my research on how [people with this professional job title] understand and deal with these kind of situations at work.
Participant (P):	Glad to be able to help – some parts of my job are pretty tricky to handle.
R:	Yes, it will be useful if we can explore that trickiness further. Will it be OK if I ask you some questions about what your job entails if we agree that you can refuse to answer any that make you feel uncomfortable in any way, or even stop the discussion altogether, without any pressure or comeback?
P:	Sure, what do you need to know?
R:	Well, first let us think about your job in general terms. How would you describe it to someone who isn't a [professional job title]?
P:	(Provides a general description, giving a short list of activities involved in it.)

This gives us a basic structure that can be elaborated by also requesting permission to take notes or record the conversation. You might also agree a signal (a raised hand perhaps) with the participant so they might indicate when the depth of probing has reached a point beyond which they do not wish to go. You could insert in the example above any professional role and later focus down onto particular activities to explore constructs further, for instance a doctor informing a patient about a diagnosis, a manager issuing a warning to a worker, a professor examining a doctoral candidate, a lawyer reviewing a client's case, or a policeman stopping and searching a suspect. For each, the researcher's goal might be to identify good practice and areas in which professionals might seek further guidance. The language might change somewhat if the participant were a less linguistically sophisticated person such as a child or other kind of worker, but the features would remain the same: transparency of purpose, process and opportunity to opt out.

The next step would be to examine further the descriptions provided, taking care not to put words into the other person's mouth. This is one of the most difficult aspects of constructivist interviewing/conversing! As we discussed in Chapter Two, one of the key benefits of well-conducted constructivist research is that it avoids researcher bias by seeking the descriptions of the participants' worlds in their own words rather than seeking their agreement or otherwise to the researcher's descriptions, none of which they might actually ever use in their own lives. Thus, as these descriptions are enquired into further, the researcher must patiently wait for the participant to articulate their constructs in their own way with no prompting with suggestions from the researcher. See Procedural Example 5.1b.

Procedural Example 5.1b

Probing descriptions provided – exploring the contrast poles

R: You said that [the activity] demands considerable expertise. How would you describe an activity that does not demand such expertise?

P: Well. Simply one which anybody can do, doesn't need a professional person to do it.

R: OK. Can you give me an example of that – perhaps something that you do at work but which you don't need to be a professional to do?

P: Ah, yes, every day I end up having to order something from stores. It's just a bureaucratic chore.

R: Tell me more about these bureaucratic chores. What is it about them …?

P: Now you have got me going – I spent years studying and then find that half my day is wasted doing stuff that a kid in school could do. Those bureaucratic things, they don't demand any professional knowledge or sensitivity, just common sense.

R: So are you saying that [the activity] demands sensitivity?

P: Certainly – it can lead to a tricky situation that needs a professional approach.

R: I see … perhaps we could explore further what expertise is needed for such tricky situations. Can you give me an example of one?

P: Let me think. … Only yesterday – you did say this would be anonymised and confidential, didn't you? – I had one that was a bit tricky (goes on to describe the situation).

From this questioning we can see that the researcher has asked the participant to provide the contrast pole to the elicited one by asking for an example of an activity that does not fit that elicited descriptor (ordering something from stores). So now they have two specific activities that fit a construct described by the poles: demands considerable expertise – bureaucratic chore. This is a simple example of a questioning technique we call **laddering down**, sometimes in the literature called **pyramiding.** It is a way of going into depth and might involve questions like 'how would you recognise that'? or 'what does it look like?'. Further, the participant has revealed the view that one aspect of professional expertise is sensitivity to deal with 'tricky situations' – the researcher has not introduced any new descriptors of her/his own but rather has echoed back the participant-provided descriptors (in this case 'tricky situation') in searching for further constructs. This could lead at this point to an examination of this construct 'tricky' when applied to a work situation. (Note that the participant has already revealed that a bureaucratic chore can be described by 'stuff a kid in school could do' as opposed to what a professional person might do, and 'requires common sense only' as opposed to 'requires sensitivity'.) Let us see how that might pan out in Procedural Example 5.1c.

Procedural Example 5.1c

Laddering up

R: That's interesting – you also referred to this tricky situation as challenging. Although it may seem obvious to you, let's clarify. Which do you prefer, situations that are tricky and challenging or situations that simply require common sense to resolve?

P: Oh yeah ...well... of course, when it comes down to it I prefer a bit of a challenge, sorting out the trickiness of it.

R: Why is that then?

P: It's as I said, it allows me to use my professional skills – do stuff I am good at that few others can cope with.

R: So why is that important to you?

P: I guess ... (pause, deep breath) I guess I like to feel respected, valued for what I can do.

As you might recognise, this line of 'why' questioning is leading us into core constructs – that is, more deeply into the core self, and is what is termed **laddering up**. The conversation shows that for this person it is important (as it is to most of us) to feel valued, and the kind of work activity preferred is the kind that demonstrates professional skills and thus engenders respect.

This excursion into core role constructs might cause the participant to feel that they are exposing their inner self, which they are, and it can be helpful to reduce the pressure following such exploration. The pause and deep breath in the participant's response give an indication that this was not easy task, revealing this personal information, and it is best not to delve further than your espoused purpose requires. In our example case of exploring 'dealing with difficult situations at work' it is useful to know that, for this participant at least, it is a professionally fulfilling task which gains respect, but we need not know further what being respected means personally. There is no need to pry, or ladder up, further with a 'why is that important' question. The dividing line between asking questions as research and prying is a 'tricky situation' in its own right – you will have to draw on your own research integrity, asking yourself 'do I need to know more of this for my research – is it essential?'

Thus the next step would be to either link into another lower-level construct that has emerged during the conversation or to begin to ladder down again. See Procedural Example 5.1d for the former and Procedural Example 5.1e for the latter.

Procedural Example 5.1d

Picking up another construct description

R: I can see that being valued is important. Earlier you talked about bureaucratic activities that only need common sense. Do you ever at work have to engage in activities that don't require either common sense or professional skills?

P: Ah! That's a good one. Let me think. Oh ... of course ... there are things like typing up notes, that kind of thing, needs a bit of brain power ... but then ... there are the things that are sort of mindless, filing notes for instance.

R: So does that mean then that there are things that need brain power and others that are mindless?

P: Yeah, yeah, the typing up is somewhere between because you need to summarise the main points but ... there's little creativity involved, but filing, that's when you can switch off and just stick the notes in the right file.

R: So this is one of the ... less challenging things then?

P: Sure, but ... I don't mind that, it has to be done and it gives me breathing space.

So, now we are learning much more – and simply by and large by repeating back what we have been told, using the same words, but picking up threads.

Procedural Example 5.1e

Laddering down

R: I can see that being valued is important. How would you describe what it is like when you are clearly not being valued?

P: That is the kind of thing, I would say ... being taken for granted - or even disrespected. So yes - there is a continuum - feeling really valued through being taken for granted to being, well, you know, being disrespected.

R: Can you give me any example of an activity at work that would make you feel taken for granted?

P. It doesn't happen often but occasionally ... when a colleague expects you to pick up something of theirs without a good reason, no 'by your leave', and probably no 'thank you' either.

R: What sort of 'something' might that be then?

Again, the echoing-back technique is being used but now the questions are of the 'what' and 'how' type. We are learning about a range of activities that are being construed using an ever growing number of construct descriptions that are being elicited from the participant rather than supplied to them. We are also eliciting rather than supplying the range of activities in which they engage at work. To get a sense of what this kind of questioning feels like from the participant's perspective, try out Activity 5.2.

Activity 5.2

Stepping in the shoes of the participant – a practice task

Earlier we said that you could apply this set of questions to just about any professional role, one of which is the researcher role. Can you identify any particular tricky/challenging/

difficult (choose your own descriptor) situations that you have experienced as a researcher or indeed as, say, a student in higher education? What would the contrast pole of that descriptor be? Which kind of activity, between the two described, do you prefer? Why is that? Why is that important to you? What would the opposite of that be like? What activity might fit your contrast description?

You may even make yourself feel a little uncomfortable if you pry too far, so do not go beyond your comfort zone but recognise the physical symptoms you might inadvertently display as you get near to your own core (perhaps shifting in your seat, getting flushed, or fidgeting with a pen). We will come back to them in the next chapter.

These apparently simple questions can, clearly, lead us through a complex exploration of a person's constructs about their different activities. In our Procedural Example 5.1a–e our participant was articulate and provided several constructs as the conversation evolved (though remember that 'construct' is our technical term – they are just providing thoughts and feelings). Sometimes it can be difficult to catch every one of them as they pop out, so it is useful to keep a pencil and paper handy to note words quickly as the conversation flows. You might find it a useful exercise to explore just how many constructs – at least the emergent poles of constructs – appear during a conversation – see Activity 5.3.

Activity 5.3

Finding constructs in conversations

To start off with, you could review the dialogue in Procedural Example 5.1a–e, noting any emergent poles. We found about 16, listed at the end of the chapter (see if you agree).

Next you could listen in to any conversation: on public transport, in a television soap opera, for instance, doing a bit of 'construct spotting'. This will make you somewhat alert to some of the ways in which you yourself reveal your own worldview constructs, which can be a little disorientating at first – even a casual comment to the postman about the weather gives information about your preferences, expectations, mood, attitude, and so on through your choice of words: 'What a dismal day, I won't be gardening today!' or 'Isn't it dull, but at least I can get on with writing without being tempted outside' or 'So glad to see some clouds, it's been way too hot, hasn't it?' or 'Hoping we get some rain, the flowers need it!'

For some construct types found in this activity, see the postscript at the end of this chapter.

Conversational construct spotting can be both illuminating and even entertaining, but it can also be subject to either random chance, if you just listen to chatter, or require skill if you are also steering the conversation with a particular research goal in mind. Thus there are times when a more structured approach to eliciting constructs can be useful, as we describe next. Until you gain confidence in steering the conversation as described, you might find it reassuring to begin with a more structured technique to exploring the worlds of others, and your own, using a constructivist approach.

Remaining flexible but with more structure

A technique that is more structured for eliciting constructs involves asking the participant to name a series of items that represent the topic of conversation that you wish to explore. In the formal theory this topic of conversation is known as the **universe of discourse**, recognising that it is a discourse or conversation on a bounded topic that is the essence of these techniques. For your participants this is the focus of your research conversation, which you should keep in mind yourself and remind them of regularly so that you both focus on the purpose of the research, and concentrate on only a particular part of their construct systems, rather than lots of parts. This choice of items, which are named **elements** in the theory, is important. The plan is to identify those elements that for the participant represent the universe of discourse so that you gain a good understanding of their constructs about the topic of interest.

When guiding your participants in selecting elements, urge them to consider items that are really representative of the area in focus, covering the full range of possibilities. For instance, if we stick with the example described earlier in this chapter in which the focus was exploring a professional job, then the items/elements would be the activities involved in that work and you would seek to have your participant select a representative set, ones that cover both the key professional aspects and the day-to-day chores that are involved. One way to help them think about their selection might be to suggest that they consider what activities they had engaged in that day, some they regularly engaged in, perhaps a couple that they seldom engaged in but are important, then ask them to make a list from which you will later ask them to choose some to work with that cover the range. These elements also need to meet some other criteria. The first one to consider is the level of specificity of the activity elicited. It is helpful if elements are at about the same level, so, for instance, if most of the elements are relatively general (such as advising clients/patients, conferring with colleagues, attending meetings) then encourage a more specific activity example to be turned into one at a similar level (for instance, 'writing up notes' could become 'dealing with paperwork'). Another criterion to consider is the homogeneity of the elements. Continuing our example, if a participant proffered as an activity 'travelling to and from work' you might explore with them, without criticising their choice, whether that fits well with the other activities listed. If it does not fit well, for instance if the journey to and from work is a time to relax and catch up with friends on Facebook, it might not be a useful element to include in the analysis. Bear in mind, though, that for some people the journey to and from work might indeed be part of the job, while for many of us it is an opportunity to catch up with essential reading or review the problems of the day. For the latter, some encouragement to explain or particularise the travel activities might be fruitful.

To help both your participants to explain and you to understand, it is advisable to try to identify elements that are concrete examples, readily brought to mind.

For instance, those active verbs given above – advising, conferring, attending – are easier to picture than more abstract ones such as thinking, feeling, reacting, or hoping. However, even they might be quite challenging for either a researcher or participant new to the research approach to deal with. It might be more helpful, before focusing in on the activities of the participant's job, to start with some much more concrete elements, say the people the person works with, as elements in an exercise to explore what and how each contributes to the work of the team or group. In such an instance again a representative set that covers the range and is relatively homogeneous could be sought. The number of elements in the final selection must also be easy to keep in mind and manipulate. Psychologists expert in the human memory suggest that we can keep in working memory between five and nine items, so that is a fair guide to how many elements might be chosen for the rest of the task (see Chapters Six, Seven and Nine for some further practical tips.)

To continue with our example, suppose that the elements chosen are: own role, direct superior, junior colleague, administrator, IT support person, peer colleague, clerical assistant. It will make the task easier and more productive if your participant thinks of the actual people in those roles rather than the more abstract job title, though they might prefer to be discreet by using initials or a pseudonyms rather than sharing actual names with you.

Now that we have identified elements, those aspects of the territory (universe of discourse) we wish to explore that exemplify its range and scope, we will take you through a process that helps you to elicit constructs using these elements. This is known as the **triadic elicitation** process. This involves first selecting three (hence triadic) of the elements, preferably at random, and asking the question 'how are two of these similar to and different from the third in relation to what they do at work?' This is to elicit an emergent pole of a construct relevant to our 'universe of discourse'. So, in our example, the triad might be junior colleague, peer colleague and administrator, and our participant might respond thus: 'well, the two colleagues are similar in that they deal directly with clients/patients/students'. Then a question would be posed to elicit the contrast pole: how would you describe the role of the administrator that contrasts with that? The answer might be: 'has only a peripheral role with the clients/patients/students' or 'never comes into contact with them'. So here we have the two poles of the first construct. Next you could explore if there are any other ways in which two are similar to or different from the third, again in relation to work activities. This might reveal further constructs, for example that the junior colleague and the administrator 'are less involved in tricky situations'! While the contrast for the peer colleague might be 'often up to his neck in tricky situations' – so we have another **bipolar construct**.

Your next intervention would perhaps be to check whether any other ways of separating the threesome come to mind. If not, you might then move on to another triad, this time IT support, clerical assistant and direct superior. The first two might be selected as similar in that they 'have rather mundane chores to do', while the superior might have 'lots of challenging activities'. A further triad could follow which elicits a construct 'makes me feel valued – takes me for granted', emerging from the triad of superior, peer colleague and junior colleague. (We will let you speculate on who might have been described by the contrast pole.)

If you use this more structured technique then there is even more reason for making a note of the constructs as they emerge because it can be very revealing to follow up, once a few constructs have been elicited, with a request that the place of 'own role' on each construct continuum be identified.

Then it is helpful also to find out which pole of each construct is the preferred one, perhaps even laddering down with 'what' and 'how' questions to find out how such behaviour or attribute can be identified or recognised, or by laddering up to find out why that chosen pole is preferred or important. You will find that each step in that process draws out more constructs.

You should continue to use different triads until you have elicited sufficient constructs. This might be when the participant begins to repeat constructs or is unable to think of new ones. To help you select elements to use as triads you might consider preparing in advance a list of possible combinations of triads for different total numbers of elements. You then have the maximum number of combinations readily to hand, while bearing in mind that any one triad could produce several different combinations of pairings and singleton (1 and 2, 3; 1, 2 and 3; 1 and 3, 2) and each of those might prompt several constructs. For nine elements, draw up the triads thus:

1	2	3
4	5	6
7	8	9
1	2	3
4	5	6
7	8	9

By following combinations across, directly vertical and at an angle, combinations of 123, 456, 789, 147, 258, 369, 159, 483, 726, etc. emerge.

However, while any combination could ostensibly produce several constructs, any one might produce no further constructs to those already articulated. Further, no matter how many triads you try, some people may have very few constructs about the topic, while others might have many. As an illustration, one of your authors can produce long strings of constructs about the topics of professional role, detective novels, gardening, and shoes, but rather few about domestic chores, sports, and cars, and even fewer about romantic novels and opera.

After a few triadic elicitations a participant might, as they become conversant with the procedure, begin to proffer triads of their own or even feel comfortable with working with all elements at once. This latter activity is known as **full or whole context elicitation**. Following our example, it might involve responding to a question such as: 'Considering all of these activities/roles, is there any way that you could divide them up so that some are similar in some way that is different from the rest?' A response could be: 'Well, yes, some of them required years of academic study while others were mainly learnt through practice on the job.' This could then lead to identification of which activities/roles fit which descriptors, which the participant deemed important and why, and so on. Thus there are several optional elicitation methods for you to follow, though they all need practice, first on yourself and then with tolerant friends and family. But before you do that, let us indicate some important cautions and limitations.

Some important notes and caveats about elicitation

Throughout this chapter we have discussed the elicitation of both elements and constructs. We have urged you to avoid putting words into your participants' mouths and to give them the opportunity to articulate what they mean, to provide their own descriptions of construct poles. One thing to note is that sometimes those pole descriptors are single words but, more often than not, participants will need a phrase or sentence, or even two, to encapsulate what they mean by the similarity or difference between elements. Remember that words are merely a code, a set of symbols, which we use to try to convey inner meanings that may be difficult to articulate. Indeed, sometimes the submerged or contrast pole might elude articulation and become 'just not X', where X is the elicited pole. It can be helpful to leave a bit of silence as the participant struggles to articulate a meaning, but not to the extent that it puts them off engaging with the task further.

We must also, as constructivist researchers, recognise that the symbols (words) we use to represent our constructs are not always used in the same way by everyone. The same word can mean different things to different people; people use different words to mean the same thing; the meanings of words change over generations and cultures. Although most people would recognise the animal 'horse', some might conjure a different picture than others from the adjective 'grey', while others might use the description 'white' for those same animals. We must, as researchers, explore individuals' meanings and resist leaping to conclusions about what others mean by the words they use.

This links to another issue you will find discussed in the literature: the researcher *supplying* elements for use in triadic elicitation tasks, whether in conversational mode, as described here, or when using a repertory grid as described in Chapter Seven. We have already noted that those elements suggested by participants should ideally be refined so that, as the participants perceive it, they best fit the criteria of representativeness, range, specificity, and homogeneity. However, in some circumstances you might want to have included a specific element such as, in the case above, own role, if it had not emerged spontaneously, or other elements that may have come to light through literature or previous research.

There may also be instances in which you might want to have your participants consider an element set with one particular element excluded, perhaps until later in the process. For example, you might consider that it would be best to consider other people engaged in an activity to bring out a full range of constructs before adding in a particular element such as 'self'. There are also instances, such as in market research or in researching a particular, confined and identified situation, in which you might find that some or all the elements must be supplied in advance. However, this may lose a little data about what the participant recognises as significant or appropriate elements and runs the risk of asking them to construe elements with which they lack familiarity or even any knowledge. In this case it would be important to ask them about their degree of familiarity with each element before you begin.

Another possibility, a process of negotiating elements, allows the participant to identify and select their own elements, but under guidance. As the researcher, you might identify a range of categories covered by things that are prospective elements and suggest that the participants choose their own examples from each category. In our example we might ask that they select a real person within their work context who fits each of the roles they have selected as categories: a senior colleague, a new recruit, and so on. The category is determined by the researcher, but the actual element is controlled by the participant and gives them an actual instance rather than an abstract category to consider during elicitation.

You may suspect from our previous discussion that our preference lies first with eliciting elements from participants and next with using the negotiation process, and you would be correct, because in those ways we give great weight to seeking meanings directly from participants. For us supplying elements or, even worse, constructs is rather like asking participants to second-guess or, indeed, to try to interpret our constructions of reality instead of the other way round. You will, though, find in the literature examples of research conducted using supplied constructs and you must evaluate their worth for yourself, using criteria derived from your own construction of good-quality research. We mention here briefly that there is, though, one kind of construct supply that can be used for special cases when eliciting a repertory grid. (Repertory grid is a widely used technique for eliciting constructs, and we will discuss it in detail in Chapter Seven. We will also discuss in that chapter how constructivist questioning as described herein can be incorporated into a variety of research designs.) It can be useful at the end of a grid elicitation conversation to supply a construct, if it has not emerged naturally, that is particularly pertinent to the research in order to see how the elicited constructs link to it. For instance, using the example of exploring professional work, you might supply at the end of the conversation a construct that relates to the key or critical aspects of the job using a question such as: 'Which of these activities would you describe as key features of your job, and which are not or less key?' When interpreting the data, always be careful to recognise the difference in 'value' of elicited elements or constructs compared to supplied versions.

In the next chapter we recognise that when espousing a personal construct psychology approach to research it is important to remember the 'personal' epithet; we are seeking to understand the world as each of our participants construes it. We are not striving to educate them (though they may learn much about themselves through the process); we are not offering, nor should we, any form of counselling or therapy. Therefore we must employ our skills judiciously and thoughtfully, supporting our participants in explaining what they deem appropriate to convey to us. Let us explore next how we can support such explorations and how we might demonstrate that we are worthy of sharing those revelations.

Summary

Having worked through this chapter, you should now understand some of the key features of constructivist research in action and be able to practise at least the rudiments of constructivist techniques. We have alerted you to the sensitivity of the techniques in order to help you, in the following chapter, to set the context and establish rapport with participants as a prelude to undertaking successful research with them.

Postscript: Some construct poles found in response to Activity 5.3

Tricky to handle; demands expertise; bureaucratic chore; stuff a kid could do; demands professional knowledge; demands sensitivity; demands common sense; challenging situation; do stuff I'm good at; feel respected; feel valued; needs a bit of brainpower; mindless; involves creativity; you can just switch off; disrespectful; taken for granted; no 'by your leave' or 'thank you'.

Suggested further reading

Denicolo, P. and Pope, M. (2001) *Transformative Professional Practice: Personal Construct Approaches to Education and Research* (Chapter 4). London: Whurr.

This chapter includes discussion, with a range of different examples, of the key aspects of establishing contract and purpose, choice of elements and construct elicitation.

Fransella, F. (2003) Some skills and tools for personal construct practitioners. In F. Fransella (ed.), *International Handbook of Personal Construct Psychology* (Chapter 10). Chichester: Wiley.

Although mainly addressed to clinicians, this chapter reflects the essence of the points made about construct elicitation described above. In particular, there is an extended discussion of the laddering process, with illustrative examples.

Pope, M. and Denicolo, P. (1986) Intuitive theories – a researcher's dilemma: Some practical methodological implications. *British Educational Research Journal*, 12(2), 153-166.

This article explores some of the challenges faced by constructivist researchers when they attempt to explore others' worlds and offers some arguments about why, despite its limitations, it can produce rich and worthwhile data deemed as authentic to participants.

Pope, M. and Denicolo, P. (1993) The art and science of constructivist research in teacher thinking. *Teaching and Teacher Education*, 9(5-6), 529-544.

This article discusses element and construct elicitation, in particular during research using repertory grids, in relation to exploring the professional world of teachers.

6

Setting the climate for effective research encounters

Key Points

- Respect, good manners and ethics
- Making contact
- Adopting a facilitating style
- Negotiating a contract
- Defining your purpose
- Language issues
- Recording and storing data

Introduction

In Chapter Five we discussed issues related to the very personal nature of our enquiries in the sense that we seek to explore the ways in which people perceive their worlds and how they respond in the light of those perceptions. We emphasised that we need to take care to avoid venturing beyond our remit as researchers, particularly when laddering up to sensitive core constructs. These points have particular salience when considering the climate you establish for eliciting data using tools that are very powerful and incisive whichever technique is employed in the process. The foundation for all good constructivist research is respect and attention to ethical procedures.

Earning and giving respect – the foundation for all constructivist research

When striving to earn respect as a researcher in order to establish trust, a crucial aspect is not just conveying 'respectability' but actually being 'respect-able', demonstrating throughout the research and dissemination process that you mean what you say about confidentiality, anonymity of sources, and appreciating alternative perspectives. Reciprocity is a significant aspect in this process, that is, participants will feel more able to grant respect if they sense or construe that they and their ideas are respected in return. (You do not have to agree with their perspectives, but must recognise that for them these reflect the world as they see it, just as yours do for you.) This is the fulcrum on which successful constructivist research balances.

It would be a rare and unwise person who shared personal values, understandings, beliefs and feelings, making explicit meanings that have previously been implicit, with a person they did not trust. You have to ask yourself under what circumstances you would be prepared to do something like that. (Think about how you reacted to your self-exploration of a core construct or two in Activity 4.1. In what contexts might you share those ideas with a fellow researcher, or a comparative stranger?) Then you can try to provide those kinds of circumstances/contexts for those who will be your research participants. The integrity and authenticity of your data depend on doing a good job in response to that challenge. Here we will take you step by step through the stages involved, noting considerations and providing some suggestions.

Ethics and good manners

You should give some thought and take some actions in relation to ethics very early on in your research, since it can take time to get full ethical approval for your research. If you will be working in the field of healthcare, no matter who your research participants are, you will have to seek ethical approval both from your university, if registered for a degree, and from the relevant local ethics committee(s). You will be required also to gain ethics approval for working with participants who in any way might be considered vulnerable, particularly children, people with disabilities and older people, for instance.

Constructivist researchers tend to espouse utilitarian ethical principles (Naidoo and Wills, 2000) in their research, which include the following concepts:

> Respect for autonomy - whereby participants are enabled to make decisions about engagement in the research by ensuring they are fully informed about the procedures and potential outcomes (or, if being cared for, ensuring that the carer takes decisions for them having been similarly fully informed);

Beneficence – whereby consideration of potential benefits of the research to participants themselves is conveyed to them;

Non-maleficence – whereby care is taken to ensure that no harm or coercion occurs to participants so that no undue effort is required of them while data are stored appropriately and confidentiality is maintained;

Justice – whereby resources are used impartially and views are given equal weight.

Researchers, in espousing these principles, also have to be alert to power differential issues by ensuring that they emphasise that, though they may have expertise in research methods and academic qualifications, the participant is the expert in matters about his or her own life and inner thoughts. The ambience to aim for is that it is the participant who owns the data they produce which they may gift to the researcher for specified purposes.

Ethics committees will expect you to provide your participants with clear and unambiguous explanations, appropriate to their nature and needs, about what the research is about, who it is for, what it is for, how it will be conducted, what their part in it will consist of and what will happen to their data over time. This is the information that forms the basis for informed consent – a formal written recognition of what they have agreed to, and without which the research cannot proceed. It may be that your organisation/institution has specific forms for this, so it is worth checking before spending time on creating your own. In the latter case, ensure that the form meets the criteria given in Further Explanation 6.1.

Further Explanation 6.1

Contents of an informed consent form

A very brief outline of the research project

Agreement that the participants have had the research project explained to them

What their involvement entails exactly

A note on how the interview will be recorded, transcribed and analysed

A promise that findings will remain in confidence, with no quotations or data attributed to them personally

Assurance that data will be anonymised, kept securely and destroyed within a set time after reporting

A pledge that they can withdraw their involvement and data at any time

Space for signatures and date

Do keep these forms safe, because ethics committees and examiners can require sight of them at any time. Once you have an ethics agreement in place then you can begin to set up your fieldwork by making contact with your participants.

From first contact

Over our wide-ranging research experience we have been surprised that most people are prepared, by and large, to at least consider sharing their constructs with us and fellow researchers. What makes the difference between their agreeing to participate in research and refusing the overture to do so is the transparency and clarity of the request. First, it must contain a well-articulated rationale. Therefore sensitive prior preparation of your initial contact medium and message is worth the effort. As in all research projects, you will be demanding participants' time and attention, but, unlike many other projects, constructivist research asks of them the revelation of inner notions, some of which they may not yet be aware of themselves, so sharp are the instruments employed. Thus you must justify the need for such a penetrating, lengthy process and reassure them about the limits they may set on how much revelation is provided, all without frightening them off before you start.

Often the first contact is in writing, by letter or email, although a personal introduction through a meeting or mutual contact is sometimes possible and often helpful. However, even in the cases in which you introduce yourself and your research interests in person, it will facilitate matters if you put in writing some fundamental details for them to consider at leisure and in private. These are similar to but may be more detailed than the consent form. They should include a brief outline of your research aims, orientated to show its intended value (in a higher education context in which 'impact' has become a by-word, this prior consideration of expected value has gained in general importance to researchers as well as to research participants), along with an overview of your credentials – why they might take your request seriously and have faith in your expertise. Following this, they need to have an explanation of what kind of commitment you would appreciate from them as your prospective research participants. This commitment will include an estimate of the amount of time you will require of them initially and an indication of whether there might also be follow-up procedures. You must be clear in this outline that the process involved will seek out their personal perspectives on the topics you present to them. Also included must be your reassurance about confidentiality, anonymity and their rights in the process, such as withdrawal from the interaction at will, and a request for permission to store (in a secure place) and use their data for the project report and for future publications. Even though at this stage this is only an outline, a prelude to the main event, it may seem a lot of information to give, but people are more likely to consider engaging, giving of their time and ideas, if they feel reassured of your professionalism. Further, you may first need to gain permission from a higher authority, such as a head teacher or even the local education authority, for work in schools, from the CEO of an organisation for speaking to workers, from carers for research with vulnerable people, and so on. They too will require the kind of information you should convey to actual participants, as in Further Explanation 6.2, with very clear indication of what amount of time and in what circumstances you wish to research with those under their purview.

Further Explanation 6.2

Initial written information for participants – checklist

- Research aim
- Intended outcomes/value of research
- Researcher credentials
- Participant's potential time commitment
- Request for individual, personal perspectives
- Confidentiality and anonymity agreement
- Right to withdraw
- Permission to store and use data
- Consent forms

These points form the basis of the contract, literal or metaphorical, that you should negotiate with your participants as you begin your building of rapport with them. We will address the building of a personal link, before going on to consider the more formal notion of a contract.

Rapport – and the key skill of listening

No matter how careful your introduction, all your potential participants will already have notions about researchers and the research process. You may be delighted to find that these are positive in orientation, but remember this caveat. The participant who is eager to please, to provide you with what you want, is as much a danger to achieving a deep understanding of a situation as one who is reluctant to engage and share and thus is either unforthcoming or intent on misleading you. Fortunately the latter are few and far between, but none of the above wear a badge declaiming their intentions. That is one reason why it is critically important to effective constructivist research to develop good rapport with participants. It is important that they recognise that you are seriously interested in their actual views and understandings rather than in finding examples of particular genres of those perceptions.

From the title of this section you will be alert to our view that a crucial skill in achieving rapport is effective listening as well as producing a cogent argument. This is not simply a matter of hearing clearly what is said (that helps too, both during a research interview and in its recorded form – see below and Chapter Nine for more on the latter). Listening is a complex act that involves intellectual and emotional engagement. It involves selection of what to attend to, which in turn interacts with the process of interpreting what is being said, or indeed not being said. You might like to try Activity 6.1 in the near future.

Activity 6.1

Listening and engaging

For this activity you will need a friend or colleague to work with. Explain to them that it is an interesting exercise about our listening skills and find a place where you can quietly talk to each other without interruption for about 40 minutes.

The idea is that you will take it in turns to describe in detail for 10 minutes, without questions or interruptions, something about yourself that the other person does not yet know. Immediately following each description the partner retells what they can remember of the story while the originator of the story takes notes about accuracy.

Only after both stories have been told should you share your notes.

Hint. If your partner is a work colleague, you could describe a vacation you have taken in the past; or your earliest recollections of school, or a hobby that has gripped you for many years. For a friend who is less familiar with your work, your story could detail some significant aspect of your job or an event that made your job feel worthwhile.

For reflections on this activity, once you have completed the exercise, see the postscript at the end of the chapter.

We hope that this activity will convince you not only of the need to listen carefully with an open mind, but also of the value of recording participants' words so that you can later reflect on the range of possible meanings they might have as you begin interpretation. One other useful adjunct to effective listening is the practice of checking back – asking 'When you said "X" I thought of "Y" – am I getting that right?' Listening is, of course, more than a hearing activity. It also involves being alert to the non-verbal 'punctuation' that suggests hesitancy, eagerness, happiness, vagueness, tentativeness, shyness, and so on. This skill is neatly but comprehensively summarised by Ekman (1964: 295):

> listening involves hearing the way things are being said, the tone used, the expressions and gestures employed. In addition, listening includes the effort to hear what is not being said, what is only hinted at, what is perhaps being held back, what lies beneath or beyond the surface. We hear with our ears but we listen with our eyes and mind and heart and skin and guts as well.

Ekman also highlights something that you may notice during the course of Activity 6.1: that in telling your story you only include certain things because of the nature of your relative roles, degree of familiarity with your partner in the exercise, and so on. Hence the need to build as helpful a relationship with your future participants as possible while also formalising the situation, or agreeing a working contract.

Defining a purpose and negotiating a contract

We noted above that your participants will more likely agree to work with you on your research if they have a clear understanding of what it is about and what their role in the process is to be. In other words, you need to define the function of any technique that you ask them to engage with and what purpose their responses will serve. This forms the basis of a contract that you should each agree to before any construct elicitation takes place. That contract should also include confidentiality agreements, and how the data will be stored and used both immediately and in the future. Some researchers like to include an option for participants to say when they would like to discontinue a specific line of exploration without necessarily stopping the process entirely (perhaps saying 'I'd rather not pursue that further' with no need for elaboration/explanation).

Certainly you should allow participants to withdraw from the process at any time. It is good practice, even when people agree in advance that you may use all that they say in, for example, a constructivist interview, to ask them again at the end for permission to use that data. Sometimes they reveal more than they expected to and thus appreciate your thoughtfulness. (Aside: it can be frustrating to you, the researcher dedicated to your project, if they do decide to withhold parts, but it should reassure your research-integrity persona nevertheless!) Another possibility is that they may suspect that the words or phrases they use might identify them to other close people. You then might negotiate a way to express the idea in a different way, perhaps using a synopsis in your words rather than theirs. Choice of language is an issue throughout constructivist enquiries.

Language – putting jargon in its place

We referred in Chapters Four and Five to the value of seeking the contrast word to that used to describe something to give a more refined idea of the intended meaning. However, it is not only important that we understand our participants; they need to understand us too so that they can engage fully in any elicitation process. Thus, like any professional talking to a lay person, it is important to avoid jargon. Jargon is useful between professionals as a shorthand – but only as long as we agree on what the symbols mean. We have, by this point in the book, begun to use the word 'construct' regularly, though we had to introduce it early on into your vocabulary, particularly in the way we use it in constructivist research. Later on, when discussing the repertory grid technique (that useful, versatile tool for eliciting constructs in a structured way), we will reintroduce the word 'element', having noted its use in the theory in Chapter Four. What does that word convey to you right now? (If you have some chemistry interest it will have a particular meaning, whereas an interest in the weather conjures up another and those knowing the workings of kettles or other electrical objects will consider yet another meaning, etc.) In Chapter One the word 'element' was described as having a specific meaning to Wundt and his pupils, while in Chapter Two it was used to convey the component parts of things. In PCP we use it as a shorthand term for an entity (person, object, or event) that represents or is included in a chosen 'universe of discourse' (oops! jargon phrase for the immediate focus of the conversation). The important point to note here is that your participants do not need to learn our jargon. You will find it more effective to use words that they are familiar with and make good sense in the context. See Further Explanation 6.3 for some examples, alongside other tips for aiding explanations.

◢ Further Explanation 6.3

Effective explanations/translations

- It is important that you feel comfortable with your explanations because clumsiness or uneasiness on your part will transmit itself to your participants. Therefore try out formulations in your own words, and practise them until they flow well.
- Your participants should know that you hope to explore how they think, feel and react to the things in their world that form the focus of your research, but usually people find that 'exploring perceptions' is a reasonable summary, at least at the start of the discussion.
- Instead of using the word 'construe' you might ask 'what are your thoughts about' and 'how do you feel about' something, or enquire what a person thinks, feels or does when that thing comes to mind.
- Of course it becomes clumsy to talk of 'things', just as it is can be confusing to talk of elements, so use the generic word that fits the particular discussion. For instance, if you are exploring constructs about fellow professionals, or about a person's actual job, or about the instruments they use in their work you could use 'colleagues', 'work activities or events', and 'tools', respectively.
- Engaging in some preliminary chat before embarking on an elicitation session can often help you judge the right tenor and vocabulary for a particular participant, bearing in mind that some words are generation-specific. However, rather than try from the start to 'fit in' to that language register, let the participant guide you: if they talk about 'chums' or 'pals' when you started off with 'friends' then you have permission to use those words without seeming to be patronising.
- When one of us was researching in a large organisation, participants talked about colleagues as 'rising stars', 'walking disasters' and 'old soaks' – terms that would not have occurred to the researcher but which formed useful 'generic elements' to add to a list to which participants could attribute real colleagues, using an initial, to gain a range of exemplar colleagues (negotiated elements; see Chapters Five and Seven).
- Going through a sample exercise with a simplified version of the instrument you intend to use, focusing on an innocuous topic, such as constructs of biscuits (a favourite one of ours), can help people get the hang of the process, especially if you bring real examples along to try!
- Even in the actual elicitation process having something to represent the things/elements (photos, drawings, or just cards with names on) can help participants to visualise and sort groups that are similar or different, or occur in a particular order or have a particular priority (for critical incidents, for instance).

All of the above illustrate the need for careful advance preparation.

Sensitive recording of data

We mentioned earlier that it is useful to record constructivist discussions of any kind to allow for repeated reflection when interpreting meaning. That is something that you can explain to your participants. However, despite the wealth of media surrounding us and the seeming insouciance of some people in relation to personal photos and opinions being displayed on such media, you are likely to find in your research that some potential participants are wary of recording equipment, audio or video, being used when they are, in effect, exploring their own, often implicit and sometimes subconscious, constructs. They need to be convinced that such a recording will be kept private and anonymised and that it is a better record than notes taken at the time. For the latter you can explain the inevitable selectivity of what is noted down which is already an interpretation of what is said. Of course you still may not convince them, so we discuss note-taking further in Chapter Nine, on the practicalities of fieldwork.

In the next chapter we will describe some of the many techniques you can use to explore with participants their construing of their worlds. Each will lend itself to a particular form of data recording, so your final choice will be a compromise between your intellectual preference, your skill in eliciting and recording data, the preferences of your participants and the nature of the technique used. You will also need to consider the requirements of your funders/sponsors, such as data archiving, and any institutional requirements in relation to your data such as its accessibility to examiners for a considerable period after the award of a degree. Further, from our exploration of ethics earlier, you will need to consider the need for the original or raw data to be stored in a safe, secure place. Thus the physical form of the data needs some thought too so that it can stand the test of time.

By now you will have recognised that constructivist research involves an intricate interplay between intellectual rigour, sensitivity and attention to practical issues – mirroring Kelly's interpretation of constructs having cognitive, affective and conative features. Before we move on to the more practical methods of Chapter Seven, first remind yourself of the activity we suggested in this chapter and consider the omissions, additions, changes in emphasis and misinterpretations provided in the reprise of each story.

Summary

We have considered the critical features which provide the best start to constructivist research: respect, ethics (good manners included), rapport building and the pervasive need when recording data to consider the limitations of the codes we humans use to communicate – language.

Reflections on Activity 6.1

Most people find that, even when listening carefully to others' stories, they interpret what is said in ways that make sense to them, filtering the words through their own prior experience. Thus their rehearsal of your tale may include some omissions, perhaps things they perceived as less salient than you did. On the other hand, they may reinterpret the story and elaborate it with their perspective, what they would expect in similar circumstances. Therefore it is not so much that they forget the actual words or details but they are actively picturing your description, populating the words with their own recollections. For example, the picture that springs to mind when you mention a beach holiday (or a grumpy boss), for instance, may conjure up for them a very different kind of beach (or boss).

Benjamin (1981: 49) expressed this eloquently:

> The empathic interviewer tries as much as he [sic] possibly can to feel his way into the internal frame of reference of the interviewee and to see the world through the latter's eye *as if* that world were his own world.

Suggested further reading

Driver, J. (2007) *Ethics: The Fundamentals.* Oxford: Blackwell.

An engaging introduction to the different philosophical approaches to ethics, laced with accessible and informative examples.

Watzlawick, P., Bavelas, J.B. and Jackson, D.D. (2014) *Pragmatics of Human Communication: A Study of Interactional Patterns, Pathologies, and Paradoxes.* New York: Norton.

Although originally written for therapists, this is one of the most famous and accessibly written books on interpersonal communication.

7

An evaluation of a range of potential research techniques

Key Points

- Adopting constructivist methods
- Conducting a repertory grid study
  - o Generating elements
  - o Eliciting the constructs
  - o Completing the grid
- Using mapping methods
  - o Relational mapping methods
  - o Eco-maps
  - o Bow-tie interviews
  - o Illuminative incident analysis
  - o Concept mapping with card sorts
- Using storytelling or narrative methods
  - o Self-characterisation sketch
  - o Mirror time
  - o Blind date
  - o Metaphors
  - o Role drawings
  - o The lying game
  - o Interview about instances
  - o Rivers of experience/snakes

Introduction: Adopting constructivist methods

We now discuss various tools and techniques that can be used in a research study. We emphasise that there is no single best method for doing constructivist research and that some techniques are better suited to some purposes and/or participants than others, as we shall note as we describe them. Several tools and techniques have evolved over many years and we share these with you so that you can assess their possible application in your study. You might use these techniques within any interpretive study, perhaps using grounded theory or action research, or using an ethnographic or feminist approach, as well as in a constructivist or constructionist study, but the principles we noted in earlier chapters should underpin this research approach. These key philosophical and theoretical principles form a bridge between the phenomenon that is the focus of your study, and the method/tools/techniques that you use, ensuring that your underpinning theory and research approach remain congruent.

We have emphasised from Chapter One the importance of gaining understanding about people from their own perspective, which will be different from anyone else's, rather than through so-called experts' observation or interpretations of them. This means that all of the techniques we note here are vehicles by which data may be elicited from the people themselves so that we gain what we have noted as a phenomenological perspective (Chapter Three). There are other key implications of a constructivist approach which are worth repeating here – see Further Explanation 7.1.

▲ Further Explanation 7.1

Reminder of key constructivist principles

- Human experience is irreducible, and any reduction impoverishes research output (Raskin, 2012). Instead we are eliciting a holistic and integrated view of a personal **life-world**.
- While acknowledging the influence of social and cultural experiences on a person or group's sensemaking processes, we also recognise that how people ultimately make sense of their experiences is an intra-individual process.
- Each constructivist study offers us a window into parts of another's life-world that is both time, and context, sensitive.
- People build a structured understanding of their world, developing layers of understanding between individual examples and generalised representations (you may recall we cited Kelly's example of mother versus motherliness to illustrate this).

For the researcher these are important because they illuminate how exploring the ways in which a participant symbolically represents a phenomenon can open the door to an exploration of the wider conceptual structures that they use to make sense of their social world and their lived experience within it. Therefore, we can understand how a person conceptualises a broad range of related phenomena (the universe of discourse) by exploring an element set of preferably concrete examples that represent it.

Although Kelly was very clear that constructs can be represented by both non-verbal and verbal symbols, constructivist psychologies are particularly interested in how people use language to shape and delineate themselves and others (Neimeyer, 2009). Ultimately, language is the key that opens the door for the researcher to the interpretation of people's life-worlds, bearing in mind the caveats in Chapters Five and Six. So, the principal aim of most constructivist research methods is to elicit a conversation or story that will provide a linguistic text for analysis, either to help elaborate results from another technique or to disseminate a narrative account. Building on the constructivist conversational approach detailed in Chapter Five (perhaps worth refreshing your memory about now) you will see in the following techniques, starting with the ubiquitous repertory grid, how each one provides a particular approach to eliciting this conversation or story, each appropriate depending on the particular phenomena being explored, the nature of participants, context and research objectives.

Conducting a repertory grid study

Repertory grids have become Kelly's most visible and popular legacy and are especially powerful for eliciting in a structured way deeply held assumptions and values that might otherwise remain untapped. By surfacing the distinctions individuals make between different people, objects or events in their experience, and the linguistic labels they give to those distinctions, you can both reveal the underlying construct systems by which participants live and engage them in a reflective dialogue about their motivations and attributions. Also, by tapping into how participants construe others' construing, the methodology can be used to understand relational dynamics.

We will provide here an outline of the grid elicitation process (and in Chapter Ten an outline of the grid analysis process). If you intend to use grids as your main data elicitation technique then you might also want to engage with Jankowicz's (2004) easy guide to grids.

Kelly created the repertory grid as an intervention-based articulation of PCP, as *'personal construct theory in action'* (Fransella et al., 2004). Unlike later practitioner derivatives that use the alternative metaphor of 'person as storyteller' (see our later design ideas) and are firmly rooted in the interpretive research domain (Pope and Denicolo, 2001), the retention of the 'person as scientist' metaphor and the mathematical basis of repertory grids means they can produce both qualitative and quantitative data.

In practice, a repertory grid is designed around a single topic (the universe of discourse) and consists of a matrix of three components – elements, constructs and ratings – which, in combination, provide a 'mental map' of how the person construes the topic in question. A sample grid is provided in Figure 7.1, showing you how to lay out the:

Elements – along the top line;

Constructs – placing the emergent pole (the similarity) down the left hand side and the contrast pole (the difference) down the right hand side; and,

Ratings – placing the numerical ratings and/or ticks and crosses in the grid boxes to align the constructs with the relevant elements.

Generating the elements

Elements are defined by Kelly (1991a: 95) as the 'things or events which are abstracted by a construct'. They are relevant examples of people, objects or events that provide

GRID PURPOSE: to explore …

Elements →	1	2	3	4	5	6	7	8	9	
HOW TWO ARE SIMILAR (emergent pole)										HOW THE THIRD IS DIFFERENT (contrast pole)

Figure 7.1 Sample grid

a balanced sample of, or occurrence within, a topic. We provided detailed guidance on the process of eliciting elements in Chapter Five, in the section entitled 'Remaining Flexible but with Structure'. This process is the same when compiling a repertory grid as when holding a conversation without the grid or matrix format; the triadic elicitation process is also the same, as we shall see in a moment. The only difference when applied to a repertory grid is that the constructs are rated against the elements. So, if you are seeking to understand how an amateur tennis player construes the game of tennis, you could ask them to think of elements, depending on your particular focus, that reflect:

> *People*, for example, the best, worst and average tennis players; or,
>
> *Objects*, for example, a range of tennis equipment and clothing; or
>
> *Events*, for example, a range of tennis competitions or venues.

If you opt for people as elements, you could also ask them to rate themselves if they have not already included themselves as one of the elements. However, it is often best to leave the inclusion and rating of self until after all their constructs have been elicited so that they do not restrict their constructs to those on which they will 'look good'.

Determining the appropriate breadth of elements is an important part of your study design. Most grid studies are usually structured around a set of between 6 and 12 elements (with more than 12 you are in danger of the participant psychologically exiting the process before the end, and with fewer than 6 you are in danger of not having enough breadth to adequately map the territory under investigation).

The nature of the examples they choose for elements is valuable data in its own right and can be informative about how they view the topic. If you are working with a group of participants on the same topic then you can consider information such as the frequency of selection of particular elements. Remember our caveats in Chapter Five about providing elements. If you do so, then you must have a clear rationale, and be able to defend how your selected elements map the territory and are meaningful to participants. Without this, you are in danger of representing your own, rather than the participant's, construct system. Whichever path you decide to follow for your study, choosing the right set of elements is essential as they form the realm of discourse in the research interview.

Eliciting the constructs

Constructs are the discriminations the person makes between the elements (Dalton and Dunnett, 1992). Kelly (1955/1991) gave several definitions of the properties of constructs which we summarised in Chapter Four. It is important to understand that each individual repertory grid only unearths how a participant construes a certain phenomenon and will only give you a tiny glimpse into how that person construes their total world.

In order to maintain rigour, it is important that you elicit constructs in a systematic manner across interviews, as we described in Chapter Five. To remind you of the key steps see the flow chart in Procedural Example 7.1 later in this chapter.

Be mindful of only exploring constructs because they relate to your own hypotheses about the phenomenon being investigated. If you fall into this trap, then you will be inadvertently exploring your own construct system vicariously, rather than exploring the life-world of your participant. Whilst Kelly acknowledged the impossibility of complete researcher independence and the influence of the researcher's own construct system on the research process (referred to in qualitative research as a recognition of the '**double hermeneutic**'), it is critical in PCP research to allow the 'provinces of meaning' to emerge from the data. Developing reflective skills to understand your role as a partner or an 'actor' in the research process is essential in order to be able to recognise and set to one side your own mental maps and sensemaking processes.

Completing the grid

Most people find the triadic elicitation method helpful in identifying their constructs about the chosen elements, only moving to the **full context elicitation** method as they become more confident (see Chapter Five). Typically, you should ask your participant to score each construct as it is elicited, although sometimes they write down a few constructs at a time as they 'spill' from memory. As the interviewer, you need to gauge the flow of conversation and the participant's accompanying narrative and try to facilitate, rather than disrupt, their reflective processes.

Scoring constructs with ticks and crosses is suitable for simpler grid studies, perhaps where you are working with a participant for the first time or with very young children, or if you only require the grid to provide you with a base-level understanding of individual or shared mental models. Once the participant has added a bipolar construct to the grid, ask them to mark the two relevant *similar* cells (in the elements columns) with a ✓ and the one relevant *contrast* cell with a × (this provides a categorical distinction). Then they can proceed to rate with a ✓ all the other elements that are like the similarity pole and with a × those like the contrast pole.

Numerical ratings offer more scalar 'greys' of a person's constructs as applied to each element on the grid, which enables the researcher to discriminate to what extent each construct pole applies to each element for that participant. Once the participant has added one or more bipolar constructs to the grid, ask them to rate the elements against that construct on a Likert scale (this provides an ordinal rating) with, we suggest, the phrase on the left (similarity) standing for the low end of the scale and the phrase on the right (contrast) standing for the high end of the scale. For a five-point scale you should explain the points on the scale:

1   matches the *similar* description mostly or perfectly;
2   generally matches the *similar* description better than the *contrast* description;
3   is no more like the *similar* description than the *contrast* description;

4 generally matches the *contrast* description better than the *similar* description;
5 matches the *contrast* description mostly or perfectly. (It can be useful to have this selection on a card as a visual prompt.)

The level of your response scale will depend upon the nature of your study, but usually a range from 1 to between 4 and 7 is sufficient. Using odd-numbered scales allows you to provide a neutral middle choice, which can be valuable in determining constructs that do not act as discriminating factors for particular elements without requiring a 'not applicable' option, which itself may be inappropriate in situations where the construct still has some relevance to the element. Forced-choice scales, with no neutral middle point, should also not be offered without a separate 'not applicable' option and may, in some situations, be too restrictive for the participant.

It is also important to acknowledge that what you are collecting through these rating exercises are ordinal data and are, in a purest sense, limited to their ability to establish how participants comparatively evaluate their constructs and, in isolation, will tell you very little about the differences between the values beyond an appreciation of high, average, and low scores and their orientation towards which construct pole. Therefore, as we will discuss in Chapter Ten when you are looking to evaluate rating data taken from a grid, or a set of grids, you should be exploring the relative nature of ratings rather than the ratings scores in absolute terms.

You may also find it useful to combine the use of categorical evaluations, using ticks and crosses, and ordinal ratings, using scale scores, across the elements. So, for example, you could ask your participant to first identify which two elements are similar using ticks, compared to which element is different using a cross. You can position these ticks and crosses in the top right-hand corner of the relevant grid cells and then ask them to use that construct to rate all the elements on the grid by applying your numerical scale. You will then be able to identify how they use that construct to evaluate all the elements, as well as identifying the particular elements from which the construct was derived.

You may find that some textbooks suggest the use of ranking rather than rating, but we have found that this adds a level of complexity to the participant's scoring that distracts from construct elicitation: whereas a rating scale allows several elements to have the same rating while some rating levels may not be applicable (there may be no element rating, say, a 4 on a five-point scale), ranking requires tied ranks and the use (probably artificial) of all the rank levels.

Sometimes it can also be useful to ask the participant to note the constructs that are important to them. See the examples of potentially 'unimportant' ones in Further Explanation 7.2, though be wary of assuming that situational or gender similarities, for instance, are less important to the participant than other constructs. A seemingly superficial construct can be quite revelatory when the data are analysed: for example, 'wears or does not wear a tie' linked with 'tidy – untidy desk' linked with 'has leadership potential or not' can indicate an unconscious bias.

You might find it useful to copy the flow chart in Procedural Example 7.1 on to a card to act as an aide-memoire until you become well versed in grid elicitation.

Procedural Example 7.1

Repertory grid elicitation flow chart

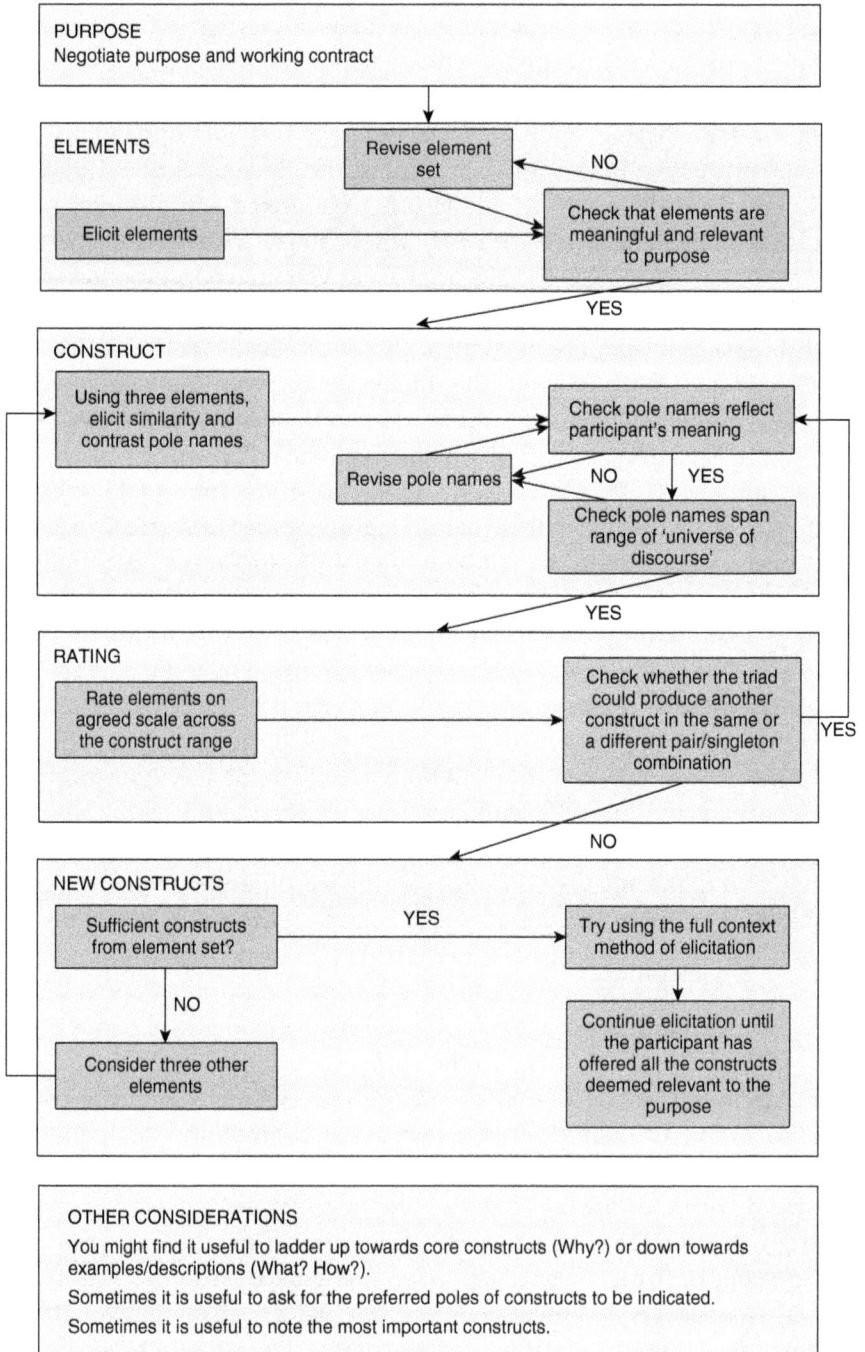

PURPOSE
Negotiate purpose and working contract

ELEMENTS

Elicit elements

Revise element set

NO

Check that elements are meaningful and relevant to purpose

YES

CONSTRUCT

Using three elements, elicit similarity and contrast pole names

Check pole names reflect participant's meaning

Revise pole names

NO   YES

Check pole names span range of 'universe of discourse'

YES

RATING

Rate elements on agreed scale across the construct range

Check whether the triad could produce another construct in the same or a different pair/singleton combination

YES

NO

NEW CONSTRUCTS

Sufficient constructs from element set?

YES

Try using the full context method of elicitation

NO

Continue elicitation until the participant has offered all the constructs deemed relevant to the purpose

Consider three other elements

OTHER CONSIDERATIONS
You might find it useful to ladder up towards core constructs (Why?) or down towards examples/descriptions (What? How?).
Sometimes it is useful to ask for the preferred poles of constructs to be indicated.
Sometimes it is useful to note the most important constructs.

Further Explanation 7.2

A final note on constructs and elements

Due to the abstract nature of the repertory grid technique, it is common for participants to give some constructs that could be less useful for exploring their worlds within the process of elicitation which the researcher can actively deal with during the interview. Kelly (1991a: 155) highlighted some to be aware of which include:

Situational – where the participant ascribes a similarity arising purely from a shared location, for example, the people elements live in the same town.

Excessively permeable – as with situational, the participant's response does not address psychological differences between elements, for example, being alike because of gender.

Excessively impermeable – the participant uses rigid, non-psychological, discriminants, such as job role.

Superficial – the elicited construct is irrelevant to topic, often impermeable, such as eye colour.

Vague – the participant attempts to take the middle ground or resist comparison, for example, by saying 'they are both okay'.

Direct product of role title or element – the participant uses labels that directly refer to the topic, without deriving deeper discrimination or meaning, for example, 'they are both leaders'.

Kelly suggested that such constructs are best dealt with by recording the response and then probing it with further questions to see if it is a peripheral construct that links to a core, superordinate construct. Some suggestions for follow-up questions include:

- 'That is one way in which they are alike. Can you tell me how [being from the same town/being female] makes them alike?'
- 'How does [their being in this role/having the same eye colour] help you [in relation to the 'universe of discourse' you are exploring]?' Using the example analogy of tennis as we did earlier, this question would be posed along the line of 'How does their having the same eye colour help you in understanding tennis?' This question type is therefore also useful in keeping participants 'on topic'.
- 'Is there something about [their being leaders/being okay] that makes them alike?'

Potential uses for and forms of grids

Repertory grids have the potential for exploring a person's constructs in depth about a particular topic, providing detailed information about how elements are grouped, how constructs relate to each other and which constructs clusters influence the element grouping (see Chapter Ten on analysis). They can be adapted for use in many different ways to suit circumstance and participants, adapting the interview language to match. For instance, although we suggested that very young children might find it easier to use the tick and cross rating scale, most children or illiterate or learning-disabled participants can readily cope with ordering things in relation to one pole or another. They can be helped by having elements as actual objects or in some pictorial form and by being allowed to move and place them between representations of the constructs, perhaps using smiley or glum faces to represent preferred and non-preferred poles. Indeed, many adults find 'tactile gridding' helpful, perhaps having cards annotated with element names to put in order, or at least being able to fill in their own grid form in pencil which they can scribble with, rub out and reorder as they organise their thoughts.

Grids can also be helpful in indicating change in construing (learning) when administered over time or before and after some intervention or event. They can be used with groups of people to demonstrate similarities and differences in construing of a particular universe of discourse; see Denicolo (1996) and Tjok a Tam and Denicolo (1997) for examples of a simplified form (overlay grids) for comparing participants' views on topics, and the SOCIOGRID facility found in the WebGrid package (see Appendix B) for comparing grids which is based on Shaw's (1980) work, noted in Chapter Twelve.

Using mapping methods

Of course, the repertory grid is a key tool for mapping people's social worlds, and this section is not intended to detract from the grid's obvious application here. Instead, we would like to widen the methodological possibilities available to us through personal constructivism by considering some alternative options focused on understanding people's internal worlds through either their relational encounters or how they mentally represent phenomena at a holistic level.

Relational mapping methods

Relational mapping methods are focused on the social and relational side of PCP, providing an understanding of how a person construes their social reality in the context of the relative positions they and others occupy in relationships, conversations or interactions (Procter, 1987). They draw on Kelly's commonality and sociality corollaries (see Further Explanation 4.2), particularly his assertion that 'social psychology must be a psychology of interpersonal understandings, not merely a psychology of common understandings' (Kelly, 1991a: 67). As such, relational mapping methods are interested in exploring the nature of different social processes and interpersonal interactions and how they give form to a person's beliefs about themselves and other people or events. We will consider three relational methods here, eco-maps, the bow-tie interview, and illuminative incident analysis.

Eco-maps

Eco-maps are a systemic tool originally developed in a social work context (Hartman, 1995). They are used frequently in counselling, coaching and qualitative research as a method of exploring and visually representing the roles different relationships play in a person's life and for quickly mapping out support networks (Baumgartner et al., 2012). Their premise is that a person's quality of life is established and sustained through their system of relationships, and that those relationships provide us with a sense of who we are (our self), with comfort and with confidence. Therefore, in order to fully understand the person, you have to understand their interdependence with other parts of their relational system, because our complex interactions with others have a great influence on our behaviours and attitudes.

The steps in Procedural Example 7.2 illustrate how to utilise the technique in your constructivist study.

Procedural Example 7.2

Eco-maps

Ask the participant to:

- Draw a circle in the centre of a large piece of paper and place themselves and their most significant others within that circle. This circle represents the people they feel most closely bonded to, perhaps the closest members of their family or very strong friendships.
- Connect themselves to the other people shown using this key:
  - Solid, double line = stronger relationship
  - Solid, single line = normal relationship, as expected
  - Dashed line = weaker relationship
  - Zig-zag line = conflict, bad relationship.
- Connect the other people shown to each other in the same way.
- Consider the level of relational influence between the people shown, including themselves, by adding arrows to the end of their lines using this key:
  - Arrows pointing from another to them = that other person is a primary influencer for themselves (same for between others as well)
  - Arrows pointing from them to another = they are a primary influencer for the other person (same for between others as well)
  - Arrows pointing both directions = each person in the dyad equally influences that relationship.
- Once this inner circle is complete, you can repeat these steps for wider relationships by asking them to add in other friends, work colleagues, work groups and social groups. By extending out to group level, you can also capture the role those groups play in forming their social identity. You can also restrict the eco-map to a specific event, such as a work project, or a specific role, such as their work role.

Bow-tie interview

This systemic interview technique is useful when conducting dyadic or group-based research, when you are interested in understanding what happens within the process of relationships and interactions between individuals. It was first developed by Procter (1987) to link the intrapersonal processes of sensemaking to the social environment of interpersonal relationships that sustain them. The bow-tie interview derives its name from the pattern formed (see Figure 7.2) when constructs and resultant behaviour are elicited from each member of a dyad or larger group. This technique encourages each individual to describe what the other person does, what they understand is motivating that behaviour and how they respond in return. Thus it reveals implicit assumptions and beliefs that orientate reciprocal behaviour and, often unwittingly, reinforce the mistaken assumptions. An example might be that a supervisor is concerned to help a new researcher to produce an excellent study and so requests regular updates which she evaluates, providing critical feedback, to improve the research and its presentation. The researcher is nervous and afraid that the supervisor does not like his work. On receiving the feedback, his worst fears are confirmed, so he is reluctant to hand over further reports and provides the minimum of information when he does. The supervisor continues to worry about the quality of the work and the reluctance of the researcher to communicate, so increases the pressure to report and the extent of her criticism – and so the vicious circle continues.

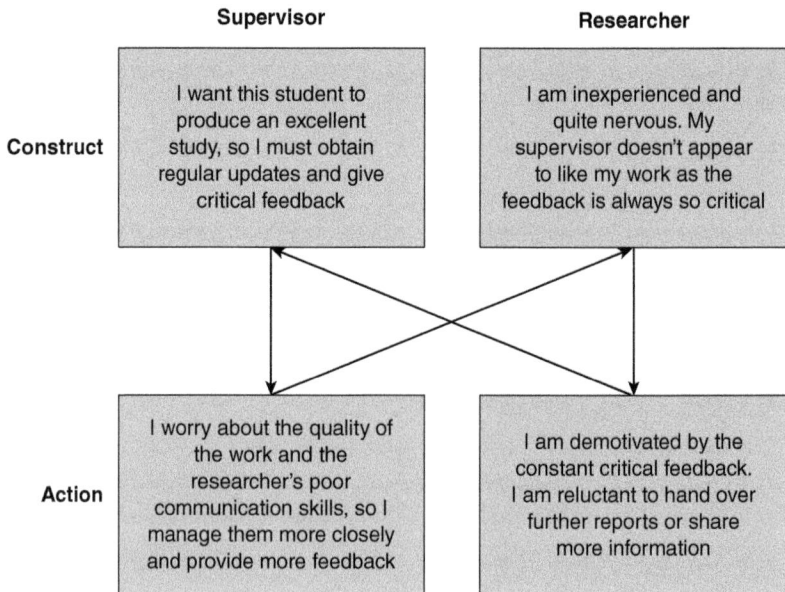

	Supervisor	Researcher
Construct	I want this student to produce an excellent study, so I must obtain regular updates and give critical feedback	I am inexperienced and quite nervous. My supervisor doesn't appear to like my work as the feedback is always so critical
Action	I worry about the quality of the work and the researcher's poor communication skills, so I manage them more closely and provide more feedback	I am demotivated by the constant critical feedback. I am reluctant to hand over further reports or share more information

Figure 7.2 Bow tie

Illuminative incident analysis

This technique uses drawings to help participants to express ideas and feelings that might be difficult to put into words because of their emotional content. It was originally devised by Cortazzi and Roote (1975) as a means of investigating the thoughts and feelings of members of teams. Drawings can be used with individuals to complement other construct elicitation techniques such as grids, or can be used in teams to help members share in a less confrontational way how they view and experience joint activities. Thus drawings are intended as a conduit from the non-verbal to the verbal. It is important to reassure participants that only rough sketches, rather than artworks, are required to represent simply how they feel about a situation.

One example is a drawing produced by a new recruit to an organisation. It shows her in scruffy clothes, seated at a table, looking aghast at the array of cutlery before her. The other diners on either side are looking relaxed, though in formal evening wear. She explained how she felt not knowing 'the way things are done around here' and how she feels out of depth in what she perceives as a much more sophisticated environment than she was used to. A slightly longer-serving staff member joined in the story by sharing her own trepidation as a newcomer, in which she felt she sat at such a banquet in pyjamas. Other colleagues offered to show them both how to use the equipment and provided 'survival tips'.

As an alternative, you can provide participants with visual prompts from which they can select to represent their experience and interpretation of an event. These can include photos, drawings, short sentences or single words that may help trigger different associations, or metaphorical connections, with the particular incident.

Analysis of participants' drawings or selected prompts requires the combined efforts of the listener and the producer of the drawing to interpret the nuances encapsulated in the accompanying commentary, to tease out their full significance. In other words, producing the drawing/mental map provides the first step in expressing ideas and feelings and acts as a catalyst to the verbal explanation.

Concept mapping with card sorts

Concept maps were developed as a tool for visually representing the structure of a person's or group's knowledge about a topic and are described as 'a schematic device for representing a set of concept meanings embedded in a framework of propositions' (Novak and Gowin, 1984: 15). They are created with the broad concept at the top of a hierarchy and show how that concept is build up by, and linked to, lower-order concepts or propositions, often using thin and thick lines, perhaps annotated with the nature of the link, and arrow heads as in the relational mapping technique to provide greater detail about links. As such, concept maps focus on the progressive differentiation and integrative reconciliation of propositions within concepts, or in constructivist terms, on how constructs are hierarchically ordered within a 'province of meaning'. Elaboration and illustrations can be found in Denicolo and Pope (2001).

Two different types of card sort exercises can develop a conceptual map of how your participant interprets a given topic, or phenomenon. You will need a table for both of these exercises.

Using card sorts as a pyramiding exercise

This method offers a simpler and more visual alternative to the repertory grid and is useful for understanding how participants differentiate between elements and how they mentally represent their constructs in hierarchical form.

For this task you will need a large blank sheet of paper (A4 or A3, dependent on the number of elements you have), a card with the topic title (or interview purpose), and a series of annotated small cards or photos to represent the elements.

As with repertory grids, identify a suitable range of objects, events or people that represent a phenomenon that you wish to investigate. Write, or draw, a simple depiction of each of these on small cards, or use photos to represent them. Make sure that you sequentially number each card, preferably on the back to avoid any response influence. These cards represent your element set and the numbers on the reverse allow you to note their relative positions on the large piece of paper as the hierarchy evolves. Start by writing the topic title at the top of the blank sheet of paper and follow the process presented as Procedural Example 7.3.

Procedural Example 7.3

Pyramid card sorts

- Lay the topic card at the top of the table; spread the element cards out randomly below it so that they are all visible.
- Ask the participant: 'Can you tell me, from your point of view, what the most important difference between these things is?'
- On the sheet of paper, capture the two distinctions hierarchically underneath the topic title; this is the first branch level and these two distinctions become the category headers for the next level in the hierarchy.
- Once you have noted the new categorisations, ask the participant to sort the cards into two piles that represent this difference (it is not necessary to sort the piles evenly).
- Make a note of the card numbers sorted into each pile, under each category header.
- Focusing on the first, or largest, pile, ask the participant: 'Looking at this group, what do you think is the most important difference between these things?'
- Again, note the distinction as the next level of categorisation, ask the participant to sort the cards into two piles that represent this difference and make a note of the card numbers allocated to each pile.
- Continue working in this way through all the piles until all the cards have been separated and differentiated from each other and you have noted down all the distinctions made.

If the participant offers more than one distinction at each stage, ask them which of these differences is the most significant to ensure that you capture the construct that has the most meaning for them. If the participant offers a distinction that you do not feel is relevant to the topic, you can check by asking them to elaborate how the distinction relates to the topic.

Your complete pyramid becomes a visual representation of how your participant construes the phenomenon as a sort of 'tree' structure. You will then be able to explore the meaning of branches further and also map attributes of different examples of the phenomenon under investigation across various branches and levels of the tree.

Using card sorts as a ranking exercise

This method can be useful for understanding the ways in which participants use common constructs to make sense of a phenomenon, and the relative order of importance they assign to different constructs in different situations. This is particularly useful for helping you understand the extent to which participants' construing is a socialised, or shared, process.

For this task you will need a card displaying the topic title (or interview purpose) that provides a description of the object, event or person that you wish to explore, a set of small cards each one displaying a relevant construct descriptor (usually the emergent pole), and some form of scale to indicate the degree to which the construct applies.

For the scale, you can use verbal descriptors if you prefer, such as from 'extremely important' to 'not important at all', or a numeric scale with however many points you deem appropriate for your study (we recommend between 4 and 7), or a visual scale, such as a series of happy to sad faces.

For the cards, identify a good range of constructs/descriptors that fairly represent the accepted universe of discourse for that topic from previous research or literature and put a sequential number on the reverse of each card. Include some blank cards for the participant to add descriptors that they deem relevant. Check that the participants understand the meaning of provided descriptors.

Lay these cards out on a table, with the topic title at the top and the scale down the left-hand side (with the highest level at the top), and follow the steps in Procedural Example 7.4.

◆ Procedural Example 7.4

Card sorts as a ranking exercise

- Explain that you wish to find out how the participant thinks about the topic and that you will do this by asking him/her to sort a set of cards along the scale. Each card contains a description/word that some people have used to explain [the topic] and you would like to understand which ways of describing [the topic] are more important or most relevant to them personally.
- Either shuffle the descriptor cards and hand the deck to the participant, or randomly spread them out on the table in front of him/her so that they are all visible.
- Ask him/her to place each card next to the appropriate scale level so that the higher up the scale the card is placed, the greater is its relevance to the topic, allowing him/her to discard any that do not apply or add their own using the blank cards.
- Provide assurance that you are not looking for a 'correct' answer, just how he/she would explain the topic using the cards. Continue working through the sorting until all the cards have been ranked or discarded.

- Alternatively, to simplify the exercise, you can dispense with the rating scale and do as Kelly himself suggested: ask the participant to select the five most applicable cards and the five least applicable cards, which you can then explore and discuss.

You can also rerun the exercise in either format using individual elements that act as concrete examples of the topic. Using the example of leadership, you could conduct a card sort for leadership at a conceptual level and then clear the table (after taking a photograph of their conceptual sort) and repeat the exercise for someone they identify as the leader who best epitomises the essential qualities. By conducting this second sort, you will have a useful triangulation of your data (see Chapter Eight).

Using storytelling or narrative methods

As Neimeyer (2009: 9) described, the main purpose of constructivist methods 'is to help reveal the meanings behind the words, the deeper themes between the lines of the stories [people] tell themselves and us'. The remainder of this chapter will focus on helping you understand how to design a study using a 'person as story-teller' metaphor (Denicolo and Pope, 2001). Storytelling sits within the research domain of narrative enquiry. Connelly and Clandinin (1990) argue that humans live innately storied lives; we use personal and social stories to construe and reconstrue our experiences, so that we not only live by the stories that we tell ourselves, adopting and conforming to our ascribed roles within them, but also use those stories to explain our lives to others. As such, the 'story' represents an account of the phenomenon being investigated, which in turn produces a 'narrative' that provides the data for analysis.

Because narrative studies focus on stories that participants live and tell, there is recognition that life changes and so do the stories when they are told. They may be modified and change direction over time. This means that the experiences are focused in different directions when they are told. They may concern:

- Feelings and reactions now;
- The setting for the telling;
- Memory of events;
- Intentions and expectations for the future.

Also, when stories are told in research settings, they are told *to you*, as the researcher. You, in turn, tell your reconstruction of the heard story or research text. It is important that you recognise these different aspects of storytelling as they can change the direction of the research. It is equally important to acknowledge that the researcher, as a particular audience, influences the stories that are being told, and that it is the researcher who interprets the narrative data, puts it into the research text and offers a re-presentation.

Unlike repertory grids, which can produce both qualitative and quantitative data, storytelling methods fit a domain of enquiry based on acquiring qualitative data. As such, their application can be more fluid and adaptive, meaning that there are fewer prescribed procedural steps to follow. Some of these methods were utilised by Kelly and others have been adapted from their original applications in other phenomenological domains, such as counselling or coaching. All of them adopt a holistic approach to personal enquiry and reject a reducible notion of human experience. We are not offering an exhaustive list of ideas here, both because there is simply not the space and because, in the spirit of PCP, we do not wish to constrain you within our own construal systems. Rather we present a range to provide suggestions of different techniques that suit the style preferences of both participants and researchers. Some examples of methods of this kind can be found in the case studies in Chapter Eleven.

Constructivist interviewing, with techniques such as laddering or pyramiding, as described in Chapters Five and Six, provide the essential methodological rigour and are applicable across all these approaches. Kelly (1991a: 241) recommended taking a 'credulous approach' during interviews, by which he meant that the researcher should accept and not ignore what participants describe as their reality, however far from your own construction of reality it may appear. At the same time, you should be vigilant to inconsistencies and conflicts within participants' narratives. When these arise, you should bring them into the conversation and deconstruct them with the participant, without simply drawing your own conclusions. Such inconsistencies and conflicts naturally arise as we evolve our life stories through the accommodation and assimilation of our lived experiences, and they may have symbolic meaning, or represent points of change, that can be lost as they are blended into the overarching script of our life.

All of the research techniques described next can stand alone or can be combined selectively either to triangulate your data, or to supplement your data if you find the participant struggles with the descriptive process in another technique.

Self-characterisation sketch

Kelly devised this narrative method as a means of exploring and understanding how an individual construes their identity in a particular context, in relation to other roles, and also as a method for inducing self-understanding as a prelude to considering personal change. The aim is to see how the person structures their social world in which they must maintain themselves in one, or a number of, ascribed roles. Self-characterisation sketches can also act as springboards to considering alternative self-constructions and, when sketches are elicited at intervals and compared, they can demonstrate change or development over time. Kelly also felt that the aim of a self-characterisation sketch is to focus the writer on the person they consider themselves to be now, in the moment, and not on the person they believe they should be or would like to be. However, it is possible to use sketches within the framework of Higgins' (1987) self-discrepancy theory, by asking participants to write a sketch about the person they believe they are now (actual self), and then follow that up with another sketch of the person they think they should be (ought self) and the person they would like to be in the future (ideal self). Steps to help a participant produce a sketch are provided in Procedural Example 7.5.

Procedural Example 7.5

Generating a self-characterisation sketch

Ask the person to write a character sketch of themselves as if they are a principal character in a play, from the perspective of a friend who knows them very intimately and who is sympathetic.

It should begin something like: 'Name (for example, Mark/Martha) is …'.

If they struggle to start, you can make the task seem less daunting by encouraging them to think about some of the following:

- What 'type' of person do they feel they are?
- How would they define themselves to others?
- What makes them unique?
- Are there any things they have been struggling with lately that are important to their identity?
- What do they value most and why?
- What do they enjoy doing most and why?
- What have they learned about themselves through their relationships with others?

Try not to interrupt their writing flow and only use some of the suggested prompts above, or others that you can think of, if they start to struggle with the task.

Kelly felt that writing the sketch in the third person from the perspective of a good friend enables the writer to conceptualise themselves holistically and purposefully. The terms 'intimately' and 'sympathetically' indicate to the writer that they need to offer more than just a superficial account. This phrasing also provides the writer with more explanatory latitude than alternative terms such as 'self-description' or 'self-analysis'; it enables them to overcome shyness about praising themselves, and helps them to contemplate foibles that others might be aware of, but which they usually prefer to ignore. This makes for a less self-conscious, less sanitised description of self in a role.

The finished sketch may be quite long and full of constructs, especially emergent poles. It will tell you about how they view themselves and their life-worlds. As well as identifying the discriminant constructs the participant applies, it is also important to consider what they have excluded from their characterisation. You can explore the constructs contained in the sketch further, perhaps using laddering techniques. You should pay particular attention to the sequence and linking of ideas, how ideas are organised, any shifts in emphasis, conflicts and inconsistencies, and the emergence of themes and their repetition.

The self-characterisation sketch and its variants in the next two subsections are useful ways of exploring their roles and relationships with participants who may find the grid technique rather too structured or formal and can provide a rather shorter, less elaborated, route to understanding as a confirmatory method in a triangulation process.

Mirror time

Mirror time was developed by Mahoney (1991) as a method of self-exploration and offers an alternative way of generating a self-characterisation. See Procedural Example 7.6.

Procedural Example 7.6

Self-characterisation using mirror time technique

Sit the participant in front of a long mirror and ask them to imagine that they had just met the person in the mirror for the first time. Instruct them to look at themselves closely and write down their answers to the following questions:

- What is your first impression of this person that you see in front of you?
- What physical features stand out about this person?
- What are you thinking and feeling as you look at this person?
- What do you like and dislike as you view this person?
- What do you see in this person that others do not?

Now ask them to imagine that this person is a good, personal friend whom they know extremely well and care about. Ask them the following:

- Spend some time describing this person's true self, the person that you know they are inside.
- Are there features about your friend's external appearance that are consistent or inconsistent with their true self, the person that you know they are inside?

Encourage them to keep looking back into the mirror as they write their sketch. The aim is to draw out the contrasts between how the person presents themselves to the world (their external appearance) and their internal self-concept (the person they believe they are inside).

Once they have completed the activity, you can explore their responses further by asking them to review what they have written and identify what stands out for them most. You can then progress onto what feelings, thoughts and possible insights have been stimulated by the exercise.

Blind date

This is another alternative to generate a self-characterisation. Ask the participant to bring to mind their best friend, that is, the person who knows their most intimate thoughts and has their best interests at heart. They should then imagine that this friend is describing the participant to someone who is a potential blind date before they meet. The procedure is described in Procedural Example 7.7.

Procedural Example 7.7

Blind date self-characterisation

Ask the participant to write down how their chosen best friend would describe them to this blind date. Encourage them to think about describing some of the following:

- What they look like;
- Their interests and hobbies;
- What their childhood was like;
- Their personality;
- Their values;
- Their aspirations;
- Attributes that make them unique.

Once the narrative has been generated, you can explore it further in the same way that is described in the mirror time technique.

Metaphors

Lakoff and Johnson (1980, 1999) graphically illustrated the metaphorical nature of language and how the use of metaphors pervades our lives, not only as descriptions of people, events and objects, but also in the way that they orientate our thinking and action. In their earlier work (1980) they used the socialised belief that 'time is money' to illustrate how this metaphor saturates everyday language in the Western world through the use of common phrases such as 'You don't *use* your time *profitably*', 'That flat tire *cost* me an hour' or ' You need to *budget* your time'. The metaphors a participant lives by can therefore offer a rich resource for understanding the meaning they attribute to their experience. Understanding how metaphors are used can provide a conduit to a participant's pervasive constructs because, as Morgan (1997) argued, a person's metaphorical beliefs represent their unconscious habits and dependencies that determine how they develop their social roles and maintain their social relationships. As such, metaphorical associations permeate language and, ultimately, underpin our unspoken social rules. Schmitt (2005) suggests three ways that you can use metaphors in a qualitative research study. These are presented as Procedural Example 7.8.

Procedural Example 7.8

Using metaphors in research

- Examine transcripts to discover how participants use metaphors to describe themselves and their worlds as part of their everyday language. These usually represent unconscious thinking patterns that are culturally embedded and therefore taken as 'givens'. They are part of our social identities and become a mantra that we live by.

- Use metaphors as a research tool by asking people to provide a metaphor to describe themselves, an object, or a situation. For instance, a participant may describe themselves as a 'bulldog' at work, and then elaborate to show how they have a tenacious approach, not letting go as problems are grappled with. Using metaphors to objectify known people, objects or events helps the participant to surface their unconscious beliefs and make new or different connections. As such, it helps them to simplify the complex and to elaborate the meanings and emotions that are embedded within their constructs. Be alert, though, that some people readily produce metaphors or other figurative language forms (for example, similes such as 'he is like a cheetah – runs fast but not for long') while others provide more down-to-earth descriptions.
- Employ metaphors as a tool for thematic analysis. In this context, the researcher can use metaphors to add richness and detail to the articulation of emerging themes and move the themes beyond a practical attachment to the data. It is good practice to check these with participants to ensure that they make explanatory sense to them.

As metaphors are multifaceted, they provide imaginative ways of communicating complex and unclear concepts, enabling the researcher to creatively conjure up an imagery of the participants' lived worlds for the reader. Used appropriately, they can help disseminate research findings in a way that connects the reader to participants' physical and emotional lives. See the Osgerby, Marriott and Gee case study in Chapter Eleven (p. 177).

Role drawings

As we saw with the illuminative incident technique, drawings are a really flexible way of surfacing core constructs by abstracting the interview method. In keeping with Kelly's fundamental postulate, this method can provide indications of how individuals construe their social role(s) and the expectancies they hold about those roles. They can, for example, through drawings of themselves in different roles or contexts, help you surface the beliefs that participants have about:

- Themselves (their identity);
- The social roles they occupy (as an expression of their identity);
- How well they believe they satisfy the requirements of those roles (as an evaluation of their efficacy in their roles).

As with self-characterisation, if we apply these notions of role relationships and anticipatory attitudes within the framework of Higgins' (1987) self-discrepancy theory, role drawings can help you explore a participant's beliefs about their actual, ought and ideal selves. Encouraging them to annotate the drawings further opens the possibility of using laddering techniques to explore what is important for them in that role. (See the Douglas case study, p. 170.)

The lying game

This method is called a game because the lies told are overtly 'pretend' – and because it provides a light-hearted way in which to reduce constraints about expressing feelings. It was initially used by Bright (1985) to help people recognise the potential for change by using Kelly's notion that we know more about a person's perspectives when we encourage them to articulate the opposite, in this case by telling deliberate lies about themselves. For the steps involved in the elicitation process, see Procedural Example 7.9.

Procedural Example 7.9

The lying game

- Focus on a particular role that is relevant to the person and your research topic: the participant as teacher, nurse student, manager, etc. The participant then lists as many lies about themselves in that role as they can think of.
- Two columns are added to the side of the page in which to insert the respondent's replies (Y or N) to these questions:

  o Would you like this lie to be true?
  o Would you like other people to believe this lie?

- This produces the following potential patterns of response for each lie: NN, YY, YN, NY.

  o An NN response indicates complete rejection of the lie, with no wish for change.
  o A YY response indicates a wish for change at a high level of awareness - a good start.
  o A YN response indicates a wish for the lie to be true but not for others to believe it - perhaps a wish for change that would be unpopular with significant others.
  o An NY response indicates a concern for image presentation rather than a desire for change - a potent source for skilled exploration.

The ensuing discussion and probing – using constructivist interviewing techniques – of these role descriptions in a relaxed atmosphere can be more personally illuminating than using more formal techniques, though perhaps not so broad in scope, depending on the range of lies revealed.

Interview about instances

The aim of this technique is to elicit everyday interpretations by using visual stimuli to orient the conversation to a concrete representation, a physical instance, of it. It has been most commonly utilised to understand and compare people's beliefs about processes or how things work and is derived from work by Osborne and Gilbert (1980), who used it to explore students' views of the world in relation to scientific concepts. They represented scientific concepts in simple stick figure drawings depicted across a range of cards (for example, force and energy depicted by a golfer hitting a ball with a club). The cards were used to elicit conversations about the concepts.

The range of visual prompts you can use includes drawings, photos, short sentences or single words. Subsequent analysis of the conversation surfaces the alternative, but coherent, understandings that participants have about the represented concepts. These layperson, or emic, views frequently diverge from experts' views.

Rivers of experience/snakes

Referring back once again to Kelly's fundamental postulate and how our sensemaking processes are based upon our interpretations of past experience, it is logical to determine that we need to look backwards in order to understand how a person's construct system has developed because our superordinate constructs are likely to be ones that have endured over time. Since much of human action is pre-reflective, our behavioural responses are often not clearly attached to our underlying beliefs and attitudes. River, or snake, drawings represent the sequential elicitation of participants' life stories and can surface both the origins and pivotal applications of these implicitly held beliefs.

The technique draws on Kelly's experience corollary, recognising that constructs evolve over a lifetime and either become more stable through reapplication across events or shift as a result of disconfirming experiences. The idea evolved from life-line methodology applied in career counselling and the metaphor of a 'snake' was devised by Denicolo and Pope (2001) to evoke a sense of a winding life journey during which events have impact by causing decisions to be made which influence the direction that a life course takes in reaching a particular 'place'. That place might be a career stage, a role undertaken or a skill achieved (becoming a research student, the head of an organisation, an accomplished guitar player). Participants are asked to draw a representation of the chosen thread in their lives in the form of a winding snake, with each turn of its body depicting a personal experience, or critical incident, that influenced the direction taken or decision made. These turns are annotated briefly as a reminder to the participant. The snake drawing then forms the focus of an interview, with the participant explaining the significance and ramifications of the annotated events for them.

The use of the alternative title 'rivers of experience' has evolved from the snake metaphor, because 'river maps' have been found to provide richer detail as they encourage participants to discuss other topographical features of their lives, such as deep and shallow points, rapids and calm sections, tributaries, blockages and surrounding environments – again demonstrating the power of metaphor in eliciting and elucidating constructs. See the Burnard and Sutcliffe et al. case studies in Chapter Eleven (pp. 165 and 182).

The subsequent discussion around the participant's snake or river generally requires little input from the researcher, other than interest and gentle probing, as participants interrogate themselves about reasons for isolating a particular incident, how it was influential and perhaps still is. They often report feeling empowered by the experience.

Summary

We have provided here a glimpse of the possible ways in which you might explore the inner worlds of your research participants. In the books we have referenced and in the case studies in Chapter Eleven you will find further examples of these methods and some other methods devised by the author-researchers. As you become more confident as a constructivist researcher, you too may well invent ways to help participants articulate their own perspectives. You will never be short of constructs to explore because they are all around us, in the words we choose in conversation, in the words and images used in public spaces, in the written words of both fiction and non-fiction authors. They are also in the missing words – the ones avoided, discarded, ignored or not recognised – in all those media. What is more, they are in the non-verbal signals given out by individuals in their physical being and in the way they organise and 'dress' their surroundings.

The choice of method to use in your research is, again, influenced by your own constructs about what constitutes good research as well as what might serve your research purpose best. It should also be guided by how your participants perceive the research process and by the means that they feel comfortable with employing. Try not to let your own constructs inhibit their potential: before they can write, children can readily organise and reorganise objects in ways that could be translated onto a repertory grid matrix – they know what for them is alike or different. Professional adults can also enjoy a game or the chance to draw. Further, most people find that they can find different nuances to share with a researcher when allowed to be involved with two or more different techniques. You might try selecting a range of methods as elements for a repertory grid on how they might be useful for a particular research purpose. As you will see in the next chapter, there is not just a plethora of potential methods but also an abundance of research designs into which to fit them.

Suggested further reading

Elaborations on these methods can be found in the following books, the titles indicating their specific focus:

Connelly, M.F. and Clandinin, D.J. (1990) Stories of experience and narrative inquiry. *Educational Researcher*, 19(5), 2-14.
Cortazzi, D. and Roote, S. (1975) *Illuminative Incident Analysis*. London: McGraw-Hill.
Dalton, P. and Dunnett, G. (1992) *A Psychology for Living. Personal Construct Theory for Professionals and Clients*. Chichester: Wiley.
Denicolo, P.M. (1996) Explorations of constructivist approaches in continuing professional education: Staff development for changing contexts. In D. Kalekin-Fishman and B. Walker (eds), *The Construction of Group Realities: Culture, Society, and Personal Construct Theory* (pp. 267-282). Malabar, FL: Krieger.
Denicolo, P.M. (1999) Exploring metaphors in the making of meaning: Art, science and PCP. In J. Fisher and D. Savage (eds), *Beyond Experiment into Meaning* (pp. 3-14). Preston: EPCA Publications.
Denicolo, P.M. (2003) Elicitation methods to fit different purposes. In F. Fransella (ed.), *The International Handbook of Personal Construct Psychology* (pp. 123-132). Chichester: Wiley.
Denicolo, P.M. (2005) A range of elicitation methods to suit client and purpose. In F. Fransella (ed.), *The Essential Practitioner's Handbook of Personal Construct Psychology* (pp. 57-66). Chichester: Wiley.
Fransella, F. and Bannister, D. (1977) *A Manual for Repertory Grid Technique*. London: Academic Press.
Jankowicz, D. (2004) *The Easy Guide to Repertory Grids*. Chichester: Wiley.
Shaw, M.L.G. (1980) *On Becoming A Personal Scientist: Interactive Computer Elicitation of Personal Models of the World*. London: Academic Press.

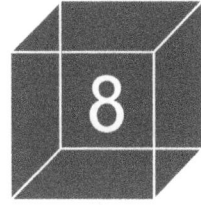

8

An evaluation of a range of potential research designs

Introduction

Having introduced you to a wide range of techniques that will help you to collect data, we now turn to how you can organise them to take best advantage of their potential. We will take you through the process from initial planning, through the various possible research designs, to procedures that can be incorporated in several designs, with a final discussion about how to balance the strengths and weaknesses inevitable in any design.

The process of planning

Whatever kind of project you are considering, whether it be a personal exploration of a situation that puzzles you, a more ambitious project for which you will seek funding, or the essence of a research degree at master's or doctoral level, the first thing you must embark on is a feasibility study. In general, the goal of any project design is to demonstrate that your purpose/aims and objectives can be achieved:

- With your research questions answered using particular techniques;
- Applied in a specified order;
- With a preselected group of participants;
- Over the time period available;
- Within a stipulated budget that considers all necessary resources, including your own skills.

This is no mean feat when you are in the early stages of research but, in true constructivist spirit, the contrast is a much worse prospect: finding out at some stage in your project, perhaps near the end when a lot has been invested, that it cannot feasibly be completed. Thus spending time and energy on checking the feasibility of your ideas by considering a range of designs for your research project is a critical aspect of constructivist research, just as it is for research in any paradigm, even though you may be planning an exploratory project that requires flexibility with the option of responding to emerging issues as it proceeds. Such flexibility can be planned into your design, as you will see as we proceed through this chapter.

Assuming that you have an idea about what your research topic will be, having refined your intuitive theories through exploration of the literature (and/or discussion with your co-researcher participants in action research, and your supervisor/adviser for a research degree), this feasibility checking process begins with a set of challenging questions which start by considering the end point. We have set these out in Further Explanation 8.1.

Further Explanation 8.1

Design questions to consider before embarking on a research project

1. What kind of data is needed to meet your purpose/aims and objectives – what will provide convincing evidence to others that you have a reasonable, credible answer?
2. What does that imply for the choice of an appropriate approach or philosophical foundation, and is this compatible with your own epistemology?
3. What is the source of your data, is it accessible and can it be accessed ethically?
4. What kind of tools/techniques/methods might provide access to those data and are you, or could you become, skilled in their use and in the analysis/interpretation of the resulting data?
5. How might these techniques be applied and in what order?
6. What resources are needed for the project? Are they available and within your financial budget?
7. How long might it take to complete the project, and do you (and those you work with, if applicable) have the time to dedicate to it?

8   How might you disseminate the results, to whom, and will they find them credible?
9   What difference will the outputs make? What might be their outcome? Is it worth the effort?

Chapters Two and Three should help you to consider the answers to the first two questions. If the purpose of the research is to gain understanding of something which may be influenced by or involves people's views, perspectives, experiences, understandings, and so on, then clearly some constructivist technique(s) will be useful at some stage, even if the aims and objectives also require some quantitative data to elaborate the final picture or to form the main substance of the results. In this chapter we will introduce a range of research designs, from those that accommodate the collection of only qualitative data to those 'mixed methods' designs that allow for the collection and combination of both qualitative and quantitative data. These designs are suitable as frameworks that might be used within any of the interpretive paradigms (phenomenology, phenomenography, hermeneutics, critical enquiry, ethnography, symbolic interactionism, grounded theory and so on; see Crotty, 1998). Although Chapter Seven discusses those techniques/methods that fit comfortably within a constructivist framework and will help you to answer Question 4, you will find descriptions of other techniques for collecting quantitative data in any number of research methods books, though we will recommend at the end of this chapter some that we have found useful ourselves or for our research students. Each of those constructivist data collecting techniques has advantages and disadvantages, as elaborated in Chapter Seven, including being more suitable for some participants than others and for some alternative data sources than others, so you will find help there for answering Question 3. Ethical aspects of working with people using this approach are threaded throughout the book, but Chapter Six addresses the trusting and trustworthy climate that needs to be established for the research techniques to realise their potential, while Chapter Nine reflects on the process of gaining ethical approval.

We will provide here and later in the book some ideas for the answers to the remaining questions, which will also particularly benefit from consideration of the case studies provided in Chapter Eleven. One caveat that I think all of our contributors would agree on is the importance of ensuring that you reflect and decide upon how you will analyse the data (see Chapter Ten) before embarking on the fieldwork – many projects have been abandoned because this preliminary stage was neglected, leaving the researcher with sacks of data they did not know what to do with. Now, though, let us look at some scaffolding designs that can incorporate a preplanned analysis method for the data revealed by each technique as it is incorporated into the design.

General research designs and processes

Research designs have been variously described/defined as: overall strategies that integrate the various parts of a project; a blueprint for collecting and analysing data; a logical plan for data collection and analysis; and the scaffolding that connects the sub-components together. Some examples are provided below, starting with case study – one of the most frequently used frameworks for constructivist research and one that can be subsumed into the other examples we provide or can stand on its own.

The most generic description of constructivist research is 'a study in which the effectiveness, value, efficacy, helpfulness, success or meaningfulness of an identified process or situation to the people involved is explored'. To give some specific topic examples: in education, we might be interested in perceptions of a new learning technique; in business, constructs might be sought about current organisational structures; in health/social care, the focus might be lifestyle activities; in travel or catering, reactions to facilities or menus might be of interest; to artists, actors, musicians, authors, poets and so on, explorations of audience responses might be salient; and in marketing, attitudes to products may be sought. We will now see how a range of such constructs can be explored using different designs, starting with the ubiquitous case study design. As you read on you might find it useful to consider what you could explore in your own discipline/professional area using each design.

Case study

Here we insert a reminder that, like many other words and phrases, the term 'case study', a particular research strategy, can be interpreted in many ways. Thus it encompasses the study of one particular bounded social entity, though that could range from an individual person to a large organisation composed of many people. Swanborn (2010: 12–23) discusses the range of definitions and how they are applied, noting that one variant can be the study of one (overarching) case that subsumes several smaller cases, while listing what common features case studies have and what features are excluded. He generally excludes those research designs that involve isolation of attributes/variables and manipulation/reduction processes (neo-positivist designs) as opposed to a study of complex attributes in a holistic, natural setting disturbed as little as is possible by the researcher (characteristics espoused by most constructivists – see Chapter Three). We would add that case studies using constructivist approaches seek to describe and understand the social entity rather than to posit causes/correlations that can be generalised, though the results of a case study can be the foundation for further studies that seek to do so (see 'mixed methods' below).

In our exemplar evaluative study, then, we might decide that our case or data source is one person whose views we can explore in depth over a specific time period using a range of techniques with their appropriate analysis potentials. These techniques could be selected from those we are already familiar with or those with which we could become competent by the time we come to apply them in the field. Using a range of techniques that complement each other helps to ensure that we capture several nuances of the participant's perspectives. Since each technique has advantages and disadvantages, using a variety of techniques helps to cancel out or at least minimise the worst disadvantages (see 'triangulation' below). This case participant is clearly going to have to be (persuaded to be) ready to give a substantial amount of time to our research as well as revealing much that is personal, and perhaps previously private. The nature and order of elicitation techniques should therefore be sensitive to: her/his availability and stamina (and our own), growing trust in us as researchers, expanding understanding of how the techniques work and tolerance of his/her own developing self-understanding, and ethical permissions and agreements, to mention but a few considerations. It is usually a good plan to set this out as a diagram, perhaps a Gantt chart (see recommended reading) or flow diagram (see examples later, Figures 8.1 and 8.2), taking into consideration such things as time to do some preliminary or even detailed data analysis between administration of different techniques as well as engage in other work, social and family commitments (researcher's as well as the participant's). We would have to factor in also resources we will need – such as recording equipment, and expenses such as travel and subsistence for us and our participant. (You can find out more about these aspects and how to deal with them in Denicolo and Becker, 2012).

Instead of a single-person case study, you might consider that your topic lends itself to a case that encompasses more than one person since the focus is a social/work activity that involves several people. Those people might be a bounded group all of whose constructs you could seek, or you might need to select views from particular examples of categories of people involved. The latter are likely to be selected on a theoretical basis rather than as a 'representative sample' as used in neo-positivist research. For instance, you may incorporate in an education setting the perspectives of pupils, teachers and parents; in a business context, executives, managers and team members; in a health context, patients, relatives, nurses and other medical staff. Although the fundamentals of the design process are much the same as those in the single-person case above, the design itself will be more complex in many respects and may need to take account of such things as gaining permissions for access (when potentially vulnerable groups are involved), diplomacy issues (suspicions about who has said or will say what about whom), and particularly costs in time (more on this in Chapter Nine). For such studies a really careful design using a chart and calendar is essential, as of course are designs using multiple case studies as described further in the next section.

Figure 8.1 is an example of a chart which illustrates how different research techniques contribute data to develop an understanding about how metaphors are presented and understood in a science classroom to explain abstract ideas (for example, chemical reactions). Each of the five techniques contribute to various information arrays, to the main topic, and to an answer to the main research question. Figure 8.2 was used as a summary of work on the same project, but this time laid out to show the relationship of the activities to each other over time. The weeks displayed represent actual working/researching weeks – the school vacation periods and researcher's breaks have been omitted to eliminate complexity for display purposes, but you should include such things in a working chart to guide your own practice. This introduces another cogent issue – in planning your design you will need to allow for such things as busy or 'down' times in the institution/organisations in which your participants work. Participants may not be available to fit into a tidy research design that fits your work times, so it is worthwhile engaging in a preliminary study of their context, culture and habits if you are not already familiar with them. In the education-based study above the researcher had to work round such things as school vacation times, busy periods for teachers (the start of term, exam marking weeks, and so on).

This example used natural groups (teachers and students) working at the same study level in the same catchment area during the same academic year, but in three different types of school. This allowed for both comparison between schools (diversity) and reinforcement of emerging views (similarity). It also illustrates forms of sample selectivity – criterion and stratified – that will be discussed in the section on processes.

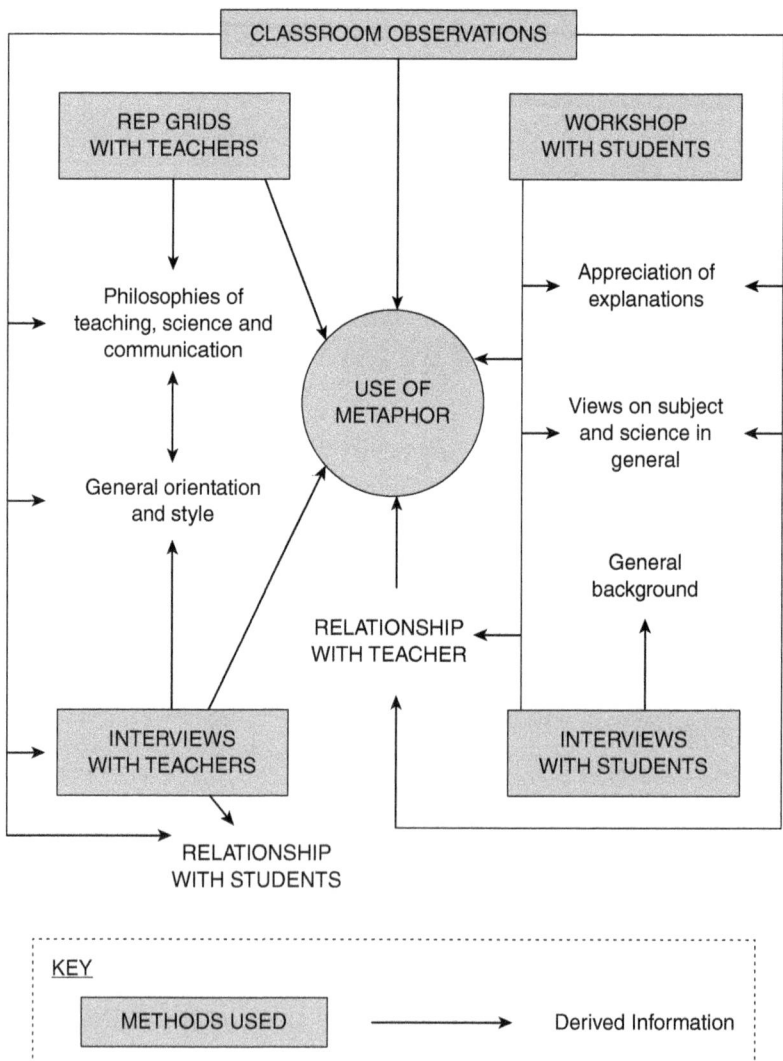

Figure 8.1 A study of metaphor use and understanding in science classrooms: relationship of data to techniques

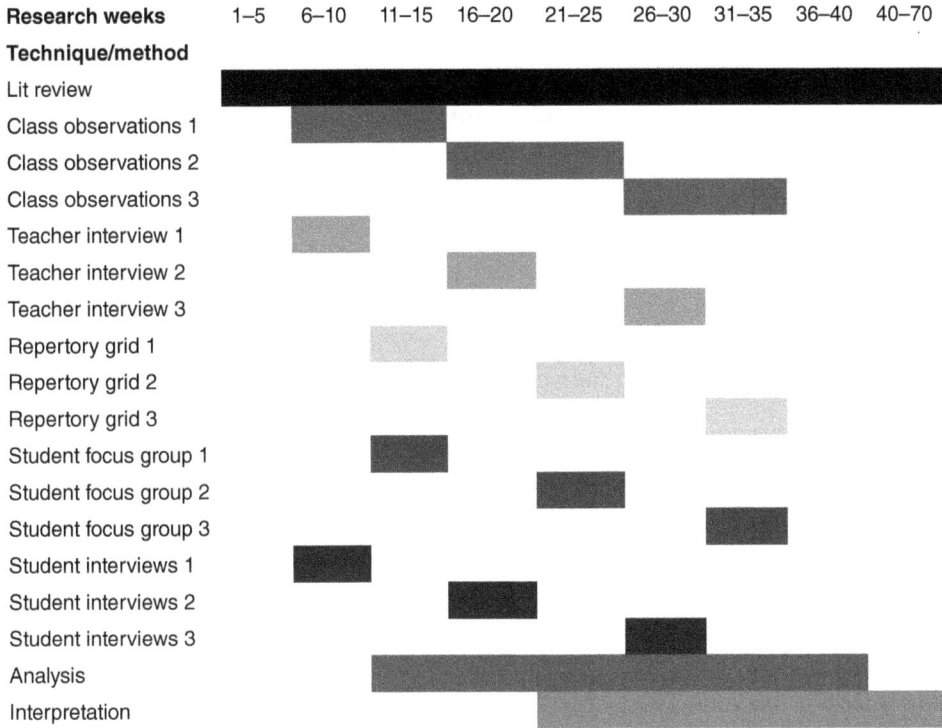

Figure 8.2 A study of metaphor use and understanding in science classrooms: time chart for research in schools 1, 2 and 3. (Shading differentiates the task type)

Cross-sectional, comparative or longitudinal designs

These designs are special instances of the multiple-case design used when you deliberately choose to compare cases to achieve aims such as identifying what factors seem to be pervasive at a particular time across groups (cross-sectional) or what circumstances seem to impact on certain groups and which phenomena are salient to different groups (comparative) or how constructs change or develop over a period of time (longitudinal).

Each of these requires particular consideration of the kinds of questions you will ask of participants, using which techniques. In other words, the kind of data sought is as important as the selection of participants who hold the data because, rather than seeking rich or thick data that describe a particular contextual world of one specific participant, you may interested in, say, how all selected participants construe particular aspects in their environment, what aspects particular individuals are especially alert to or influenced by that others may not be, or which of their constructs remain stable and which are challenged at different points in time. Thus your research is more focused and requires very careful consideration of what you are really looking for and which instruments or techniques might help you to access it.

Some examples of research purposes that would lend themselves to these designs might be that you want to find out more about how people of different gender or status or role differ in their perspectives, or how the views of similar people vary according to different circumstances/contexts, or you may wish to follow up the development of understandings or changes in attitudes/opinions over a particular age range, circumstance or time span and so on. A study of construct development is also the aim of the next example.

Before and after study

One particular form of evaluative study concerns how people's constructs are changed as a result of a particular intervention. This kind of study involves exploring constructs about a relevant issue before the intervention and then afterwards, either immediately and/or after a period for reflection and/or practice. In an educational setting, say, we might evaluate the potential of a particular curriculum development by eliciting the constructs of students or teachers or examiners (or any combination thereof) before the development process and then after it has been in place for a month or so. For example, we might work with schoolgirls to find out about their interest in and attitudes towards science in terms of a future career, then take them on trips to various workplaces to meet and follow 'a day in the life of' women scientists. Perhaps we could use the repertory grid technique using a range of career roles including scientist as elements, with a construct finally provided (if it does not occur naturally): 'I would be interested in – this is not for me'. We could instead, or as well, ask them to draw a picture of a scientist to demonstrate any personal attributes scientists have. We might then repeat the exploration of career interests the day following the visits and then six months later to get a sense of the stability of any construct change. At this point you might like to contemplate what kind of before and after study might be appropriate in your particular field or discipline, including what techniques you might choose.

As well as constructivist techniques, your study might be enhanced by the collection of some specifically quantitative data, perhaps extending your study to a larger group of participants than is viable using data-rich but time-consuming methods. This brings us to the next potential design, mixed methods.

Mixed methods

We suggested in the early chapters that interpretive research seeking rich descriptions does not preclude the use of quantitative data, although qualitative data generally predominate in such studies. This sort of design is usually referred to as 'mixed methods' because different kinds of techniques are used to collect different kinds of data. Such studies differ from 'multi-method' studies, as described above and in Golsorkhi et al. (2010), in that multi-method studies investigate complex phenomena using several qualitative data collection techniques, rather than several techniques each collecting either qualitative or quantitative data or both. In the arts, for instance, individual members of an audience may be interviewed about a performance/work of art using constructivist techniques to produce qualitative data, while the audience as a whole might be surveyed with some questions seeking yes/no answers, others seeking answers to 'how often and how much' questions and yet others allowing open-ended responses. The qualitative data might satisfy the artist about why people respond in the way they do, while the quantitative data may well satisfy the 'angels', that is, the people providing financial support, who are more interested in how many people will attend or view or buy the art work and how often. Together the data can provide information which will be useful to many stakeholders about detail and about how generalisable responses are.

Österlind, who also provides a case description of another project in Chapter Eleven, worked with her colleague Aili on a large project studying teacher work (Aili and Österlind, submitted). They had to satisfy several stakeholders: the teachers themselves, their head teachers and the local authority, as well as the funders of the research and themselves, researchers with a vested interest in interpretive enquiry. They provided us with a chart of their research (Figure 8.3). This research was an investigation into teacher work tasks that have to be done to support teaching, such as ordering materials and fixing computer links. From this chart you can see that in the two phases of the exploratory study teachers first completed e-diaries, over a fixed time period, that were shared with the researchers, and then took part in focused team discussions guided by the researchers. Originally it was intended that the next stage would be the contextualisation and collation of those first two phases (now ongoing phase IV), but the data produced were so rich that it was worth developing a questionnaire for phase III, using learning derived from those

Research Design Overview		
Phase I	Phase II	Phase III
Exploratory studies: Illuminating professional tasks		Expanded study: Checking generalisability
Individual task-focused e-diaries	**Focused team discussions – supported by a task-focused web team reflection protocol**	Web questionnaire focused on hindrances and support for specific tasks
Directed to 60 teachers from two school districts		Directed to 1050 teachers in the two school districts
Daily notations on work tasks, during ten workdays	The same 60 teachers, in their natural teams	Questions about the three latest workdays
	Twice over two weeks	
Phase IV		
Process study: contextualisation of phases I–III and new knowledge about the ongoing processes in the two school districts and in the teacher community, and their implications for the teachers' performance of quality-driven professional work		
The same teacher teams as in Phase II.		
Principals [head teachers] of the selected schools in phases I and II		

Figure 8.3 Mixed methods research design overview from Aili and Österlind (submitted)

first two phases, that could be distributed to a large number of teachers in the same school districts. The details and meaning of daily practice felt genuine and authentic to the teachers involved, while the generalisable data of the third phase satisfied the funders' needs for 'scientific' data, as they understood the term.

Within research fieldwork using that design, which demonstrates flexibility in response to emerging data, and those other designs above, other strategies or processes were embedded that could be used in your research. These are described briefly next. As you read, try to identify how they were manifest in the previous research examples.

Processes that can be incorporated within designs

The following processes can all be used independently, on their own or in combination in constructivist research designs, while some, such as pilot studies, can be used in any form of research.

Pilot study

Pilot studies can serve many purposes, not the least of which is a practice of planned techniques to gain confidence in their use and to check their suitability as methods for helping participants articulate their understandings. To gain confidence in a technique you can persuade a range of people (friends and family or peer students, for example) to work with you, giving feedback on your performance until you are ready to 'go public'. Next you can try out your new skill on a person or two within your target participants' age and background range to check that you are using the most appropriate language register and personal approach as well as whether your explanations are clear of what you would like them to do and why.

Pilot studies can save a lot of the kind of heartache that comes from finding that you are not getting the data you expected, especially when there are only a few suitable participants available. It is preferable not to 'muddy their thinking' by skipping the pilot stage but instead to build your own confidence in what you are doing and how you are doing it.

Other reasons for including a pilot study in your design are included in Further Explanation 8.2.

◢◣ Further Explanation 8.2

The value of pilot studies

A pilot study can help you ensure that:

- Your participants are able to provide the data you need to collect to answer your research question(s);

- Your materials/instruments are presented in an attractive way that helps the participant(s) to engage with the task;
- The language used for eliciting constructs is age and culture appropriate;
- The questions you will use are couched at a level of difficulty that encourages reflection but does not discourage engagement;
- You are prepared for the kinds of questions that you may be asked and have, say, examples to hand to aid explanations;
- Any ambiguities or redundancies have been eliminated;
- Any potential threats or undue intrusiveness either have been removed or have appropriate reassurances built in;
- The time needed to elicit good-quality data has been identified both to inform participants when recruiting them and to incorporate into the main study design;
- The best sequence for presenting a range of techniques has been ascertained;
- You have confidence in using your data collection tools.

Sampling strategies and participant numbers

We now consider which people, among those able to respond effectively to your data-eliciting questions, you might choose, why and how many.

Like many aspects of research design your sampling procedure is heavily dependent on the purpose of your research. Unlike neo-positivist research in which the gold standard for sampling is the randomised controlled trial, there are a number of sampling protocols for constructivist or any kind of interpretivist research, each suiting different purposes. To be a skilled constructivist researcher you need to be able to tolerate that diversity and the tension of wondering if your selected sampling strategy is the best within the limits of your resources, particularly in relation to the most effective use of the participants' and your time.

The range of sampling strategies that can be categorised as 'purposive' rather than probability sampling is summarised in Further Explanation 8.3. You can find more detail in the general textbooks recommended below.

⚠ Further Explanation 8.3

Sampling strategies

Criterion sampling. Used when participants must exhibit specific attributes, for example, having had a specific experience or being engaged in a particular bounded activity (say, as members of a work or sports team).

Typical case sampling. Used to illustrate what is common, or average, within an attribute range, but this requires good knowledge of what the extremes of the range are and what constitutes normal – could be useful as the second stage of in-depth data collection following a stage in which a survey demonstrates the range of responses in a mixed methods study.

Critical case sampling. Like the typical case version above, the use of this case can exemplify what constructs are likely to emerge from a particular group of identified people but the actual members of that group need to recognise that the chosen case is a 'critical' case from their perspective for resulting data to be credible to them.

Intensity sampling. Selects participants who exemplify well a particular attribute or set of attributes; often used for comparison studies such as full-time and part-time students/workers or good team players and loners; can be used to identify people who form a homogeneous selection in some respect, such as early career researchers, actors or musicians.

Maximum variation sampling. Participants demonstrating a wide range of one or more particular attributes chosen to show either common patterns despite diversity or the different responses to a common experience, for example all the competitors in a challenging situation.

Snowball sampling. After identifying a key informant, that person identifies others with similar attributes or experiences, and so on, to source information-rich data, for example a professional with expertise in a particular field might introduce colleagues with similar expertise to whom access may not previously have been easy for you.

Extreme or deviant cases sampling. Used to demonstrate the views of unusual or outstanding or exceptional people, or those who hold special positions or have potentially unique perspectives, such as a Nobel Prize winner, a prime minister or a hermit.

Stratified sampling within, say, the criterion group. Can facilitate comparisons between subgroups.

Opportunistic sampling. Involves following up leads as they emerge; requires flexibility built into the design so that advantage can be taken of opportunities.

Convenience sampling. Engaging people who are handy and willing as participants – not easy to defend since it has no rationale and is likely to produce poor data.

Another critical aspect of sampling is how many participants is 'enough'. The answer is invariably that the number is contingent on your purpose, what you want to find out and how credible your results will be. Of course it also depends on your resources, but remember that the nature of your research question, not the number and nature of participants, should be determined by what you can manage, albeit that it is usually what you can manage when pressed. So if you only have time or funding for a small number of participants then focus your research question on what their data can tell you rather than deciding the question and then trying to stretch your resources and data beyond their elastic limit. Sometimes a small number, even only one person who provides data through a range of elicitation techniques, can deliver richer data than many people surveyed about an experience. This illustrates the trade-off between large numbers and rich data that we frequently meet in research. The use of multiple techniques to provide different or supporting perspectives on a topic is one form of triangulation, as we shall see next.

Triangulation

The first important point to note is that in research the term 'triangulation' does not mean that you have to have three of anything. It does derive from surveying where bearings from three positions pinpoint a location, but in research you can gain advantage, if not a fixed point, by using two, three, four or any number of perspectives. As noted above, those perspectives can come via:

- The use of several different elicitation techniques with one or more people (methodological triangulation);
- Comparison and contrast of the constructs from several different participant people or groups (data triangulation);
- Interpretation of the data through the lenses of different theories (theoretical triangulation).

It is also possible to triangulate using different judges to review the data or different researchers to collect the data. These are all ways in which you can guard to some extent against a variety of potential flaws such as bias due to the questions themselves or the questioning technique (each technique or theoretical perspective asks a slightly different question in a different way), or the skill and nature of the questioner or the ease with which participants can express themselves or their experience with the topic under scrutiny. Triangulation can act as a test for consistency, but more often than not it provides additional, deeper or wider insight into your topic. Some of that insight could be that certain aspects of the world are indeed inconsistent.

We have already provided some examples of triangulation; for instance, the study in Figures 8.1 and 8.2 used data triangulation (the teachers' and the students' perspectives from three different schools) and methodological triangulation (observation, interviews, focus groups and repertory grids). The study described in Figure 8.3 also used those two triangulation forms since data were collected from teachers and principals via e-diaries, team discussion groups, a process study and a web-based survey. Viewing and analysing the data from different theoretical perspectives, perhaps through a sociological theory and a psychological one, or a political one perhaps, can uncover hitherto unconsidered dimensions that perhaps send you back to your hypothetical drawing board to revise your own constructions of that particular reality, if you are up for that challenge.

Iteration

Another challenging way to design your project is to use the process of iteration. This is particularly useful for truly exploratory studies in which the answers are mysteries yet to be solved because the questions have not been asked before. It is perhaps the most challenging design process for those who prefer a set, well-rehearsed and planned approach because it requires great tolerance of uncertainty. Yet it is an approach favoured by those who like to follow a puzzling phenomenon, such as unpredictable consumer, patient or student needs, or implicit understandings, to see to where it leads them. It involves trying out one technique on a test model or prototype, then testing, analysing and refining the model, in a cyclical process in which new information is generated at each round of the cycle. At each turn this new information is then used to interrogate and refine the data from previous stages. What emerges from each cycle informs the focus and sampling decisions for the next cycle, and the cycles continue until no new data or perspectives emerge – the point of saturation.

For example, you might have intuitive theories about what is happening in a particular context that results in particular outcomes but decide to set those theories aside while you do some in-depth observation of the situation. You do a preliminary analysis of the results which seems to indicate that some people have more influence than others on the outcomes. You therefore decide to select a stratified sample of informants from both criterion groups (influential and non-influential) to take part in a repertory grid interview that focuses on roles in the context with a disclosed purpose of exploring with them who does what and why. On a preliminary analysis of that data you find that there are three particular key people who determine the outcomes. At this point you could return to the observation technique but focus only on what interactions those three key people have, and/or you could conduct some further investigation with those people, perhaps using a river of experience to explore the critical pathways that influence their behaviour in the context. Another possibility is to ask them to provide an illuminative incident to demonstrate to you what their role in proceedings is, or even design another instrument to follow up your findings. At each stage you use the findings to reanalyse your previous findings in order to elaborate your understandings until you find that you are gaining no more useful information.

Progressive focusing and pyramid designs

The iteration example above is also an example of progressive focusing. This is a process whereby the researcher starts out with the equivalent of a wide-angle lens (Parlett and Hamilton, 1976) to gather data. Then, step by step, the researcher analyses and reflects on results to isolate significant components, explores those components in greater depth, again analyses and reflects, and identifies the crucial component. Thus the data collection and analysis progression acts as a funnel from the general to the particular. In constructivist research this could take the form of applying a questionnaire survey about a topic (perhaps based on documentary analysis of books and articles on the topic) to a large population, using the resulting general responses to identify a sample of respondents to take part in a focus group to debate and delineate more detailed information on aspects that emerge as salient to the majority. Thereafter perhaps one or two of those participants could be identified as being particularly knowledgeable about or involved in those aspects. They would be invited next to take part in a constructivist in-depth interview to elaborate as exhaustively as possible their perspectives on the aspects.

Conversely, you might start with an in-depth constructivist technique to gain an understanding of a situation, event or role from a small number of selected key informants in a specified population, analysing the results for both the issues they deem critical and the language they use to describe them. Ultimately, language is the key that opens the door for the researcher to the interpretation of people's life-worlds, and the principal aim of most constructivist research methods is to elicit a conversation or story that will provide a linguistic text for analysis, either to help illuminate results of another technique, such as a repertory grid or an experiential river drawing, or to design a really relevant instrument to collect more generalisable data. For a pyramid (or inverted funnel) design the next stage could employ a focus group technique with a wider section of people involved with the situation, event or role (maximum variation sampling would perhaps work well) to investigate which topics were universally important and which might be more minority perspectives, with an indication of whether the category labels remain homogeneous or had variation across the group. The results of this exercise could lead to the design of a large-scale survey with the questions derived being on aspects selected by participants as the most salient and couched in the language of that community or population.

Both of these design processes, upright and inverted funnel, acknowledge reflexivity – the mutual interdependence of accounts/descriptions, analyses and interpretations, as do the other strategies and processes described in this chapter, each of them with their own strengths and weaknesses.

Advantages and limitations – a balancing act

We have emphasised the importance of planning your research project. This is especially significant when investigating the very complex and messy world of people's constructs or meaning systems, using tools that are all inevitably limited in what they can achieve. Thus the researcher is wise to recognise those limitations by incorporating checks and balances into their plan or design so that the advantages of each technique are maximised while their limitations are complemented by the advantages inherent in another technique (see Chapter Seven).

However, each design and the potential procedures within them, such as sampling processes, will also inherit the benefits and constraints as outlined above so the whole process of research is one of choosing designs in which component parts complement and compensate for each other. An informed researcher can then liberally lace appropriate caveats into the analysis, interpretation and dissemination stages to recognise and make explicit the limits to the understandings presented. The perfect method in the flawless design to produce an impeccable truth is a holy grail. When learning science at school we were introduced to 'laws' that were said to apply 'under standard conditions of temperature and pressure' and 'within the limits of the measuring device', and the same maxims apply in constructivist or any other form of research, for the conclusions we draw are within particular conditions of time and space (circumstance) and are restricted by the limits of our research methods/instruments and design, as well as by our own skill or lack of it.

Summary

In this chapter we have urged you, rather than imitating the procedures and designs adopted previously by others or those that seem relatively simple and easy to accomplish, to take time to reflect on what you want to achieve and the best way to order and balance techniques to gain the best outcome within your resources. Then build in some flexibility, because when a well-thought-through design meets the trials of the fieldwork world there are inevitably further challenges to manage, as we shall reveal in the next chapter. Either before or after you investigate those next considerations, you might like to review some of the case studies in Chapter Eleven to see further examples of some of the many design ideas presented here.

Suggested further reading

Office Tool Tips (2015) *Creating a Gantt Chart*. Accessed 17 April 2015, from: http://www.officetooltips.com/excel/tips/creating_a_gantt_chart.html

A practical resource:
Bryman, A. (2007) Barriers to integrating quantitative and qualitative research. *Journal of Mixed Methods Research*, 1(1), 8-22.

A practitioner's perspective:
Yin, R.K. (2006) Mixed methods research: are the methods genuinely integrated or merely parallel? *Research in Schools*, 13(1), 41-47.

The following books introduce in accessible ways a range of techniques compatible with and complementary to constructivist ones:
Cohen, L., Manion, L. and Morrison, K. (2011) *Research Methods in Education* (7th edition). Abingdon: Routledge.
Gray, D.E. (2009) *Doing Research in the Real World*. London: SAGE.
Patton, M.Q. (2002) *Qualitative Research and Evaluation Methods* (3rd edition). Thousand Oaks, CA: SAGE.

9

Realities and practicalities in managing fieldwork

Introduction

The many publications on how to do research provide important insights, but there is nothing quite like being on your own in the driving seat of your research study to develop those personal and technical skills to carry it out most effectively, safely and ethically. As with learning to drive a car, the lessons are critical but it is only once we have passed the test and are set loose on the road that we really learn to drive.

In this chapter we move from principles of effective research to explore tips and considerations relating to the realities of conducting constructivist research – those issues and practical concerns often ignored by theory but that tend to arise in normal circumstances. We share what we have learnt from the many years we have spent working in different contexts in the hope that our mistakes and bits of wisdom will at least save you time, but might make the difference between a dependable outcome and one that is undermined by the burden of inappropriate actions or missed opportunities. Some of these realities will be trivial, or at least might appear to be, while others will be more substantial, and we will discuss each in an order typically followed as a research project unfolds. To this end we pick up on many formal aspects of research from other chapters, but in particular from Chapter Six. We start with those subtle, often hidden, issues that influence us as researchers as we seek to clarify our research focus, and then move on to those issues of a more interpersonal and practical nature.

In the beginning

Reasons for carrying out a research project are many and varied – a requirement of a master's degree programme, or an aspect of your internal consultancy project work, for instance. You may have only some, or possibly complete, control over the topic itself or at least the approach to take. Whatever the motive, you want to make an impact, to do something that has real value and will be applied widely, that will change things significantly for the better. Be careful. In your drive to create new knowledge or practical insights, be aware of two key considerations. The first is to select a topic and approach that you genuinely expect could be carried out within the time, resources and abilities that you possess (see Chapter Eight). Depth versus breadth is always a dilemma. Of course, the balance will depend entirely on the nature of the project. An internal consultancy or practitioner project may be served best by a broad understanding of key issues, whereas a master's or doctoral study would require more academic, theoretical depth. However, in general, especially in academic research, you are most likely to make an impact when you tackle a topic that is sufficiently narrow to allow you to develop deep, rich insights. For example, the broad topic of 'leading change' might be better focused as 'leading people through particular change projects in a selected set of small and medium enterprises'. This is more than just a resource or impact issue. In a similar vein to our discussion on quality of research in Chapter Three, there is a minimum level of depth of research necessary in order to contribute anything at all. There is a sort of tipping point. Broad, superficial research can be so lacking in rigour or insight that it not only lacks dependency but also can be misleading. We need to be sure that our research extends beyond this point. Think about depth versus breadth and make sure you focus sufficiently to make a dependable contribution.

The second key consideration when selecting your topic is to be aware of existing understandings and insights. We have emphasised the importance of reviewing current thinking, largely through peer-reviewed journals or other credible sources. However, there is a more subtle, but perhaps more important, dynamic that can influence your interest in a topic. We have personally experienced occasions when a potential researcher, for whatever reason, has such a deep commitment to a research question that it blinds them to its broader value. Commitment to a topic is important, but deep belief that stirs emotions may not be a good basis for maintaining independence in the research process. In one research supervision case, a psychology master's researcher had come to academic life late in a career that was deeply rooted in objective, quantitative, positivist analysis and decision-making. Then, as he explored the literature and reflected on his experience, he 'found' emotions. This was such a profound revelation to him that he felt it his calling to research and teach the importance of emotions in leadership. Whilst aspects of emotions may well form a relevant research project for a master's programme, the depth of commitment he had to this topic created an underpinning fantasy-like perspective which masked its real nature, and masked openness to learn from established theory and practice. As you approach your research topic, adopt a degree of humility – albeit a confident humility. As in the Buddhist tradition, adopt a 'beginner's mind', or as Kelly (1991a: 241) notes, a 'credulous approach'. Recognise that just because you have discovered a phenomenon for the first time, it is almost certainly not the first time it has been discovered and there may be deep existing insights for you to explore.

However, having said this, one of the most important criteria you should use to select a research topic is to do something that interests you, that is intrinsically engaging and meaningful for you, and that will add value by advancing knowledge to make a real difference.

Refining the focus

Throughout we have noted that the approach you take in your research should be consistent with the nature of the phenomenon you wish to explore and the research question you wish to address. If you were adopting a positivist perspective, experimenting with natural scientific phenomena, your research objective, focus and scope might be clearly established at the start and remain in place over the course of your project. But this is rarely the case in social sciences and especially when we wish to explore internal human phenomena, as we constructivists do. The problem lies in the iterative nature of discovery: we most often do not know enough about the phenomenon or what to research until we have begun to explore it.

Whilst in positivist, deductive research (see Chapter Three) we might well start our research with a hypothesis, in exploratory constructivist research we do not, because implicit in hypotheses is assumption. We remain open to where the research takes us. Apart from a strict grounded theory approach, it is often most helpful to start with a general understanding of the nature of the topic, phenomenon, problem or issue of interest. You might read around it, talk to experts and search the internet to gain broad insights. In the jargon we tend to use, you might take a hermeneutic approach. This approach recognises that understanding develops through two distinct but interrelated dynamics: broad understanding of the nature of the topic and its context, coupled with in-depth insight into specific elements. As you initially explore a topic area, reviewing the literature, you might move iteratively between big picture and focused detail, each cycle allowing you to develop deeper comprehension about the phenomenon and the specific focus you wish to take. With such a careful cyclical development, you will find it much easier to refine your focus and gain deep insight into what research into the topic might entail. Thus you can progressively focus your literature review and/or your research design.

In summary, you need to start your research with some clarity, to the level of identifying an area requiring deeper exploration. You should not have a refined research question or objectives at this stage and should not expect to clearly understand the nature of the phenomenon until you have carried out your initial research enquiry. However, by the time you start to design your research in detail, you should be clear about the topic you are exploring and what your research aims are. This leads to the next practical consideration.

What the topic really is

In Chapter Three we noted the importance of distinguishing between cause, symptoms and effect as we clarify research focus. Here we take this a little deeper as we consider focus in practice. What researchers *think* they are researching and what they actually *are* researching can be very different, especially in constructivist research involving people.

Let us take the topic of communication to illustrate this issue. You wish to research reported problems of communication between two of your organisation's departments. First you will need to determine if there really are communications problems or if the reports are symptoms of personal or political agendas. Once you are content that there really are communication problems, you then need to consider the medium and the message to discount dysfunctional formal process, technology or other systemic obstacles. If it is not politics or technology you might then consider the 'objective' information that passes between the departments. It might just be that the systems work well but the information communicated is inadequate. Only once you have resolved these questions might you get into constructivist territory. So, people are reporting problems with communication. Is it perceived communication issues that are of most interest? Is it about interactions and relationships? Or is it something to do with what is transmitted versus what is received that you wish to address? Or is it something even deeper than this? Are you most interested in the feelings and attitudes that people have, which are externalised as complaints about communications but are really expressions about not feeling valued, listened to, treated equitably or given credit? Keep challenging yourself, and ask others to challenge you, until you are absolutely clear about what it *really* is that you *wish* to research.

Now you can get on with the detailed design of your research. We have discussed many different alternative tools and techniques (in Chapter Seven), and designs for constructivist research (in Chapter Eight) and here we continue with our discussion around practicalities that you need to consider as you design your research approach.

Let us start with the importance of establishing a good foundation with key parties involved with you in your research.

Building relationships

Your research will involve a number of different stakeholders. Of course the most important relationships are between the researcher and participants. But there are others who may have a keen interest in your research and its outcomes. As you immerse yourself in the intrinsic draw of collecting data, make sure you take time to address stakeholder needs and interests.

Think about your sponsors. You may have received financial support for the research, and with it come obligations and expectations. It is only too easy to lose sight of the supporting organisation/people once the funding has been secured. Be proactive, keep in touch. You may have other sponsors, perhaps not so formal, but those who have given resources, time, equipment or other inputs to help you succeed. Let them know you appreciate what they have done and keep them informed of progress. Do not neglect the support you gain from friends and family. It may seem strange to include these in a section on sponsors, but it does no harm, and a lot of good, to recognise each one's role in ways that are appropriate and personal to them.

The research process often involves people who would otherwise be working. Some participants will feel they are making a real contribution, while for others involvement might be a distraction or novelty. However, for the employer, it is a cost, which is acceptable if they are a sponsor, but you need to recognise the time, disruption and other sacrifices or losses they might incur. Of course you will thank them, but take care to honour your agreements, only extending your intrusion by timely agreement with key contacts.

Recall our observations in Chapter Six about first contact. You may need, perhaps, to negotiate permission to speak to participants in work time or, indeed, contact them in their professional capacity in any way at any time. Most managers will be predisposed to help you if they can, so be positive, and again, confident humility can go a long way. Showing how the research will benefit them will help, but do not lose sight of simply appealing to their goodwill. Remember that you are not actually asking an organisation, you are asking a person, so your appeal will need to reflect the person's needs and interests, not (just) the organisation's.

The degree of 'imposition' on an employer can go far beyond costs associated with participants. You might address topics and issues that could be sensitive, possibly to the business but more likely to the individual. Maintaining integrity, an ethical approach and confidentiality is important, and these have been discussed in Chapter Six. However, be sensitive to more informal issues, to those that you may not have been aware of initially but which come to the surface as you explore personal meanings. Be ready to back off or change tack if necessary – never take the view that you have a right to be there; always show deepest respect for the people you meet and their organisation. The same caveats apply if your participants are children, vulnerable adults and those who give ethics permission for such research.

In essence this comes down to a single concept – relationship. Try not to be so tied up with your research project that you lose sight of accountabilities, responsibilities, courtesies, sensitivities and contributions towards stakeholders. You should do this because it is right but also because it builds the relationship for those times when you need to return for more data or to check your findings. How you establish these relationships depends on you and them, but keep in mind a useful principle – the lagniappe. A lagniappe is something you do that is not required or expected but adds value – it is a way of investing goodwill into a relationship and helping to balance the value that has been extended to you. See what *you* may give as stakeholders contribute to make your research a success.

Further Explanation 9.1

Responding to sensitivities

An interesting coincidence has just occurred! Exactly at the time the author was completing the previous paragraph, a researcher under his supervision Skyped. He is setting up an in-company research project, as a requirement for an MBA programme, on internal communication. He was worried. The HR department had rejected his first proposal because it overlapped with a survey study they wished to carry out. We discussed a different perspective, and how to gain the support of HR – in particular to carry out a project that had no political sensitivities or overlaps. The new approach we discussed would effectively form a **lagniappe** for HR because it would add triangulation data for their survey!

Engaging participants

Participants are key stakeholders, and all that we have noted above about developing a relationship with them will help to ensure that they not only agree to take part but also are willing contributors to a successful process and outcome.

A person is most likely to agree to take part if they can see how the research will add value that they also align with, and if they can see a benefit for them – which may be simply feeling valued, or wanting to contribute, not necessarily a direct tangible benefit. We have discussed initial information that should be given and agreements that need to be made with participants (Chapter Six). Once they have consented to be involved, their ongoing engagement will need to be managed carefully. It is counter-productive to persuade people to be involved if they really would rather not, especially with constructivist research that requires open collaboration between you the researcher and the participant, without impediments of resentment or watch-watching. Always be honest. Say exactly what their involvement will entail, and if you expect a repertory grid interview to take 90 minutes, do not try to gain co-operation by saying it will take only 60 minutes. It is better to ask for too much time than not enough.

Whilst being honest, you will also need to be careful in an early contact not to discuss any aspect that will compromise the research. For example, if you wish to explore, say, ethical leadership, you might not wish to use the adjective (construct) 'ethical' in your recruitment documents because this is likely to prime participants and influence the way they respond in the interview. So, develop relationships with integrity, but be careful not to undermine the exploration of the phenomenon of interest.

You may encounter the question of payment for participants. It is normally better to avoid any form of payment for their time since it establishes unhelpful expectations and sets a precedent for future researchers. You will gain the best involvement if they are willing volunteers. You should offer to cover any costs they incur, although an interview in company time is unlikely to incur any. You might also consider a gift, as a token of thanks. Though not absolutely necessary, it can help to balance an otherwise imbalanced relationship where you may well be viewed as having superior expertise or power. We have given a good-quality pen sporting our email contact at the start of an interview to help build rapport, or at the end of an interview as a thank you. This is a lagniappe, and is a courtesy recognition of the time and contribution that participants give. Equally, we have conducted many interviews without offering more than a sincere thank-you for the participant's time.

The importance of gaining written consent was noted in Chapter Six. If your research is into an uncontroversial topic with adults in a normal professional environment, it is likely that you would face few barriers in gaining permissions and voluntary involvement, and few issues with the data collection activities. However, your research might not be so straightforward, as is often the case in constructivist research, which by its nature often involves topics and participants that require careful management. There are many participant populations who require particular care, including children, people with disabilities and others who are vulnerable. We should be meticulous in maintaining strict standards of care to ensure, first, that no harm is done and, second, that we maintain dignity and respect, ensuring as far as we can that our participants' experience is a positive, enjoyable one. Researchers should never take advantage nor place participants under pressure or embarrassment. Having said this, constructivist research, by its nature, often addresses deep issues, and the tools and techniques, as 'sharp' instruments, can access constructs that can provoke difficult emotional responses, even with people who are not otherwise vulnerable or disadvantaged.

For example, consider the questioning approach of laddering up that we use to elicit core constructs, discussed in Chapter Five. Here we take an elicited construct descriptor and attempt to explore what lies behind or underpins this construct using 'why' questions. For example, in the apparently uncontroversial scenario in Further Explanation 9.2, about approaches to teaching young adults, what starts as a straightforward data elicitation process between the researcher (R) and a participant (P) quickly becomes emotionally charged. What starts as a conversation about a teaching technique quickly, by laddering, exposes an evident reluctance indicative of a difficult personal, emotional issue. As we noted previously, if we had recognised this early we might have backed off at that point and considered a different questioning tack, but it is a fine line between seeking deep meanings and delving into difficult emotional issues, so we may find we inadvertently enter sensitive territory.

Further Explanation 9.2

Danger of inadvertently exposing sensitivities

R: You have said that you enjoy interactive discussion.

P: Well, exploring different views helps to develop their breadth of insight and critical analysis ... and it always nice to know what they feel.

R: Why else is it nice to know what they feel?

P: Well, I like to think they are enjoying a discussion.

R: Why is it important that they enjoy the discussion?

P: Of course, when they enjoy the activity they learn better ... but also, not that's it really ...

R: ... also ...

P: Nothing really ... I ... er ... well, I like to know that they appreciate what I'm doing ... er ... appreciate me really ...

R: Is that especially important to you?

P: I guess so, I'm, I often feel that I'm no good and not valued ...

This is important to manage in research like this, which, as we noted, we would expect to be uncontentious, but it is much more important with those who are vulnerable or have particular special needs. As a constructivist researcher, aim to develop a sense of empathy that enables you to recognise the non-verbal signals emitted when you are touching sensitive personal constructs, and then learn how to manage these occasions. In particular, as we have noted, change tack when you are creating pressure with your questioning, but if you sense that you have already exposed something deeper that is potentially problematic, consider how you may most effectively deal with it. Never attempt to go into an issue that is outside of your expertise. Even if you have empathy and want to help, or have experienced something similar, you are not there to be a therapist. Be ready to refer the person on to an expert who could help, outside of the context of your research.

Not every unexpected revelation is negative, though. Indeed, they are easily outnumbered by the number of positive revelations that occur during the process of exploring people's constructs. Our own experiences, those reported in some of our case studies in Chapter Eleven and those that can be found in journal articles attest to participants finding the process: helpful, in setting out their ideas clearly; illuminative, in allowing them to express previously unrecognised perspectives; and stimulating, in urging them to find out more or review perspectives or change responses for the better. A few examples include: a participant who realised what his real interests and talents were and then went on to further study and eventually a new career; an employer who recognised that she was underestimating talent in her organisation because of a construct that biased her views (people with tidy desks indicates tidy minds and are worth promoting); a student who identified that an irrational, unfounded fear was limiting their aspirations; a doctoral researcher who acknowledged that being an 'attentive wife' (in her view of what that entailed – giving lots of time) was limiting her research activities and who persuaded her husband to take on further study too so that they could be in each other's company while both studying. There are also the majority who feel that someone has listened attentively to their views, valued them and put them to useful effect.

The need for ethics permissions was discussed in Chapter Six for people who are young, or disabled or otherwise vulnerable, and in particular in any sector where personal details may be exposed, for example, in contexts that are medical or military, in which health and safety issues predominate or where personal or national security is at stake. We would like to add here that the review process can take a long time, possibly several months. One of the case study authors in Chapter Eleven, Sarah Dentry-Travis, in another study, took over 18 months to gain permissions to collect constructivist data from serving soldiers because of the complexity of the military system.

Collecting the data

Having discussed those often subtle but complex personal and interpersonal issues that are especially important in constructivist research, we now, in the last section of this chapter, turn our attention to those more practical considerations to ensure that your research progresses without incident.

Research venue

It is common practice that the researcher travels to a venue convenient to the participant and arranges meetings at times convenient for them. You need a comfortable, relaxed, secure location that is private, cannot be overheard, facilitates a co-operative climate, and provides ready access for equipment use and refreshment. This might require a preliminary visit to establish the best meeting space for your purpose. Being in participants' place of work can create problems, however. For example, they may be deemed interruptible by their work colleagues. More subtly, unhelpful social dynamics can arise. For example, during her research into emergency services, Barbara Richards (2011: 258–262), interviewed participants in their place of work. She noted how her presence appeared to shift the equilibrium of normal routines and relationships. Whilst arriving early afforded her the opportunity to gauge the working atmosphere, on one occasion, striking up informal conversations with a participant's colleagues led to unhelpful banter, black humour and undercurrents of tension. Clearly, you should make the best of the opportunities you have to collect data, but do be aware of the practical and subtle factors that can influence the situation and aim to establish clear understandings about needs and relationships in your research activities.

Take health and safety seriously. Your personal safety is paramount. Whilst you would not expect potential problems in normal work environments, be aware of any locations or buildings that appear hazardous in any way. For instance, never meet participants in a place that is not designated work accommodation or where you would be totally isolated from other people. You should also be careful about equipment. Never use equipment that is suspect and, of course, never engage in activities or behaviours that are dangerous.

Research equipment

Whether this is just a pen and a pad of paper, or as involved as a set of cards for sorting, a recording device or a laptop, every researcher will make use of some equipment during data collection activities. The key to an effective and efficient process is to ensure that you are prepared for all possible eventualities. Here we discuss some of the most likely; however, to ensure that you are as prepared as you can be, do rehearse every step of the data collection process, make sure that you are familiar with every detailed step, and take spares.

To advise researchers to have a spare pen, extra paper, or new batteries would seem too trivial and obvious to mention if it were not for the many times that researchers have experienced embarrassment, lost time, or even loss of data due to the most basic equipment failing. Carry a kit containing all the spares you might possibly need, including extra stationery, spare cables and batteries, a compact (preferably wireless) mouse, headphones, a memory stick, external microphone and more personal items like tissues and even breath freshener and deodorant! Carry the kit every time you collect data, and check it often to ensure it remains complete.

For constructivist research, amongst other approaches, you will nearly always wish to audio-record conversations wherever you can. You might even wish to video-record, especially where non-verbal behaviours are of interest. You will, as noted, need to gain permissions and as a precursor be clear about confidentiality and use of the data. Some potential participants will still be wary of being recorded, as noted in Chapter Six, so whilst you will need to practice an empathic but clear approach, do not take it for granted that they will agree, so be prepared to take comprehensive notes if necessary. Practice taking notes from, say, news broadcast on television. When you take notes you are not paying such close attention to the participant, so learn how to note key points and, following the interview, allow time to quickly add detail. Some researchers learn how to take notes without looking down at the paper, but this takes a lot of practice.

Recording is nearly always preferable over note-taking because you can maintain attention and eye contact with the participant, but it does have some disadvantages. First, make sure you are actually recording. You would not be the first researcher to press the wrong button and not record at all, or to set the volume incorrectly or site the recorder too far from the participant to gain an audible recording, or even record over a previous interview. Practice going through each step exactly as you would in an interview.

Another issue with recording interviews is the analysis of data. Thematic analysis of conversational data, for example, can involve verbatim transcription that can take 5–6 hours for each hour of recording. It is possible to use a professional transcription service, but then you will need to gain permission again from participants and ensure that the transcriber has a confidentiality agreement in place. Best practice is transcribing recorded data yourself so that you immerse yourself in the data and can note the tone, emphasis and so on that gives specific meaning to words, but this is not always practicable. Whoever transcribes, when analysing recoded data, it is often helpful to simultaneously read transcriptions and listen to the interview, which allows you access to expressions and unwritten verbal data that help you to elicit meanings. A foot-activated control for the recording playback can be really helpful.

It is worth reiterating here that the process of analysing qualitative data to elicit personal meaning involves interpretation. You wish to get as close to the actual meanings intended by the participant as you can. Accordingly, wherever you can, check your interpretations with participants. This not only ensures that findings are dependable, but also has the benefit of participants themselves maintaining a sense of ownership of findings. You may need to do this after data collection activities, but it is often possible during the application of some techniques to check interpretation as you go. You might even transfer the data collection to participants, for example by asking them to complete a repertory grid form or producing a pictorial representation of their views (see Chapter Seven). In Trevor Long's case study (Chapter Eleven), he notes how he handed a laptop to participants with a web-based grid program running so that his participants could complete the grid themselves, prompted initially by questions from him until they got the hang of the process. Again, managing this effectively in real time required rehearsal, which includes rehearsal of recovering after losing an internet connection or other technical fault, as well as rehearsal related to immediate analytical outputs and effective segues between different parts of the interview.

Summary

Our previous chapters emphasised the need for a clear, rigorous process in constructivist research. In this chapter we have taken a step back to recognise that in all research, but especially that involving people's inner meanings, informal problems, mishaps and difficulties can easily occur, ruining your best intentions. We have highlighted the requirement to convey clarity of purpose and focus and, in particular, the need to challenge and clarify your own constructions of the phenomena and research context, while building effective relationships from the outset and maintaining integrity throughout. Finally, make sure that all the practicalities relating to the venue, equipment and research process are planned down to the smallest detail. Visit venues, prepare equipment, take spares, and rehearse the process exactly as you plan to do it in the data collection activities. Such investment pays dividends!

Suggested Further Reading

All of the research books referred to in this book provide some guidance on the realities and practicalities in managing fieldwork. The following three books add to this list, but are noted here as suggested further reading because they are especially helpful to the topics of this chapter.

The first book reviews the use of many different qualitative method and techniques in practice:
Cassell, C. (2004) *Essential Guide to Qualitative Methods in Organisational Research*. London: SAGE.

The next book is a pragmatic approach to the key stages in applied research projects:
Marshall, C. and Rossman, G.B. (2006) *Designing Qualitative Research* (4th edition). Thousand Oaks, CA: SAGE.

Finally, a book covering fundamentals for the novice researcher or for the more experienced researcher to dip into on key practical as well as philosophical issues:
Remenyi, D., Williams, B., Money, A. and Swartz, E. (1998). *Doing Research in Business and Management: An Introduction to Process and Method*. London: SAGE.

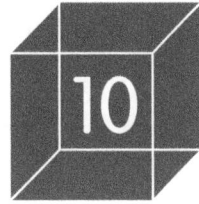

10

Data analysis, meaning interpretation and management/ presentation issues

Introduction

> Much of the purpose of constructivist assessment methods ... is to help reveal the meanings behind the words, the deeper themes between the lines of the stories [individuals] tell themselves and us. (Neimeyer, 2009: 9)

Personal constructivist methods can deliver rich research results because they enable researchers to go deeper than quantitative surveys and broader and deeper than qualitative interviews. Their abstract nature is valuable for surfacing peoples' implicit beliefs and tacit knowledge. In this chapter we consider what you can do to derive meaning from the wealth of data they generate. We start with repertory grids and, using a real research example, take you through a series of practical steps to manually analyse both single and multiple grids. Then, using the same real research example analysed in RepGrid 5, we demonstrate how computer packages can facilitate the creation and interpretation of grid data. The second part of the chapter deals with the analysis of elicited texts, and we offer practical advice on how to utilise the three most common interpretative approaches that are methodologically congruent with PCP, as well as exploring how you can use computer-assisted qualitative data analysis (CAQDAS) packages to help you manage your research project. Finally, we offer some advice on how to present the narrative of the elicited data to your research audience.

Repertory grid analysis

Generally, repertory grid analysis is based on a 'least sum of differences' technique, whereby rating scores are compared across individual elements and constructs and then with each other to determine the relationships between elements and constructs: which constructs and elements cluster together and which ones are distinct and different. Comparisons can range from simple eyeballing techniques through to computer-aided cluster analysis, factor analysis or principal components analysis. In determining the appropriate analytical technique, it is important to remember that grid data are ordinal and, as such, not necessarily appropriate for advanced statistical analysis, even though some researchers attempt it. Kelly (1991a: 102) himself saw 'constructs as providing ordinal axes in psychological space' and advocated the nonparametric analysis of grid data.

Denicolo and Pope (2001: 90) also raise an important caveat regarding how numbers are treated in repertory grid analysis. Repertory grids are not psychometric tests and their numerical scores do not represent an absolute measure of a person's construct system. Instead, they argue that 'it is important to recognize that the grid only provides information and a basis for structural/content analysis – it does not provide solutions to problems'. Therefore, numerical analysis in this context must be undertaken with caution, and within the epistemological context of the study.

There are many and varied ways to numerically analyse grids and we are unable to cover them all in this chapter. Our aim is to provide you with sufficient knowledge to be able to manually analyse a rated grid (if only so that you can understand the kind of process that occurs with electronic analysis), and a broad level of understanding of how computer packages can assist you in a deeper analytical process. If numbers are daunting for you, be reassured that for your normal research purposes there will be a computer package available to suit your needs (see Appendix B). For more detail on various forms of analysis, we refer you to the additional resources listed at the end of the chapter.

Manual analysis

We draw and expand on explanations given in Pope and Keen (1981) and Fransella et al. (2004) to describe some basic techniques for manual grid analysis, bringing them to life with an abstracted example taken from recent grid research into leadership perceptions by Bradley-Cole (2014a, 2014b); see Figure 10.1. The element set (L1–L6) is different leaders the participant has worked with over time, rated on a scale of 1–5, with a mid-point of 3.

Manual focusing

Kelly suggested that an initial judgement of the extent and flexibility of a person's constructs can be made by looking at: the number and nature of constructs elicited (whether they are more psychological or physical-situational); how similar they are in their application to elements (whether they overlap fully or partially); their permeability (how usefully and flexibly the construct is applied across elements); and the uniqueness of certain elements (for example, elements that are likely to be associated with contrasting poles only).

This initial stage of visual analysis enables you to identify relationships between elements and between constructs. Had we simply used a tick and cross rating in

Emergent (1)	L1	L2	L3	L4	L5	L6	Contrast (5)	Sum of scores
Advisor	2	1	5	1	1	5	Let you sink	15
Expressive	2	4	1	1	5	5	Unemotional	18
Freedom	1	1	5	2	3	5	Controlling	17
Creative	2	3	5	2	3	5	Destructive	20
Listening	2	1	5	1	2	4	No voice	15
Inspiring	2	3	5	1	3	5	Demotivating	19
Sum of scores	11	13	26	8	17	29		
Mean scores	1.83	2.17	4.33	1.33	2.83	4.83		

Figure 10.1 Grid example: leadership perceptions

Figure 10.1 you would see immediately that L3 and L6 receive similar ratings on all constructs except how expressive/unemotional they are. You might also spot that the construct creative/destructive has similar ratings across elements to inspiring/demotivating, so it is possible to begin to make sense of these data without any complex statistics being involved.

Relationships between numerically rated elements

To identify which elements the participant construes as being most similar, you need to isolate pairs of columns with the closest match by counting up the number of constructs with equivalent scores across both. For larger grids, or those with more scalar ratings, you can:

- Copy the grid, cut up the copy version into its component columns and lay each side by side to identify matched scores for constructs. L3 and L6 have four matching scores out of six, so are construed in similar, largely negative ways because these matches converge towards the contrast pole.
- Identify the elements that overall converge more to the emergent or contrast pole, by calculating the mean score for each element. In Figure 10.1, we can see that L1 and L4 have lower mean scores and converge more to the emergent pole. So, even though none of their scores match, they are construed in similar, more positive ways.

Through this matching process you can reorder the elements by the similarity of their ratings.

Relationships between elements and constructs

Taking the reordered element grid, you can inspect the rows of constructs to isolate higher matches. You should follow these steps:

- Rewrite the reordered element grid obtained from the first part of the exercise.
- Add in new lines for reversed scores for each construct (as shown in Figure 10.2). Because constructs are bipolar, this step is needed to check for matches between the emergent poles of constructs and the contrast poles of other constructs.
- Copy the reordered element grid and use it to horizontally cut up the construct rows and match them up. Calculating the mean score for each construct can help you identify possible matches more quickly.
- Manually cluster the constructs so that those which are similar to each other are grouped together. See Figure 10.2.

Sum of differences

This approach offers slightly more detailed analysis and can be used in conjunction with manual focusing. The aim again is to create a matrix to identify the most

Construct pole	L1	L2	L3	L4	L5	L6
C1: Advisor	2	1	5	1	1	5
C2: Expressive	2	4	1	1	5	5
C3: Freedom	1	1	5	2	3	5
C4: Creative	2	3	5	2	3	5
C5: Listening	2	1	5	1	2	4
C6: Inspiring	2	3	5	1	3	5
C1R: Let you sink	4	5	1	5	5	1
C2R: Unemotional	4	2	5	5	1	1
C3R: Controlling	5	5	1	4	3	1
C4R: Destructive	4	3	1	4	3	1
C5R: No voice	4	5	1	5	4	2
C6R: Demotivating	4	3	1	5	3	1

Figure 10.2 Adding in reversed constructs

Elements	L1	L2	L3	L4	L5	L6
L1		2	15	3	6	18
L2			13	5	4	16
L3				18	9	3
L4					9	21
L5						12
L6						

Figure 10.3 Sum of differences between elements

similar elements, which are those with the smallest difference in ratings across constructs. Using our grid in Figure 10.1, you can create a sum of difference 'element matrix' by following these steps:

- Sum the total ratings for each element (these are shown as 'sum of scores' in Figure 10.1).
- Calculate the differences between the total ratings for each element pair (as shown in Figure 10.3).

You can now cluster the elements together based upon their least sums of difference, as shown in Figure 10.4.

Emergent	L1	L2	L4	L5	L3	L6
C1: Advisor	2	1	1	1	5	5
C2: Expressive	2	4	1	5	1	5
C3: Freedom	1	1	2	3	5	5
C4: Creative	2	3	2	3	5	5
C5: Listening	2	1	1	2	5	4
C6: Inspiring	2	3	1	3	5	5

Figure 10.4 Elements ordered by sum of differences

Now that we have ordered the elements, we move on to ordering the constructs using the same calculation process to create another sum of difference 'construct matrix' (Figure 10.5), except that this time you need to work through the grid in paired rows, adding up the differences between each pair of construct scores for each element. So, start with comparing C1 with C2, and add up the differences between the scores given for each element (L1, L2, etc. in our grid). Place the sum of those differences in the corresponding matrix cell and move on to the next comparison. Remember to add in the reversed constructs as before.

Construct Pole	C1	C2	C3	C4	C5	C6
C1: Advisor		11	4	5	2	4
C2: Expressive	11		11	8	11	7
C3: Freedom	4	11		3	4	4
C4: Creative	5	8	3		5	1
C5: Listening	2	11	4	5		4
C6: Inspiring	4	7	4	1	4	
C1R: Let you sink		11	20	17	20	18
C2R: Unemotional	11		13	12	11	13
C3R: Controlling	20	13		15	18	16
C4R: Destructive	17	12	15		15	13
C5R: No voice	20	11	18	15		16
C6R: Demotivating	18	13	16	13	16	

Figure 10.5 Sum of differences between constructs

There are many insights we can draw from Figure 10.5. Some key highlights are as follows:

- The leadership attribute C6 (inspiring) overlaps almost entirely with C4 (creative), which is also strongly related to C3 (freedom), suggesting that these three constructs are very close in personal meaning.
- C1 (advisor) is strongly associated with C5 (listening), which also partially overlaps with the leader creating a sense of freedom, being inspiring and being creative.
- C2 (expressive) appears to be a unique construct, with less overlap and a different application profile.
- The reversed construct of expressive, C2R (unemotional) has the same level of association with the strongly associated C1 (advisor) and C5 (listening), suggesting that these qualities are no more associated with the leader being, or not being, emotionally expressive.

We can then use this sum of difference matrix to work through the reordering of the constructs, which produces a clustered grid as shown in Figure 10.6.

At the end of this process, you have another form of clustered grid, with the most similar elements and the most similar constructs grouped together. Although we have used the emergent pole more in this analysis, it is worth remembering not to lose sight of the contrast pole in explaining the meaning of constructs. For this participant we can see which constructs are related and how they differentiate the different leaders.

Content analysis of grids from groups

To content analyse a group of grids sharing a common purpose, you need to have supplied all participants with at least one common construct or one common element to rate during grid elicitation.

Construct	L1	L2	L4	L5	L3	L6
C6: Inspiring	2	3	1	3	5	5
C4: Creative	2	3	2	3	5	5
C3: Freedom	1	1	2	3	5	5
C1: Advisor	2	1	1	1	5	5
C5: Listening	2	1	1	2	5	4
C2: Expressive	2	4	1	5	1	5
C2R: Unemotional	4	2	5	1	5	1

Figure 10.6 Reordered grid, clustered by elements and constructs

Constructs are usually supplied after you have freely elicited their own constructs and must correspond with the grid topic. So, using our example grid of leadership perceptions, we may offer the construct of 'is an effective leader–is an ineffective leader'. After the participant has scored the construct in the normal way, you can then calculate sum of difference matrices between the element ratings for this supplied construct alongside the freely elicited constructs to determine which constructs cluster more closely with leader effectiveness.

You can also follow the same procedure with a supplied element. So, for our example grid where participants selected their own leaders as elements, we could supply an element of 'effective leader' and then content analyse the grids to determine which leader elements sit closest to the effective leader prototype and what behaviours or characteristics of those leaders are most valued.

Content analysis can also be used where groups have used the same elements or negotiated specific examples across shared categorical elements (as in our example of different leaders). This multiple grid aggregation method involves identifying commonly used constructs across the group to give frequency counts. For grids focusing on leadership you might find that 'inspiring' – with a range of contrast descriptions – appears frequently whereas, say, 'joins in office banter' is less so. You need to be aware that you are making assumptions about meanings when aggregating what seem to be constructs that are similar, for instance that 'inspiring–lets you sink' means something similar to 'stimulating–dispiriting'. You can also sum the scores for each construct across the grids and aggregate them into highest, middle and lowest across all grids. This will enable you to identify similarities and differences in how participants apply their constructs across common elements.

Computer analysis

You have probably noticed two things about the manual analysis of repertory grids covered in the previous section. First, there is a vast amount of data held in the simplest of grids. We have managed to do some quite detailed analysis with a grid of only six constructs and six elements. Second, manual analysis can be very time-consuming and, with more complex grids, you can very easily become overwhelmed by the volume of data and lose sight of the objectives of your study.

Fortunately, there are several computer packages available to constructivist researchers to analyse grids, some of which can be found free online (see Appendix B for more details). Additionally, some analysis can be undertaken in Excel, SPSS or its freeware version (PSPP). However, it should be recognised that manually analysing your grids really helps to ground you in the life-world of your participants, and also, should you decide to use the assistance of a computer package in your analysis, knowing how to cluster your grids by hand enables you to interpret computerised grid outputs more effectively.

There are numerous alternative methods for statistically analysing grids advocated by different researchers. More common methods include cluster analysis, factor analysis, principal components analysis and multidimensional scaling. A full review of all these methods is beyond the scope of this chapter, so we refer you to Appendix B for ideas on further reading, and will focus our attention here on how RepGrid 5 can be used for cluster analysis of one or a group of grids. As we write, a newer version is being developed but the principles will remain the same.

About RepGrid 5 and other analysis tools

The RepGrid suite of programs was developed by Brian Gaines and Mildred Shaw to enable researchers to create, elicit and analyse single grids (RepGrid) and groups of grids (RepSocio). Use of these packages not only provides researchers with more advanced analytical capabilities, but also enables participants to complete grids on a computer, if that is appropriate for your study. Alternatively, participants can complete grids by hand, and you can input them into RepGrid afterwards for analysis. At the time of writing there are two versions of RepGrid available: the free personal version, which allows you to analyse simpler, single grids; and the subscription enterprise version, which offers more extensive analytical capabilities across grids. It is a standalone package, and therefore you cannot export its data to other packages such as Excel or SPSS.

In Appendix B, in addition to the wide range of analysis tools already mentioned, you will also find contact details of fellow constructivists so that you can discuss with others the benefits and limitations of each within your discipline or professional area.

Cluster analysis – single grids

Hierarchical clustering is based on measures of association between constructs, and this forms the basis of the focus plot output in RepGrid, in much the same way as the manual focusing process described earlier. The focus plot visually demonstrates the relationships between constructs and between elements by reordering them to sit closest to those with which they share the strongest relationship, depicting the comparative strength of those relationships through the use of dendrograms (tree or branching diagrams). In Figure 10.7, we provide the focus plot for the full grid that was used as our example extract in Figure 10.1 onwards. The dendrogram for constructs is shown on the right-hand side, and the element dendrogram is shown beneath the focus plot.

From inspection of the focus plot we can see that it has produced similar associations to those obtained through manual analysis of the reduced example.

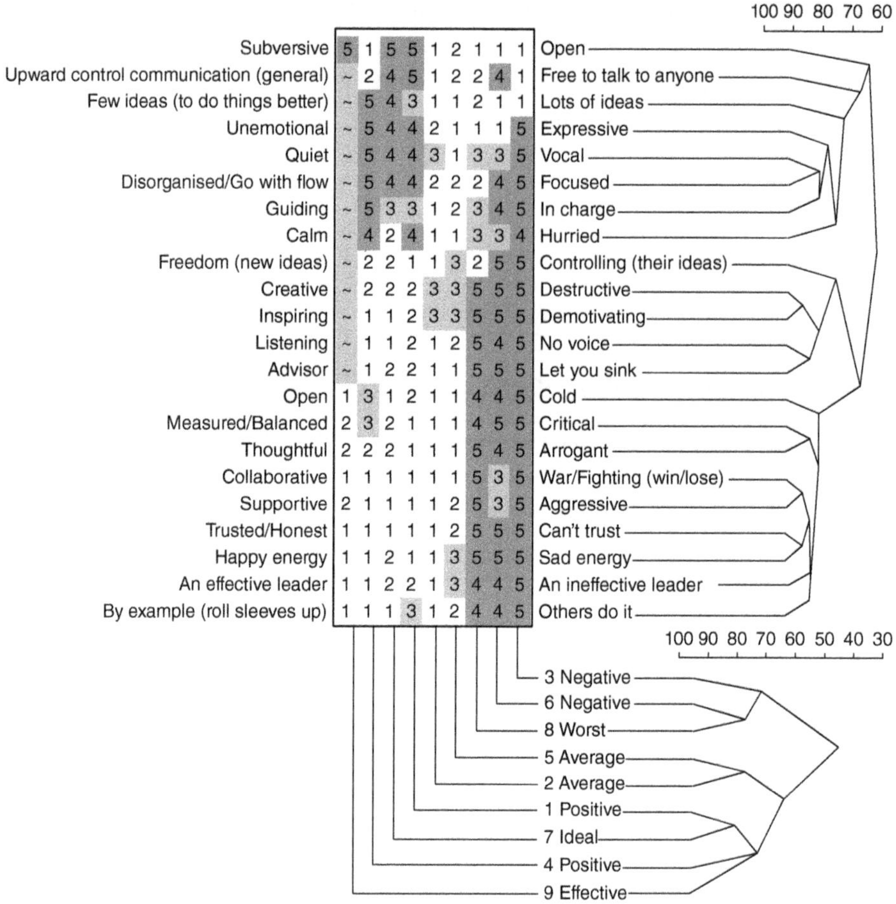

Figure 10.7 Focus plot for full grid

For example:

- The element dendrogram shows that L3 and L6 are more negative leaders who are closely associated with each other and with the prototypical representation of a 'worst leader'.
- The plot shows close relationships between the leadership attributes of 'inspiring' and 'creative', and between 'advisor' and 'listening', along with their collective associations with 'freedom'.

The more detailed analysis of the full set of constructs provided by RepGrid offers a clearer picture of some insights, including:

- The element dendrogram more clearly positions L1 and L4 as positive leaders, more closely associated with the prototypical representation of an 'ideal leader'. This association was not as readily visible in the manual analysis, where L4 was more closely related to L2 than L1 because of the absence of direct matches between L1 and L4 scores, even though the mean score calculations placed them closest together.
- In the manual analysis we found that 'expressive-unemotional' stood out as being something that is not strongly associated with other constructs, with both poles offering as

much explanatory power. However, the plot, having clustered this construct with all the other constructs, has reversed it and more clearly clustered 'expressive' with 'vocal', 'focused' and 'in charge'.

- We can also see from the provided 'effective leader' element and constructs that this participant associates effectiveness with more positive expressions of leadership (element cluster), evidenced through attributes of 'collaborative', 'supportive', 'trusted/honest' and 'happy energy' (constructs cluster).

Cluster analysis – multiple grids

To explore the associations between different participants' constructs, you can compare single grid outputs manually or use the RepSocio package to analyse groups of grids that share the same elements and/or the same constructs. Both approaches can help you unpack similarities and differences in the application and meaning of constructs, but with RepSocio those similarities and differences are more easily identifiable. There is an important caveat for comparing dendrograms across single grid outputs. These relational trees are useful for visualising the distances between constructs within a grid, but, because of the ordinal nature of grid data, they are asymmetrical and, as such, only the associations between constructs and not their absolute distances are comparable across grids. This caveat is mitigated somewhat by the use of RepSocio, because all the constructs are clustered within a single grid.

Such analysis gives us the basic associations between constructs but, even though this grid data set is itself rich, even more information can be derived from the ensuing conversation around a grid, as we shall see when we discuss text analysis.

Interpreting and explaining grid data

It would be unusual if your participants did not want you to give them an indication of 'what you can see in their grids'. Indeed, if you take the time to explain your interpretation to them you may well find that they provide reinforcement and/or elaboration of your interpretations. As you do so, remember to take a questioning approach, exploring interpretations together and being open to participants elaborating or clarifying their own meanings. In the research carried out by Trevor Long, included as a case in Chapter Eleven, during interviews in which participants completed repertory grid activities directly onto a laptop, the immediately generated analyses formed the basis for further exploration and clarification.

Remember that the raw data are still visible in your reordered, analysed grids. It is reassuring for participants that you have not put their words into a 'magic statistical box' and churned them into unrecognisable form. The only thing you might need to explain is any reversing of constructs. A simple example should suffice such as: on a construct about degree of softness/crunchiness in relation to fruit, a banana might score 2 and an apple 4 if the poles were soft to crunchy. If the poles were instead crunchy to soft, then apple would score 2 and banana 4.

You might then view the element tree, showing how some elements cluster together, noting the degree of similarity and number of elements within each cluster. For instance, there might be a tightly related pair, a group of three in which two are more similar with the third being more like those two than elements in other clusters. Then, as you check the links between clusters, there may be groups of clusters separated from other clusters, showing which clusters are similar and which are different, or less similar. See if you can identify examples of this in Figure 10.7. You can explain this by saying that these elements (objects, people, events) appear to be most like each other and different from the other groups. You could point out on which constructs the alike ones differ but how they are described most similarly by the majority of constructs.

You can then do something similar with the linking and clustering of constructs. You can say something like: 'It seems for you that the descriptions (taking examples from Figure 10.7) collaborative–war/fighting and supportive–aggressive are used in a similar way: people who are collaborative also tend to be supportive, and vice versa. Those who are trusted/honest generally generate for you happy energy while those you cannot trust produce sad energy, and they tend also to fit well the aggressive and war/fighting poles. Also they have a tendency to be ineffective leaders.' You would then go on to discuss the links, though increasingly less tight, with other constructs within and between construct clusters. It can be illuminating to explore some links that are less obvious, for instance why, for them, the 'expressive, vocal, in charge' people also have a tendency to be seen as 'hurried', perhaps even considering, if a new person arrives and seems to be calm and quiet, whether they might automatically be perceived as potentially having few ideas. Your participant may not have recognised that possibility previously but then be able to provide other examples, or indeed contradictory ones to that possibility. Whatever the outcome, we suggest that they will be intrigued by how revelatory the grid can be.

For your own research purposes you may need to go further into the analysed data than looking at the clusters and relationships between them. You may find it useful to inspect more closely the array of ratings, perhaps noting tendencies to score towards the positive pole if you have asked the participant at the end of the elicitation to annotate which poles are positive for them. Certainly you will want to study how other constructs relate to any you have provided, or how other elements relate to a provided one, such as 'effective leader' in Figure 10.7.

When working with multiple grids you could explore not only which general construct descriptions they have in common and which constructs are unusual, but also the range and variability of construct production for a given topic produced by different participants, with perhaps some noting many differentiations and others noting only a few closely linked descriptions. Similarly, it can be relevant to some purposes to note whether individuals use the full scale when rating elements or only part of it, whether they discriminate subtle differences or only extremes, and so on.

All of these explorations should be tempered by the caveat we have often repeated – that the ratings produce only ordinal data – but they can be better understood by combining the cluster analyses with analysis of the discussion or conversation occurring during grid elicitation as we describe next.

Analysing elicited texts

We now move on to considering ways in which we can analyse textual data elicited from the elaboration of constructs in a repertory grid exercise, storytelling method, diary account, focus group, or even through responses to open-ended questions in a survey. In PCP, the interview transcript represents the participant's 'province of meaning', their view of the world, in relation to the phenomenon explored.

It is important to acknowledge the double hermeneutic (Smith et al., 2009) within PCP analysis, that is, the acknowledgement that the research output represents the researcher's interpretation of the participants' interpretation of their life-world. This interpretative stance is linked to symbolic interactionism (Blumer, 1969; Mead, 1934), where it is acknowledged that we are embedded in a linguistic world where meanings are symbolically derived and shared (see Chapter Six), but not always exactly. So, in order to understand the lived world, researchers must understand how such symbols are used to create shared meanings and drive human action.

Many researchers, with whom we broadly agree, advocate that good practice involves the researcher checking their interpretations with the participants. However, if there is a time lag between elicitation and checking of interpretations then be aware that subsequent rumination by the participant can result in construct revision, especially for constructs that are peripheral or loose. You might present, then, both interpretations with this rationale for readers of your research.

Formatting transcripts for analysis

When transcribing interviews from recordings it is important to establish, and follow, a set of standardised principles. From our own experience, we offer here some suggestions in Procedural Example 10.1 that will facilitate comparative analysis across cases and also help you optimise the analytical support provided by computer packages such as NVivo and ATLAS.ti.

Procedural Example 10.1

Transcribing interview recordings

- Use an anonymised code to clearly differentiate who is speaking: interviewer (I), participant (P), note-taker (N), and start a new line for each speaker.
- If you are using Microsoft Word, use the Heading Styles feature to section any semi-structured questions (you can auto-code and/or run word counts on specific question/question-type responses in Nvivo/ATLAS.ti).
- Record verbatim and do not correct grammar.
- Listen carefully and note down all unspoken data (sighs, emphasis, groans, laughs, etc.) that help convey meanings not captured by spoken words. As long as you are consistent

across cases, you can develop your own system to suit you, or you can follow this one from Bradley-Cole (2014a):

- o ... (three dots) to indicate a short pause, usually less than 3 seconds.
- o [pause] to indicate a definite break in conversation, usually more than 3 seconds.
- o [long pause] to indicate a prolonged silence of 10 seconds or more.
- o [sigh], [err], [um] to record short, non-lexical utterances that interrupted speech.
- o [chuckle] to indicate a short, contemplative type of laugh.
- o [laugh] to indicate a definite outburst of laughter.

- In NVivo/ATLAS.ti, you can use these non-verbal utterances to add richness to your analysis, for example, by exploring incidences where participants displayed different types of emotional responses, or where they needed to be more reflexive or considered in their responses.

Finally, before you start your analysis, it is useful to format each transcript as follows:

1 Provide reasonably wide left- and right-hand margins so that you have space to annotate lower-order themes in the left-hand margin and higher-order themes in the right-hand margin.
2 Number each line, if you are analysing by hand. This will allow you to locate the data extract in memos and as you abstract your analysis to higher-order themes/concepts. You do not need to do this if you are using a computer package.

Selecting the appropriate analytical lens

The appropriate method of data analysis will typically be determined by your research question, which in turn will also determine how you collect your data. Delivering high-quality research is recognised as being dependent upon methodological fit, which is achieved through 'congruent', 'integrated' and 'mutually reinforcing' research elements (Edmondson and McManus, 2007). Therefore, as we have emphasised previously, decisions on the appropriate analytical method should be made at the start of your research design.

Broadly speaking, transcripts elicited through PCP methods are open to any interpretative methods of analysis that recognise the integral role of the researcher in the sensemaking process. We offer three common alternative approaches here: grounded theory (GT) to build a theory inductively; interpretative phenomenological analysis (IPA) to understand the meanings attached to personal, lived experience; and the 'theoretically neutral' method of thematic analysis offered by Braun and Clarke (2006). For each method, we offer only a partial picture within a varied and contested landscape. Our aim is to help you quickly identify the differences between these approaches, understand where each is compatible with the essence of PCP, and give you an initial view on their key analytical stages. Other methods to investigate include narrative analysis, content analysis, conversation analysis and discourse analysis, which can be found in general methods textbooks.

Although Kelly continually argued against subsuming PCP into another philosophical or epistemological perspective, it should be recognised that, at the time of his writing in the 1950s, qualitative research was not as well developed or accepted as it is today. He was forging an argument for PCP within a paradigm of positivism that was dominated by behaviourist and psychoanalytical approaches. None of the methodologies that we offer in this chapter had yet been written. From a contemporary standpoint, we can see that both IPA and constructivist forms of GT share with PCP an acknowledgement that most of human behaviour is pre-reflexive, that a relationship exists between what we think and what we do, and that emotions are intertwined and inseparable from perceptual processes. They also acknowledge the impossibility of researcher neutrality, so their interpretations of 'bracketing' relate more to the need to recognise and set aside preconceptions throughout the research process, not just at the start, and to remain open to new ideas emerging from the data even if they contradict your own or socially established perspectives. Ultimately, it is your role as a researcher to act as the voice of your participants in your interpretation of their stories.

Grounded theory

The primary purpose of GT is to build a theory inductively from the data, that is, to develop or construct theories that explain social-psychological processes by exploring lived experiences within relevant contexts. It was originally developed by Glaser and Strauss (1967) who challenged the prevailing negative views of the time towards qualitative research and maintained that hypotheses could be derived inductively and systematically, from a grounded theory, and tested. Although they adopted a positivist standpoint in respect of there being a straightforward relationship between objects in the world and our perception of them, they argued that what we ultimately determine to be 'truth' is a matter of perspective and consensus. Today, there are several different versions of GT available, which vary in their epistemological perspectives. The more recent works of Charmaz (2000, 2006) and other authors, such as Clarke (2003), offer us a constructivist perspective that is compatible with a PCP approach. These authors acknowledge both the contextual relativity of perceptual knowledge and the role of the researcher as an active interpreter of the data. Charmaz (2000: 521) argues that by 'adopting a constructivist grounded theory approach, the researcher can move grounded theory methods further into the realm of interpretive social science consistent with a Blumerian (1969) emphasis on meaning, without assuming the existence of a unidimensional external reality'.

GT is particularly appropriate for studies where there is an absence of existing theory, or insufficient depth of knowledge, or where existing knowledge fails to adequately explain all manifestations of a phenomenon.

How to do it

In terms of the analytical method, Charmaz (1995, 2002) identifies a number of features that all versions of GT share:

- Simultaneous collection and analysis of data;
- Creation of analytic codes and categories developed from data and not by pre-existing conceptualisations (theoretical sensitivity);
- Writing analytical memos as the stage between coding and writing;
- Inductive construction of abstract categories;
- Theoretical sampling to refine categories;
- Integration of categories into a theoretical framework.

Individuals or groups are sampled theoretically based upon concrete criteria concerning their content. This form of purposive sampling also involves the active sampling of new instances to meet evolving criteria as the analytical stages develop. Starting with the transcripts from your first two interviews, and holding no pre-existing hypotheses or beliefs about the phenomenon under investigation, you develop a theoretical framework through the systematic coding, comparison and conceptualisation of your participants' stories. There are three levels of coding in grounded theory (Strauss and Corbin, 1990, 1997):

1 Open coding is the starting, close coding stage where the aim is to generate initial concepts from the data in each case (line by line).
2 Axial coding is where you begin to abstract and interpret the data, by developing and linking concepts across cases into conceptual families – this is your coding paradigm.
3 Selective coding involves the refining and formalising of conceptual relationships into an overarching theoretical framework.

During the coding process, you keep the codes active by asking comparative questions across cases and by writing memos. Pidgeon (1996) explains the notion of 'constant comparison' as being a continual shifting between, and comparing of, data codes and theoretical concepts. As the researcher, you should adopt a reflexive position and remain 'open' to new ideas throughout the analysis process. The continuous writing of memos, as both notes to yourself as the researcher, and also as explorations into tentative conceptual explanations, is a key part of enacting a reflexive approach.

Each case comparatively builds on the codes and concepts derived from previous cases until reaching 'saturation', in other words, until you are learning nothing new. Your aim is to move beyond a descriptive account of the topic and derive a theoretical conceptualisation that adequately explains the collective findings.

Interpretative phenomenological analysis

IPA was developed by Smith (1995) and is concerned with acquiring an 'insider' or lay perspective through the idiographic understanding of lived experience and 'how individuals make sense of the world, from their point of view' (Bryman, 2008: 15). It is phenomenological in that it is interested in the perception of experience, rather than in deriving an objective or factual account of experience. It is interpretative in that it adopts a hermeneutic viewpoint and acknowledges that our ability to understand another's personal world is complicated by our own conceptions of that world. The aim of IPA is to derive a close and nuanced understanding of each participant's personal world and to understand in what ways the perceptions of participants are both shared with and different from each other. As such, it positions participants as experts in their own lives and in the phenomenon under investigation. As with grounded theory, IPA is inductive and interpretative, and must be approached as an exploratory endeavour, with no prior hypotheses.

IPA is strongly idiographic, meaning that it is built on the detailed examination of each and every case. To achieve this, IPA studies are usually conducted with a relatively small number of homogenous participants who share specific and relevant attributes and can, therefore, be purposively sampled as exemplars in the context of the topic being explored. IPA samples can also be stratified for comparison purposes within the study, for example, if you are interested in comparing perceptions of different age groups or gender, and this may necessitate slightly larger sample sizes to achieve, although, overall, IPA samples are usually smaller than grounded theory samples.

IPA is particularly appropriate for studies where depth of understanding is needed. For example, where the issue is complex, controversial, personal, or related to a process or processes, and also where existing knowledge has been derived purely from positivist, or **nomothetic**, methods (as opposed to **idiographic** methods).

How to do it

Smith is keen to encourage innovation in the application of IPA and points out that, rather than being a prescriptive theoretical approach, IPA is more of 'a repertoire of strategies [that offer] considerable room for manoeuvre. The route through them will not be a linear one, and the experience will be challenging' (Smith et al., 2009: 80). A key aim of the analytic process is to engage the researcher in an open and reflective dialogue with each participant's story. Here is a summary of the principal steps:

1 Taking the transcript from the first case, read the whole transcript several times to familiarise yourself with the participant's story. This stage helps you immerse yourself in the participant's world.
2 Start initial coding by moving slowly and carefully line by line, making close annotations in the left-hand margin to build up a detailed commentary on the case. This stage is about exploring the data and drawing out how you think the participant is construing the topic under discussion.
3 Begin organising the data by drawing the initial annotations up to within-case generalisations, or emerging themes or constructs, in the right-hand margin. At this stage, your aim should be to thematically organise aspects of the data in ways that best explain them psychologically but can still be clearly connected back to the text that each is seeking to explain. This is where you seek to hermeneutically interpret and demonstrate your understanding of their lived experiences.

4   Once you have completed the analysis of your first case, you should draw up a thematic table that lists each emerging theme, quotations to support it, and your comments and observations. This is an important part of your **audit trail**, and helps ensure that you remain connected to your participants' voices.

5   Now you can start building a thematic hierarchy for your first case by clustering themes that are conceptually similar. This is the second level of abstraction where you start to distinguish between superordinate and subordinate themes, either by drawing up similar emerging themes into one superordinate theme, or by recognising an emergent theme as being superordinate and deconstructing it. Themes with a poor evidence base are likely to be discarded at this stage. It is useful to make separate notes, maps and/ or diagrams to cluster your themes and start creating a hierarchical thematic structure that organises and explains the data.

6   Then you can move onto the next case and follow these steps in the same detail. You should set aside previous findings and interpretations and allow the themes to induc- tively emerge. This is part of the idiographic process and needs to be retained for all subsequent cases.

7   When you have completed the analysis of the second case, you can start looking for patterns and connections across cases, paying particular attention to thematic and contextual similarities and differences between the cases. These cross-case relation- ships and idiosyncratic differences will help you abstract the data further to evolve and develop a thematic hierarchy that explains the topic under investigation. As you add more cases, your findings from your earlier cases can be used to iteratively shape your interview guide.

Smith et al. (2009) also advise that, when working with larger samples, you can look to assess emergent themes at a group level by identifying recurrent themes across cases. In such instances, the individual case analysis will not be as deep and it is up to you to determine and argue the criteria for measuring recurrence and to retain individual case examples as thematic illustrations.

Thematic analysis

Thematic analysis (TA) is an epistemologically flexible methodological tool for categorising qualitative data and identifying patterns across data sets. Like grounded theory and phenomenology, it comes in a variety of forms, includ- ing template analysis (King, 2004), and approaches focusing on the systematic and rigorous application of qualitative techniques offered by authors such as Boyatzis (1998) and Joffe (2011), versus the relativist ontological approach offered by Braun and Clarke (2006), which is the method we focus on here. Braun and Clarke's (2013) approach fits well with PCP because they emphasise the association between meaning and context, and embrace the integral role of the researcher as an active interpreter of those meanings within the research process. A theme in TA 'captures something important about the data in relation to the research question, and represents some level of *patterned* response or meaning within the data set' (Braun and Clarke, 2006: 82).

How to do it

Braun and Clarke (2006) outline six key steps in their approach to TA:

1   Familiarisation and engagement: immersing yourself in the data by repeatedly reading transcripts, listening to recordings and making initial analytic notes to move beyond descriptive observations and identify patterns across the data set. Within this stage, transcription is seen as a key interpretive act and should be undertaken as an active process of sensemaking, rather than just passive recording.
2   Initial coding: starting with an initial list of ideas generated from step 1, systematically code the data in a uniform and equal way that is relevant to the research question and that identifies patterns across cases. Make notes as you go and generate as many codes/thematic ideas as you can.
3   Searching for themes: with your list of initial codes, sort them into potential themes and collate the corresponding data extracts. Consider different ways of organising your themes hierarchically and experiment with different visual representations such as dendrograms, tables, or mind-maps. Decide on an initial thematic map.
4   Reviewing themes: this involves reviewing and refining the themes until they represent a 'good fit' with the coded data and offer an accurate reflection of the meanings held within the entire data set. This step may well require you to go back to step 2 and code themes differently. Your aim in this step is to generate an overall story about your data, organised around a central concept.
5   Defining and naming themes: with a refined thematic map of your data, further define and refine your themes to identify their 'essence'. This stage is about ensuring that each theme is coherent and internally consistent and requires you to focus on the meaning of themes, rather than just a representation of their contents.
6   Writing the report: here, your goal is to tell the story of your data in a convincing narrative that demonstrates the merits and validity of your interpretation.

Computer analysis

Computer-assisted qualitative data analysis (CAQDAS) packages, such as NVivo and ATLAS.ti, offer useful functionality for both project-managing your qualitative study and keeping an audit trail of your interpretative journey that you can use to evidence the internal rigour and validity of your analytic process. These packages do not do the interpretation for you, but they help you to organise, interrogate, visualise and reflect on your data in ways that facilitate deeper exploration, inductive conceptualisation and wider interpretations of data sets. As such, they are especially powerful tools in the coding and thematic development stages, because they facilitate the ability to switch between the different abstraction levels of data and model alternative thematic hierarchies. They are also extremely useful collaborative tools when working as part of a research group. We provide some tips for working with computer analysis in Further Explanation 10.1.

Lewins and Silver (2014) provide a thorough overview on the use of CAQDAS packages in qualitative research and how they enable a cyclical and iterative process of data analysis across the key qualitative tasks of integration, organisation, exploration, interpretation and reflection.

◤ ◢ Further Explanation 10.1

Some tips for computer analysis

- Manage your whole research project within a CAQDAS package, not just your transcript coding and thematic development. You can improve your literature review by coding and analysing journal articles, book chapters and your own notes in the same way as transcripts.
- Prepare transcripts in Word and import them. The functionality in Word is superior.
- Speed up the coding phase by making use of Heading Styles when transcribing in Word to section your transcript and then use the CAQDAS auto-code feature to isolate those sections for analysis.
- Import repertory grids and/or focus plots as pictures for analysis alongside transcript data.
- Import interview recordings (or hold as external files if too large), so that everything is together.
- Speed up the familiarisation stage by running word counts and data queries.
- Export data to external packages (such as Excel, mind-map or word cloud packages) if the functionality in the CAQDAS package is either too complicated or too rudimentary. You can still resave these outputs as files within your CAQDAS project.
- Scope out your project before you start building it in the CAQDAS package, and keep within that scope. There is a lot of functionality in these packages that you will not need, even for complex projects.

Managing the wealth of data

You may, by now, be feeling excited by how much understanding you can derive from constructivist techniques, and also a little panicked about how you will keep track of the vast amount of data you may produce. The solution is strong project management skills and we recommend that, before you collect your first crumb of data, you devise for yourself a convenient filing and storage system that complies with all that you promised yourself and others when you considered ethics (Chapter Six) and designed your research (Chapter Eight). Using a software program, such as NVivo or ATLAS.ti, can help you store and manage your data, but the tips offered in Further Explanation 10.2 will work as well with or without them.

◤ ◢ Further Explanation 10.2

Some tips for managing data

- Set up a secure, independent filing system for primary data. A lockable filing cabinet for paper records and a password-protected, non-networked hard drive for electronic records are essential. It is also essential that all electronic data are held in accordance with the Data Protection Act 1998, hence our recommendation that you use non-networked storage.

We would also recommend that you also have a back-up storage system that you keep up to date.

- Set up a data management spreadsheet in Excel recording the storage location of data and any cross-references between data sets. It is useful to collate in one place all of the information you collect for each participant, and you may also find it helpful to be able to bring together all of the data collected by a particular technique, especially if you are triangulating data or doing a comparative study.
- Set up folders for data analysis, including all stages of your interpretations and analysis, from memos to thematic hierarchies. For an effective audit trail, remember to date your files and record their content in the data management spreadsheet.
- Some people find it useful to keep a separate reflective diary as they work through the research process, and this can help you keep track of how your interpretations and thematic hierarchies evolve over time.
- Caution is required too in ensuring that your interpretations of data remain as close to the source as possible. The grounded theory ideas of iteration and constant comparison are useful techniques whatever approach you take. Each analysis step away from the raw data is a form of data degradation, so checking back to your original notes as you go through interpretation cycles is good practice, while best practice is to check your interpretations with the original participants.
- Keep records of each stage in the process between raw data and the final interpretation to illustrate to readers/examiners a clear data trail.
- Remember, though, that your final presentation should include both your own and your participants' interpretations (for example, your themes supported by their quotes), since each presents an informed perspective on the topic at the time.
- If you plan to use a software program to aid your analysis as we suggested above, it would be wise to learn how to use it before collecting your data and to input your data as soon as you have it so that it does not build up to unmanageable amounts.

Presenting your data

As we said at the start of the chapter, your goal is to act as the voice of your participants, and how you decide to present your findings is a critical part of telling their stories. You will also by now appreciate that whatever form your dissemination takes, be it a thesis, dissertation, journal article or report, you will not be able to include all of your data, or all the possible interpretations; a compromise has to be made.

This is where your data trail is especially important, because readers need reassurance that your discussion is based on the data elicited from participants. By weaving a dialogue through your interpretations, which are supported and brought to life through the raw data, you must demonstrate to the reader how what you heard/recorded evolved into your final interpretation so that they can follow the logic and consider whether it fits with their own potential interpretations. For a thesis or dissertation, examples of each step can be included in the appendices, where you can also demonstrate differences between participants and between data derived through different techniques. For shorter written or verbal presentations, a sample grid or illuminative incident drawing, or similar, with selected quotations from the conversation that accompanied the elicitation activity, may suffice to demonstrate the quality of your data and interpretations.

One particular benefit of a repertory grid is that the raw data, the ratings attributed to elements/constructs by the participant, are still visible in a focused grid. A limitation is that the few words recorded as the poles of constructs do not necessarily do justice to the views of the participant that might be better conveyed in the grid conversation. Readers/listeners need to be alerted to that. Pictorial representations or metaphors can be striking in their own right, but again the participants' elaborations are also crucial for understanding.

We provide in Further Explanation 10.3 some tips on presenting your results and discussion to readers.

Further Explanation 10.3

Some tips for presenting your data

Presenting findings

- When elaborating your thematic hierarchy, discuss each theme in order of its explanatory power, in other words, how well it explains the overarching or central idea.
- Define each theme in the hierarchy and present short extracts to support your interpretative argument. You can provide more direct data through the use of tables or by linking to the appendices.
- Discuss links between themes and overarching observations throughout.
- Think carefully when selecting examples. They should contain no material that would identify participants personally to other colleagues taking part in the research or to other more remote readers.
- Spend time explaining to the reader the nature of your data. Whether it is derived from a repertory grid, a metaphor or a drawing, it is participants' elaborations that are crucial for understanding the intended meanings of the symbols or labels applied in any method, and the reader should be able to understand the nature of the elicitation and surrounding discourse.
- You can present count/frequency data for how often themes or linguistic labels occurred in your data, provided that you understand the nature of numbers in constructivism and do not subject them to inappropriate analysis.
- Use colour and visual presentation if you can; it will bring the narrative alive for the reader.
- You should consider any interviewer and other context effects on data collection and interpretation, and include these in your reflection.

Presenting the discussion

When discussing your findings, remember to:

- Relate them back to any existing research presented in your introduction or literature review.
- Introduce additional theories that can help explain your findings (rooting your findings back to the wider theoretical field).
- Generate predictive models/theories if you are using grounded theory or thematic analysis, or generate explanations of how people make sense of their worlds if you are using IPA.

Also remember that, in all constructivist research, findings may be transferable, but are not generalisable, so you should reference the option for further research to test conclusions more widely if appropriate.

Summary

In this chapter we have offered an overview of how to manually analyse both grid data and elicited texts, along with an explanation of ways in which computer packages can be utilised to broaden, deepen and bring additional clarity to your data analysis. Our aim has been to give you enough practical guidance to feel confident in analysing your data. To achieve that, we felt it was also important to help you understand the basis for repertory grid analysis, and how to identify and employ an appropriate method for analysing your participants' discourses, or, as we have previously referred to them, their 'provinces of meaning'. In the suggested further reading, we offer a range of additional reference sources that will help you build your expertise in the different analytical methods.

In Part III we present a series of cases (Chapter Eleven) and a PCP biography (Chapter Twelve). Severe length restrictions were imposed on all of the contributions to fit into our book rubric, yet they present compelling evidence for the power of a constructivist research approach.

Suggested further reading

Designing and analysing repertory grids

The following three texts provide different, but detailed explorations of the design and application of repertory grids in research:

Jankowicz, D. (2004) *The Easy Guide to Repertory Grids*. Chichester: Wiley.

Fransella, F., Bell, R. and Bannister, D. (2004) *A Manual for Repertory Grid Technique* (2nd edition). Chichester: Wiley.

Pope, M. and Keen, T.R. (1981). *Personal Construct Psychology and Education*. London: Academic Press.

Grid analysis tools

See Appendix B for a list of resources and other sources of support.

Qualitative approaches

We recommend the following text as an accessible overview of a range of qualitative research practices:

Lyons, E. and Coyle, A. (eds). (2007) *Analysing Qualitative Data in Psychology*. London: SAGE.

For more detailed explanations of each of the specific methods covered in this chapter, you can explore the authors' principal texts:

Braun, V. and Clarke, V. (2013) *Successful Qualitative Research: A Practical Guide for Beginners*. London: SAGE.

Charmaz, K. (2006) *Constructing Grounded Theory, A Practical Guide through Qualitative Analysis*. London: SAGE.

Smith, J.A., Flowers, P. and Larkin, M. (2009) *Interpretative Phenomenological Analysis. Theory, Method and Research*. London: SAGE.

Qualitative data analysis

We suggest the following texts as good handbooks for using CAQDAS packages to help you manage your qualitative projects. Lewins and Silver offer a general 'how to' guide, and we recommend either of the other two texts depending on which package you choose:

Lewins, A. and Silver, C. (2014) *Using Software for Qualitative Data Analysis: A Step-By-Step Guide* (2nd edition.). London: SAGE.

Bazeley, P. and Jackson, K. (2013) *Qualitative Data Analysis with NVivo* (2nd edition). London: SAGE.

Friese, S. (2014) *Qualitative Data Analysis with ATLAS.ti* (2nd edition). London: SAGE.

For practical advice, you can also access support online at http://onlineqda.hud.ac.uk/.

PART III

How others have
used PCP – sample
research cases

This part of the book provides a range of examples drawn from recent research, to stimulate readers' imaginations about how they might design and conduct their research, including how they might amend, redesign or invent their own tools to suit particular participants.

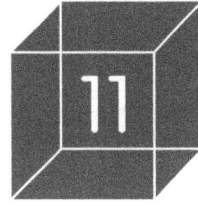

11

Cases using different designs

Introduction

Throughout the preceding chapters we have emphasised the breadth of applications of constructivism and the different tools and techniques that could be used in such research projects. In this chapter we include case studies, each written by different researchers who have designed a particular constructivist research study using those techniques most appropriate to the phenomena they wished to explore and their research objectives.

Figure 11.1 shows, for each case, the nature of the study and techniques applied, to help guide you to those cases that relate closest to your research interests. The 14 cases included are ordered by surname. Most cases are formatted similarly, including the focus and purpose, methodology, findings and the benefits of personal construct psychology. However, the uniqueness of each individual author's style and research project adds particular colour.

For more case examples in the broad field of education, see Pope and Denicolo (2001); for more case examples in other professional arenas, see Denicolo and Pope (2001). Details of the application of constructivist methodology can also be found for research conducted by each of Bradley-Cole (2014b), Denicolo (2013), Dentry-Travis (2014), Long (2014) and Österlind (2013b), amongst others, on the SAGE Methods Cases website: www.methodspace.com/page/SAGE-research-methods-cases.

TOPIC	AUTHOR; COUNTRY	TECHNIQUES USED
Assessment of students by teachers as meaning-makers	Apelgren, Britt-Marie; Sweden	Repertory grid Conversational interviews Questionnaire survey
Communication with people who have learning disabilities	Apraiz, Elvira; UK	Viewing pictures of paintings Triadic card sorting Conversational interviews

(Continued)

(Continued)

TOPIC	AUTHOR; COUNTRY	TECHNIQUES USED
Knowledge transfer across national boundaries	Bourne, Dorota; Turkey	Ethnographic interviews Repertory grid Laddering
Meaning of authenticity and authentic leadership	Bradley-Cole, Kim; UK	Repertory grid interviews
Using critical incident charting for reflecting on experience	Burnard, Pam; UK	Critical incidents Rivers of experience
Mental and physical durability	Dentry-Travis, Sarah; Canada	Meaningful artefact Laddering Validation cycle
Beliefs about success and work–life balance of working mothers	Douglas, Bethan; UK	Drawings of constructs Conversational interviews Interpretative phenomenological analysis
Mental models of leadership by men and women in the armed forces	Dunn, Michael; UK	Critical incidents Conversational interviews Thematic analysis
Understanding effective supervision of student teachers	Ilin, Gulden; Turkey	Repertory grid Interviews conversations Observation
Engagement, disengagement and meaningfulness	Long, Trevor; Javes, Stephen UK	Repertory grid Metaphor Card sort Conversational interviews
Personal development planning for accountancy students	Osgerby, Julia, Marriott, Pru, Gee, Maria; UK	Visual metaphors as meaningful representations
Professional role exploration: social care managers and head teachers	Österlind, Marie-Louise; Sweden	Personal diaries Group discussion
Student meaning-making and academic identity	Simmons, Nicola; Canada	Life mapping Snakes and ladders
Exploring people's relationship with nature	Sutcliffe, Jamie, Burr, Viv, King, Nigel; UK	Rivers of experience Conversational interviews

Figure 11.1 Summary of cases

Construing language assessment: the teacher as meaning-maker

Britt-Marie Apelgren PhD EdM

Purpose and focus

The purpose of this research was both to gather information about and to explore the nature of a group of teachers' attitudes to and experiences of different forms of assessment in foreign language teaching. In short, it concerns the teacher as meaning-maker. The project was part of a larger Swedish national study also including a questionnaire survey, classroom development work and field testing of assessment techniques (Apelgren, 2010; Oscarson and Apelgren, 2011).

Methodology

The study was designed as a repertory grid interview study. The participants ($N = 20$) had previously participated in a questionnaire study ($N = 600$). All the interviews were conducted at the individual teacher's school and were audio-taped and later transcribed. The Rep IV research program was used, with the elements and constructs being entered into the program during the actual interviews, which took 60–90 minutes each. Both elicited and provided elements and constructs were used, with the aim of being able to compare and aggregate interview data. The teacher was asked to write down different forms of assessment that s/he uses when assessing students, which became the elements, together with three provided elements. The teachers each listed between 6 and 11 elements. The supplied constructs were put together so as to give a broad picture of the teachers' construing of assessments and student development with the intention to represent different kinds of constructs: perceptual/sensory, behavioural, inferential and attitudinal.

Some findings

A total of 173 elements were generated by the teachers, and a cluster analysis of the data gave 23 types of assessment sources.

The results indicate that:

- Teachers' used a huge variety of assessment data, both formative and summative, when grading their students.
- There was mainly assessment *of* learning and not much *for* learning in so far that the teachers highlighted mostly product-oriented assessment.
- None of the teachers mentioned student-centred elements such as 'self-assessment' or 'peer-assessment'.

The benefits of using the PCP tool of repertory grid

The repertory grid procedure together with taped interview transcripts deepened understanding of what lies behind individual elements and constructs. The use of direct computerised entering of elements and construct of the grids made it possible to further explore the teachers' experiences and attitudes. The participants were shown their own repertory grid analyses after the actual elicitation and asked to comment on patterns they saw in their grids or issues they wished to comment on further. This gave both a structure to the original responses and a basis for the following discussion. In addition, the teachers were asked to comment on their own development of assessing language proficiency. This is when the participants often recognised particular aspects of their assessment practice that they had not before been aware of. For example, one teacher realised to her surprise that, although she used very varied assessment tools, she never allowed types of assessment that included student self-assessment. Her own comment was that she needed to be in control all the time, but that she now wanted to learn more about and eventually introduce learner assessment. This shows that the constructs are open to reconstruction if and when a person encounters new experiences and sees his/her pattern of constructions, and it highlights the importance of elicitation tools that promote choices of continuous revision. Computerised repertory grid programs such as Rep IV allow this, and make it possible for participants to change both the wording of the bipolar constructs and the ratings.

I have tried to bring forward the complexity of allowing for both the individual teacher and the generic teacher to be heard. As a sub-study of a larger project, it was found that interview data reinforced grid findings and made it possible to 'listen to' individual teachers through their statements. By using quotations, the teachers' voices are heard, which helps to provide explanations and clarifications of both questionnaire answers and repertory grid data. Hence, it is important that the repertory grid tool used in interviews does not become a means in itself, but a way forward in understanding the person's constructions.

Using pictures of paintings as aids to communication with people who have learning disabilities

Elvira Apraiz PhD[1]

Purpose and focus

'A review of the literature showed that some people with learning disabilities may have psychological problems which worsen, or even are caused, by communication problems of external origin, such as social isolation and expectations of failure.' Elvira was convinced that such people could be helped to communicate in a therapeutic setting if only professional therapists could learn how. Having, as a counsellor, taken some learning disabled clients to art galleries and observed their

---

[1] Sadly, Elvira died not long after obtaining her doctorate. This case summary was written by Pam Denicolo (her supervisor) from Elvira's writings and a book of her thesis compiled by Pam, Maureen Pope and Elvira's sister. Direct contributions from Elvira are in quotation marks. Comments from Pam are marked [PD] and from her external examiner Prof. David Sines [DS].

reactions to paintings, she sought to explore how works of art might act as catalysts to facilitate communication [PD].

Methodology

'The research explores some of the ways in which six adults of mixed gender, with moderate and severe learning disabilities, made sense of the experience of viewing pictures of paintings.' Using PCP questioning techniques with an array of pictures of paintings, 'the participants and their experiences of viewing the pictures were studied and analysed ... also included are my reflections during the research process ... and some examples of data triangulation are given'. Elvira had, of course, to design her project very carefully with such vulnerable people and gain ethical approval before conducting her pilot and main study, but she used that time to become a familiar figure to her participants on social occasions, visiting their home and liaising with their carers, learning about their normal daily activities and backgrounds. Her main research, conducted in short episodes with each participant to suit their needs, included playing with the cards on which there were individual pictures of a wide range of famous paintings. First the notion of selecting three cards and indicating which were similar and which was different was introduced. In the next session they chose pictures they liked, those they did not, and those that were similar in some way, so that later Elvira could elicit their ideas about in what ways pictures in triads were similar or different [PD].

Findings

Whilst the fieldwork was undoubtedly extremely demanding, the resulting discussions and revelations of the participants, beautifully presented in the thesis, were revelatory – for themselves, their carers and those who read the work [PD]. Her examiner, DS, said: 'Analysis of the findings from her innovative study demonstrate that visual art has a beneficial influence on the way in which people with Learning Disabilities communicate and interact, both with regard to how they appreciate and demonstrate concern with the aesthetic propositions of the paintings ... and the facilitation of personal responses and increased disclosure which enabled people to make specific self-directed decisions regarding their lifestyle and choices'.

The benefits of personal construct psychology

'Focusing on the participants' constructs illuminated their concerns at the time and was trustworthy in that my interpretations were constantly checked with the people concerned in order to reflect their ideas ... These constructions allowed me to explore their view of the world through their own frameworks ... The expression in language of constructs with highly emotional content is difficult for most people so it was always likely to be more so for people who are unused to being asked for their reactions. That the participants were able to convey such a range of constructs as they did is very encouraging regarding the use of PCP tools ... I found particularly useful some of Ravenette's (1998) methods for eliciting constructs from children.'

Elvira has provided her participants with a new voice – the techniques she has used have had a direct influence on that achievement [DS]. Her passion and skill helped her to do what others deemed impossible [PD].

Knowledge transfer of the idea of quality within General Motors from western Europe to Poland

Dorota Bourne PhD MA

Focus/purpose of the research

The research explored the process of transfer of knowledge and ideas across national, cultural and linguistic boundaries. In particular, it examined the transfer of the idea of quality in the car manufacturing industry from western Europe to Poland. It also explored the cultural change which was part of this process and the factors determining its success/failure.

Methodology

Different techniques were adopted in the service of triangulation: the ethnographic interview and methods derived from personal construct psychology, that is, the repertory grid interview, followed by laddering, and the resistance to change technique.

Brief outline of results

The case revealed the process of international transfer of quality to Poland as consisting of two strands: the concepts of lean manufacturing and 'hard' quality which arrived from Germany, and the built-in or so called 'soft' quality which travelled to Poland from the UK. The meaning of quality was analysed and reconstructed in these locations, with a particular focus on England and Poland. The study revealed contradictory notions of quality existing in the UK and Poland and outlined the institutionalisation of quality in these two locations explaining the factors that led to the success of this process in Poland and its failure in the UK. The values embedded in each organisational culture were analysed, which enabled a more critical appraisal of the factors shaping the transfer of ideas across cultural boundaries, including culture-clash management, creative development of new working practices and norms, and mechanisms of managerial control in organisations.

Why constructivism suited the project and added value to the research

When we attempt to get to the roots of organisational culture and identify people's shared assumptions and values, the ethnographic interview might not give us sufficient in-depth opportunity for this. The repertory grid interview and laddering technique proved to be great complementary tools to aid this process.

This research demonstrated that the role of the ethnographer can complement that of the psychological observer and that the combination of ethnographic techniques and the research tools derived from PCP can aid the exploration of the values and shared assumptions embedded in the culture under scrutiny. Moreover, the repertory grid technique played a crucial role in the identification of the contrasting pole of the core constructs, which shed a new light on the behaviour of the people we were trying to understand. Additionally, the repertory grid interview proved to be a very useful tool, enabling the elicitation of tacit knowledge, such as 'soft' quality and its explicit definition.

What really constitutes authentic leadership? Using the repertory grid to unearth and explore leaders' implicit beliefs and attributions

Kim Bradley-Cole PhD

Purpose and focus

Authentic leadership, as it is currently conceptualised by Luthans and colleagues (see Gardner et al., 2005), stands before us as a potential false prophet. On the one hand, it purports to offer the solution to the ethical and social crisis in modern leadership practices, and is held aloft almost evangelically by practitioners and organisational decision-makers. On the other hand, it is condemned by academics such as Ford and Harding (2011), Algera and Lips-Wiersma (2012) and Lawler and Ashman (2012), who argue strongly that the theory is flawed, represents an unrealistic, idealised view, and is potentially harmful to employees if pursued by organisations. The purpose of this research was to bring clarity to this contested field by determining how the meaning of authenticity and authentic leadership is construed, and attributed to others, by leaders themselves. Twenty-five senior managers, working in large, mostly multinational organisations, across a breadth of sectors, functions and reporting levels, were purposively recruited for the study, which was funded by the Economic and Social Research Council.

Methodology

Previously, authentic leadership research had asked leaders to report on their own sense of authenticity, an approach that had been criticised in the literature due to potential issues of self-serving bias. This study adopted a different perspective to directly address this criticism and explored leaders' beliefs about their own leaders. Selecting subordinate leaders situated the topic of authentic leadership in its relational and perceptual context, something that was missing in previous research, and because these managers were leaders themselves, I was also able to explore the impact of authentic leadership on their own in-role behaviours and on the performance quality of these high-level work relationships. Participants were asked to report on their direct working relationships with their two best, two worst, and two average leaders from across their career span, along with rating prototypical views of their ideal, worst and authentic leader. This spread of leaders represented a uniform element set across all participants, and constructs were elicited using the triadic method, and laddered/pyramided as required during the interview. Participants were also asked to rate all leader elements against one supplied construct of 'behaves authentically–behaves far from authentically'. Participants were advised that the purpose of the study was to 'explore positive working relationships with managers that have enabled you to work at your best', and this statement was visible throughout the interview and used to orient the discussion. The grids were analysed using RepGrid 5 and Excel.

Findings

The grids elicited 494 constructs in total. Of these, 326 clustered with the 'authentic leader' element, and can be considered as the enabling behaviours implicitly expected of an authentic leader, and 247 were associated with the 'behaves authentically' construct, and can be considered as the leadership behaviours that are more explicitly associated with authentic behaviour. By exploring authenticity as both a common behavioural construct and a leader prototype, a difference was discerned between leaders' socialised beliefs of how an authentic leader should act, versus what they implicitly expect of a leader they attribute as being authentic. Additionally, it identified the pivotal contribution of leader authenticity to the subordinate's perception that the leadership relationship is enabling. By comparing the ideal and authentic leader elements, it was also possible to isolate what leader attributes/behaviours facilitate manager and team performance, but are perceived as separate or distinct from the leader's authenticity.

The benefits of personal construct psychology

Adopting a PCP perspective enabled me to focus on the subjective experiences of authentic leadership as a received phenomenon, and the abstract nature of the repertory grid offered me a unique opportunity to explore the schematic, tacit representation of authenticity and authentic leadership that would not have been accessible through interviews or surveys. Through this approach, I was able to offer a reconceptualisation of a hitherto contested field, based upon lived experiences that ground the findings in context. Authentic leadership as a construed, attributional phenomenon is a narrower idea than claimed by the incumbent theory, but is essential to the formation of high-quality managerial relationships and team identity.

Using critical incident charting for reflecting on experience

Pam Burnard PhD MEd

Purpose and focus

The ways in which educators and researchers freely employ certain terms (such as 'learning' or 'creative') are not necessarily the same as practitioners whose habits of being and living most embody inclusive representation of the action or the practice. The act of naming enables them to give an interpretation, a definition, a description and often requires developing tools for reflecting and researching. Tools without sharp edges are crucial. Critical incident charting (adapted and referred to here as 'rivers of experience') refers to one such tool that has been used in counselling and psychotherapy, educational research and teacher education.

Critical incident charting originated as a clinical tool used in personal construct psychology (Kelly, 1955/1991) and was later developed, alongside other labels, as 'career-rivers' by education researchers (for example, Denicolo and Pope, 1990; Pope and Denicolo, 1993). The term 'critical incident', however, has been used widely in the research literature on classroom teachers and, indeed, has a long tradition in ethnographies of other cultures. In many cases, its use has been synonymous with periods of strain, beginnings and endings of teachers' careers and turning points that are brought about by surprise or shock. The path to understanding what we do and why we do it is through reflecting and acting on those reflections.

There are several types of critical phase that mark times of change and choosing. For example, 'extrinsic' phases include historical events, conditions that force decisions or act as obstacles. 'Intrinsic' phases usually involve a natural progression of a career, whilst 'personal' phases bring to the forefront particular issues relating to, for example, family. In relation to detailed charting of classroom teaching, the critical incident does not necessarily introduce anything new into the practices of the teacher, but rather acts to crystallise ideas, attitudes and beliefs, which are already being formed. A critical incident may create a turning point, which is confirmed by a subsequent 'counter-incident'.

In my own research, I have adapted the use of critical incident charting for reflecting on the experience of a particular phenomenon, such as creativity, creative teaching and learning, and teacher career paths.

During interviews, or on sheets of paper, respondents annotate a winding timeline with key turning points, critical incidents or significant episodes. As a tool for reflection, creating 'rivers of musical experience' encourages active involvement from participants in an emancipatory and democratic way. Like rivers, the words start to flow since the participants draw them in ways that they own and that they feel are appropriate.

By tracking usage of terms such as 'creative' and 'learning' we may elucidate how these terms have the power to create, augment and reinforce learner identities.

Methodology

I have used three different methods of critical incident charting:

- Participant self-report charting – participants write down specific instances that they consider have influenced the direction of their outlook and identity.
- Interviewer/researcher charting – the researcher uses an interview to construct a chart or river which is then verified or adapted by the interviewee.
- Interviewee-interviewer charting – where a narrative is co-constructed around incidents that both interviewee and interviewer consider highly influential to their identities.

Findings illustrated

For many school children, not taking part in musical activities is the norm because they often do not see themselves as being sufficiently musical. Children assume they are expected to be able to automatically read and play music. What follows is an example of a 12-year-old girl, with no formal training on an instrument nor instruments at home, whose negative musical identity and perceived absence of musical ability can be tracked in key moments identified as significant in her life (Figure 11.2). It is evident that, despite her musical focus and enthusiasm, musicality is an attribute she does not see in herself.

In contrast, Tim's recollections of critical events in his life (Figure 11.3) clearly reflect a positive musical identity identified in terms of musical progress, achievement and specialism.

From this type of charting we clearly see how individuals come to label themselves and are labelled (in this case as being 'musical' or not).

The benefits of critical incident charting (or use of 'rivers')

We can use critical incident charting to reflect on and research:

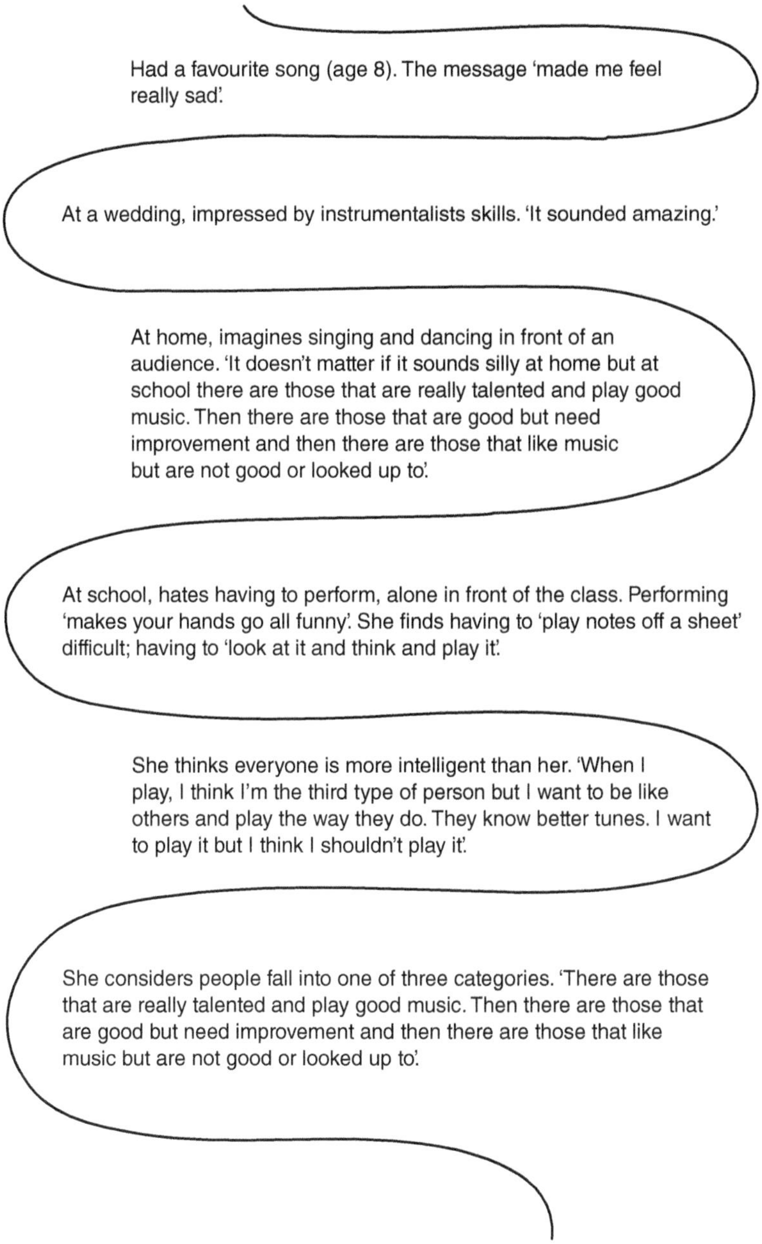

Had a favourite song (age 8). The message 'made me feel really sad'.

At a wedding, impressed by instrumentalists skills. 'It sounded amazing.'

At home, imagines singing and dancing in front of an audience. 'It doesn't matter if it sounds silly at home but at school there are those that are really talented and play good music. Then there are those that are good but need improvement and then there are those that like music but are not good or looked up to'.

At school, hates having to perform, alone in front of the class. Performing 'makes your hands go all funny'. She finds having to 'play notes off a sheet' difficult; having to 'look at it and think and play it'.

She thinks everyone is more intelligent than her. 'When I play, I think I'm the third type of person but I want to be like others and play the way they do. They know better tunes. I want to play it but I think I shouldn't play it'.

She considers people fall into one of three categories. 'There are those that are really talented and play good music. Then there are those that are good but need improvement and then there are those that like music but are not good or looked up to'.

Figure 11.2 Sidin's musical river

Source: Initial Interview reported in Burnard (2000).

- Beliefs, by identifying critical moments in our lives and the strength of emotion attached to those moments;
- Why and how our thinking has changed, by identifying patterns and particular sequences of events;
- Who we are and how we come to perceive ourselves and others.

Recalls playing simple pieces, 'but now I play proper pieces like Allegro by Bach'.

Has had two violin teachers. 'The first one really frustrated me. He kept me on the same old pieces until I'd memorised them without mistakes'.

At one point gave up piano. 'I got sick of preparing for exams and being criticised for not practising'.

Sometimes doesn't practise violin, loses interest. 'The sticky bit is in lessons when you get seriously struck ... It's embarrassing and frustrating'.

Performs in many concerts. Best part is the applause.

Enjoys every time he is asked which grade he has reached. 'Though I am looking forward to getting Grade 8 on piano and violin out of the way, this will be a big moment'.

Plays for Mum's friends. 'I usually rattle off the same old piece ... something quite fast like Bach's Allegro'.

Dad records his pieces. In a recent recording, couldn't get it perfect. You can only 'play perfect' when you're messing around ... When it's 'not serious'

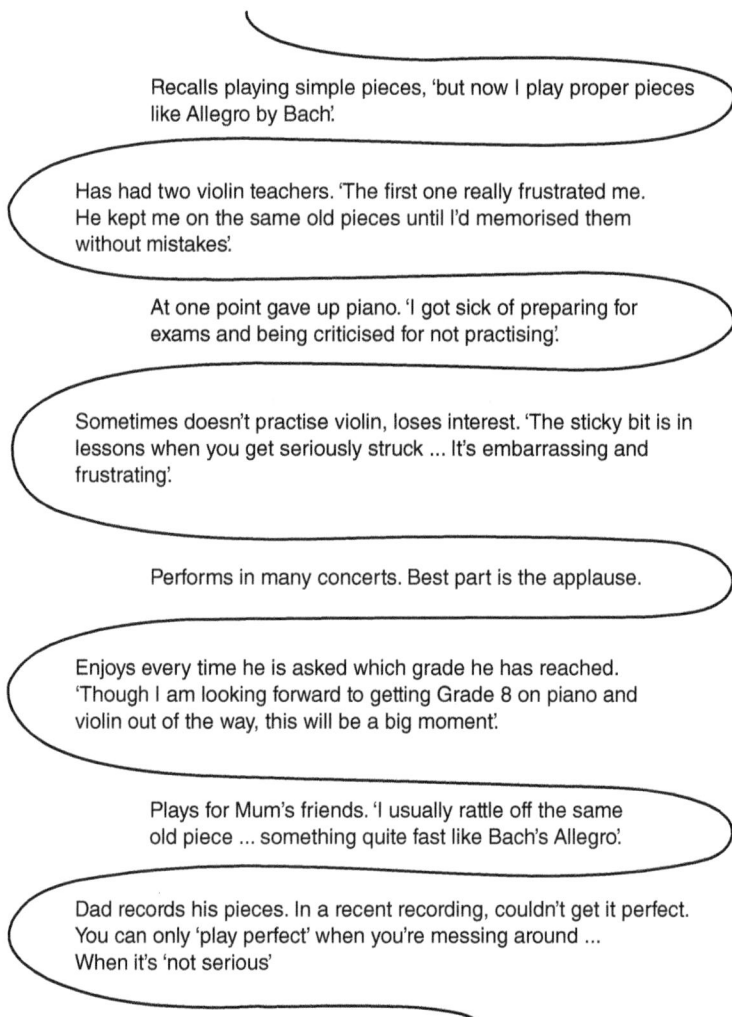

Figure 11.3 Tim's musical river

Source: Initial Interview reported in Burnard (2000).

Constructs of mental and physical durability in elite circus artists

Sarah Dentry-Travis PhD MA

Focus/purpose

Although stress is typically perceived as a negative experience, a person needs to experience stress, challenge and failure in order to acquire knowledge and confidence to expand their abilities. Positive growth through challenge is an area that is under-researched, and as such this project explored perceived components of mental and physical durability in extreme challenges. Its aim was to help shape positive interventions amongst populations that push themselves to the limit, such as elite military personnel, ultra-athletes, and elite circus artists, but it is also informative to the general population.

Resiliency is increasingly being conceptualised as not simply an absence of pathology after a stressful event, but instead as a positive process that differentiates those who may have heightened vulnerability (Bartone and Hystad, 2010; Friborg et al., 2009). This study explored elite circus artists engaging in long hours of extremely physically demanding tasks requiring mental fortitude, along with the necessity to push themselves further than others, physically and creatively. It concentrated on the positive side of the stress spectrum, looking at 'when things go right' during mentally and physically challenging scenarios.

Methodology

Participants in the study were students ($N = 21$) and teachers ($N = 7$) from the National Circus School, the premier circus arts school in the world, as well as professional circus artists from Cirque du Soleil ($N = 10$), in Montreal, Canada.

The participants were asked to bring an artefact to the interview that they perceive best describes mental and physical durability. The artefact could be digital media, such as a video or an image taken from their smartphones, twitter or Facebook account. The personal construct laddering technique was used in conjunction with the artefact to elicit the participants' constructs surrounding 'challenge and durability'.

The validation cycle, where constructs are tested and revised in accordance with a person's experience (Walker and Winter, 2007), was especially interesting with respect to the National Circus School and Cirque du Soleil. Construals from artists at various levels within the circus world regarding mental and physical durability were explored and compared to create a list of constructs that the artists felt were central to mental and physical durability in their specific environment. The resulting construct lists will form the basis for future research on durability in the elite circus population as well as within other extreme populations, such as elite ultra-athletes and military personnel.

Why PCP?

At first the project intended to use survey instruments. Problems with this approach became apparent when it was noted that the pre-existing personality psychology surveys on mental and physical durability were not adequate for the task, as they used researchers' preconceived theories on what mental resiliency was, and they were overwhelmingly designed for team-sport populations and were not necessarily transferable to other populations. It was then thought that perhaps the pre-existing surveys could be revised to be more inclusive of non-team-sport populations; however, the investigators felt that the questions were becoming contrived.

The project demanded that its method provide an unbiased approach that would enable the participants to speak for themselves, as experts in the area of mental and physical durability. Using PCP allowed a better understanding of how certain individuals construe aspects of the world around them and allowed for various mechanisms involved in durability to come to light, rather than forcing components of durability into a pre-existing theory.

The insights gained through the PCP approach to the project will guide further investigations with the circus population, allowing the investigators to be confident that the constructs being discussed are meaningful to the participants rather than taken from another population and made to fit. The circus is an innovative population, and PCP provided an excellent avenue for them to show their creative individualistic flair.

Further reading

Dentry-Travis, S.J. (2013) Canadian soldiers' constructions of their role-sets. *Personal Construct Theory and Practice*, 10, 28–39.
Dentry-Travis, S.J. (2014) Survey Research and Focus Groups Using Personal Construct Psychology. In *SAGE Research Methods Cases*. London: SAGE. doi: 10.4135/9781446627305014527685.

The impact of women's implicit beliefs about success on their experience of being a mother and being in paid employment

Bethan Douglas MSc

Purpose and focus

The purpose of this project was to gain an understanding of how six women experienced their concurrent roles of mother and employee. The extant literature included qualitative and quantitative studies, but none that looked at women's conceptualisations of success in each of these two roles. A homogeneous group of six women in senior roles were involved in the study. All six worked at least 75 per cent of a full-time contract, had children of primary school age and were continuing in similar employment to that held before having children. These characteristics were felt to be important because a key aspect of the study was to look at perceptions of the possibility of 'having it all'.

Methodology

Participants were identified through purposive sampling and then asked to complete a pre-interview questionnaire designed to gather demographic and job information. Interviews comprised three parts: the first explored the participant's idealised conceptualisation of their professional role; the second their idealised conceptualisation of their maternal role; and the third the participant's experience of working and being a mother. Interviewees were invited to draw their prototypical constructs in relation to their conceptualisation of an idealised mother, an idealised person in their job and then to draw a picture of themselves as a working mother. These pictures were explored using semi-structured interviews which were analysed using interpretative phenomenological analysis.

Findings

This study found that culturalised beliefs about maternal and professional prototypes may conflict with working mothers' self-constructs. These conflicts appear to be eased through reflection and conscious processing. Failing to do so may leave in place a barrier to working mothers achieving their potential in the workplace. Several of the working mothers interviewed appeared to simultaneously hold different and fundamentally conflicting mental models. The interplay of these cognitions impacted negatively on their day-to-day experience and their perceived ability to fulfil the characteristics of one or more of their prototypical constructs. A notable consequence was that they felt psychological tension due to the impossibility of achieving their implicit theory of a successful mother.

The benefits of personal construct psychology

PCP was useful in two specific ways in this study. Firstly, during the interview process itself, consistent with Festinger's (1957) theory of cognitive dissonance, participants experienced discomfort with their prototypical constructs as they became aware of incongruence between them and sought to think and talk it through. The process of reflecting on and working through psychological tension experienced between their conceptualisations of maternal and professional roles appeared intrinsically useful to participants in helping them recognise and reduce the tension. A number of participants commented on this specifically. Secondly, the study signposts the fruitfulness of a hitherto uncharted area of study in relation to work–life balance. PCP enabled the exploration of the interplay of personal constructs, cognitions and the experience of work–life balance.

Gender and leadership in the UK's armed forces

Michael Dunn EdD MBA

Purpose and focus

My research question, in the context of the UK's armed forces, was: 'Do women and men lead in different ways?' I conducted two studies, using PCP, one in the British Army (Dunn, 2007), and the second in the Royal Navy (Dunn, 2015).

Methodology

Participants were officers of middle rank; half were men and half were women. They were asked in their interview preparation to pre-identify four female and four male leaders with whom they had worked. Of these, two should be good leaders and two poor leaders, on the basis that both categories would produce a normative model of leadership. The research was mixed method and used the critical incident technique (Flanagan, 1954), so respondents were asked also to identify an incident of either good or bad leadership they had witnessed.

I listed the constructs as they were articulated; with practice, I found that I could do this without spoiling the flow of the process. Participants frequently found it stretching to articulate their complex and abstract conceptualisations of leadership, and there could be long pauses before they found the right form of words. I found it important not to prompt the respondent during this process because, on a number of occasions, their eventual descriptors were completely different than those I had anticipated. Participants then rated each leader, or element, on a scale of 1–5 against the poles of the constructs, using the lists I had built up during the interview.

Findings and use of PCP

The research interviews were revealing in terms of both the research and the participants. In both studies, participants very quickly grasped the PCP element. The triadic elicitation process provided a fruitful response. On average, each interview yielded 20 constructs for male leaders and slightly fewer for female leaders. Because there is a major gender imbalance in both services, some participants had not had experience of four female leaders.

A common post-interview response from respondents was that they had found the process of elicitation and rating very challenging, but rewarding and enjoyable. A number also commented that they had surprised themselves with what the process had revealed about their own mental maps. This response is important for research, where often the researcher is not able to offer much in exchange for the respondent giving of their time. With PCP, there is payback for the respondents. It was also helpful in that respondents then had the confidence to identify colleagues who might also participate.

I suggest it is good practice to identify a star construct after each study simply to acknowledge that respondents will often articulate their thoughts using unconventional, but powerful, turns of phrase. For example, my star construct for the RN study was:

> common sense, brightness, practical application ... knew cubic capacity of jam-pot but not how to get the lid off.

Analyses of statistical variance for each construct were calculated using the principle that high variance is a proxy for the significance of that construct in the respondent's mental map of leadership. Using content analysis, the constructs were brigaded into factors and independently verified. Content analysis was also used to identify key themes from the critical incidents and a comparative analysis done with both sets of data to triangulate a common model.

The data produced were often rich and nuanced, an indication that the PCP method is both powerful and effective in accessing respondents' mental models, in this case, of leadership.

A model for effective supervision from the student teachers' perspective: a social constructivist approach

Gülden İlin PhD

Purpose and focus

This study was conducted in order to provide a general description of the teaching practice experience in the English language teaching department of a Turkish university with a specific reference to two fundamental components of the process: the supervisors and the student teachers. Initially, the study focused on how six supervisors in the department perceived the qualities of an effective supervisor, and how their perceptions, if any, showed themselves in their practices. The probable consequences of the supervisors' feedback on the 15 student teachers' conceptualisation of an effective teacher were the second major enquiry of the study.

Methodology

The repertory grid was the main technique for gathering data. In addition, views about an effective teacher at the beginning and at the end of the study were elicited, in addition to recordings of supervisors' feedback sessions, interviews, feedback forms, contact summary sheets, observations and stimulated recall activities.

Findings

Findings revealed no consistency in the supervisors' views regarding the qualities of an effective supervisor, and no mutual approach was found for the practices of supervisory duties in the department. The supervisors elicited 104 constructs, but only 75 of these were concretely observed in practice.

Analyses of the two grids completed at the beginning and at the end of the study revealed, for nine of the 15 participants, significant structural changes in student teachers' personal theories. The changes were both thematic and hierarchical. The 68 constructs about teaching behaviours, personal qualities and academic qualities elicited at the beginning of the study were reduced to 52 construct themes. Seventeen new constructs were added to the grids through the other techniques, and changes in high-priority constructs were detected. Most participants were able to state the rationale behind these changes. Based on their rankings, classroom observations and feedback sessions, their supervisors as models, mentors, peers and personal experiences respectively played a role on this change.

The overall findings revealed that the practice period, with its ability to provide a thought-provoking environment for student teachers, was clearly influential in teacher development, and the study indicated the importance of reflection, interaction, collaboration and a supportive environment.

The benefits of personal construct psychology

Detecting change was the general objective of this study. Knowing that change does not necessarily have to show itself in behavioural terms only, going deep inside my participants' minds and looking for conceptual change seemed plausible. Using personal construct psychology and the repertory grid technique contributed significantly to the study as they uniquely served to reach the content and structure of the participants' personal theories without directing their answers in any way. This would not have been possible with any other data collection instrument. As a component of the repertory grid technique, interviews held on the basis of each of the participants' grids clearly led to better understanding of the meanings the participants attached to their constructs as well as how they construed their experiences at the practice schools. All these led to more elaborate and profound interpretation of research results. As a secondary benefit, repertory grid use and follow-up interviews raised the student teachers' awareness of their personal theories and the underlying reasons for their teaching behaviours.

Further reading

İlin, G. (2003) A model for effective supervision from the student-teachers' perspective: a social constructivist approach. Unpublished doctoral thesis. Çukurova University, Turkey.

İlin, G. (2014) Sendan: a case study. *International Journal of Language Academy*, 2, 3-13.

İlin, G., Kutlu, Ö. and Kutluay, A. (2013). An action research: using videos for teaching grammar in an ESP class. *Procedia - Social and Behavioral Sciences*, 70, 272-281.

Personal work engagement, disengagement and meaningfulness

Trevor Long PhD MBA and Stephen Javes MBA

Purpose and focus

The purpose of this research project was to explore the key factors that would help leaders to design work so that employees' performance and personal well-being could be enhanced simultaneously, despite these being often conflicting objectives, especially in commercial organisations (Long, 2013). The literature revealed personal work engagement as a broad theoretical underpinning for this exploration. As the research required depth of insight into people's internal experiences, and in order to maintain contextual consistency between participants, it was carried out in a single organisation. A housing association was selected because varied personal engagement dynamics were expected to be especially salient in such an environment.

Methodology

Seeking to build insights into deep individual experiences, an inductive, phenomenological paradigm was adopted, collecting primarily qualitative data about personal meanings from representative participants at different managerial levels. This relativist philosophy underpinned the choice of conversational interviews, supported by tools and techniques that elicited personal constructs, including repertory grid, concept card mapping and metaphors, based on 'critical' or illuminative incidents. This was an exploratory study, so, following an in-depth literature review, it progressed iteratively, with outcomes from one phase of interviews informing the next. A total of 41 interviews were carried out in four phases over 16 months, interspersed with further literature reviews, analyses, and the introduction of refined techniques. Because interpretative analysis of data was essential, care was taken to bracket personal views, triangulate from different data sets and immerse myself in the data sufficiently to elicit credible identifiable patterns and trends through iterative hermeneutic exploration.

Findings

Literature indicated that the notion of engagement, which is understood as the personal employment of discretionary focus and effort, establishes the prospect of designing work that enhances the sense of self whilst also enhancing work quality. Literature also suggested that disengagement and engagement were two ends of a single spectrum and that leaders can manage work factors to help move people towards a more engaged experience. Findings from this study contribute to the literature by eliciting evidence that engagement and disengagement are actually two distinct constructs, operating on different spectrums. This reconceptualisation of engagement has major implications for leaders. First it means that both engagement and disengagement can be experienced simultaneously, in the same mental frame, creating the potential for deep inner conflict. Second, leading people out of disengagement requires a fundamentally different approach than leading people towards higher positive engagement opportunities. Further, the research revealed that the metaconstruct of meaningfulness plays a central role in the experience of both disengagement and engagement.

The benefits of personal construct psychology

It was not the initial intention in this study to use PCP. It started with a broad research interest and possible research question. Once the nature of the phenomena was understood the value of PCP as an underpinning theoretical perspective became clear. In early interviews, just asking participants for contrasts to their inner experiences, such as autonomy, involvement and contribution, created clarity that would not have been available otherwise. Eliciting participants' own words was especially important in order to explore their inner sense of reality. The use of repertory grid provided a structure to quickly elicit constructs, which formed the basis of discussion and the development of depth and breadth of insight through pyramiding and laddering. Using a computer-based repertory grid application (RepGrid 5) in interviews enabled direct input and 'ownership' of the process by participants, and immediate analytical feedback and further clarification on outcomes. During interviews, asking participants to metaphorically associate particular construct issues to a shape allowed deeper exploration. As engagement and disengagement as distinct constructs became clear, the use of construct card mapping against critical, illuminative incidents of engagement and disengagement elicited greater clarity around distinguishing key constructs that related to each. This in turn revealed patterns of constructs that converged to uncover meaningfulness as the central phenomenon. In conclusion, whilst other theoretical perspectives and methodologies would have elicited data to allow exploration of aspects of engagement dynamics, their inability to explore inner realities with such depth as was possible with PCP makes it unlikely that engagement and disengagement distinctions would have been revealed, at least with such clarity, nor that the role of meaningfulness would have been so prominent.

'Say what you see': Using visual metaphors as part of personal development planning

Julia Osgerby MSc, Pru Marriott PhD and Maria Gee PhD

Purpose and focus

The literature reports that students:

- find the type of reflection required by personal development planning (PDP) difficult;
- often dislike the experience;
- find it difficult to evaluate themselves and to articulate the generic skills that they possess.

In the area of career coaching, counselling and planning, research suggests that the use of visual metaphors, such as drawings, icons and artefacts, gives voice to personal experiences which may otherwise be difficult to express. We wanted to use visual methods in the undergraduate curriculum to help students engage in PDP and to assist them in the preparation and development of personal development plans in an enjoyable and novel way.

The subsequent research into the use of this pedagogic approach explored the notions that using visual metaphor supported both thinking skills and critical reflection, and aided the PDP process. Establishing the benefits, or otherwise, of this pedagogic approach helps to inform the debate on introducing new ways of engaging students in more meaningful learning.

Methodology

This exploratory case study involved first-year undergraduate accounting students studying a compulsory year-long module entitled 'Academic and Professional Skills'. During the first few weeks of the module, we introduced students to the notions of learning styles, visual methods, and PDP.

We asked students to create a personal development plan, including the production of a visual metaphor covering 'their aspirations during the next five years'. The purpose of the visual metaphor was to encourage students to express their thoughts about the developmental journey they are likely to undertake from new student to successful graduate employee using meaningful imagery. Examples of visual metaphors were discussed with students, but they were left free to use any technique, format or image of their choice to create an illustrative product that assisted them to think about their personal developmental needs.

To investigate the students' perceptions of the approach, we developed a questionnaire with both closed and open-ended free text questions covering cognition, learning styles, enabling skills and engagement. Additionally, there were questions relating to students' opinion of the purpose of the visual metaphor work, their likes and dislikes of the approach, their chosen visual method and their perception of the utility and future use of the approach in the PDP process.

Findings

The evidence from the study suggests that the negative and bewildering encounter that students have with PDP was replaced, through the use of visual methods, with a positive, engaging, enjoyable and productive experience. The use of visual tools enabled the students to articulate and reflect on their knowledge and experiences, and to present their personal goals and aspirations. However, the visual approach to PDP was not appropriate for everyone; for some students the requirement to use imagery to express their views was challenging, and some considered it to be a waste of time. Nevertheless, two-thirds of the students expressed a preference for more tuition to be given on personal development planning with the use of visual methods.

The benefits of personal construct psychology

Our case study is about the use of constructivist techniques within the academic curriculum (student as scientist) rather than the use of constructivist techniques for the 'academic' research of phenomena. The findings of our study support the use of visual metaphor in helping students to explore and construct their own knowledge. The technique encouraged and motivated students to think more deeply, critically, creatively and proactively about their personal goals and future plans. The use of visual tools as part of PDP in the curriculum has encouraged students' creativity, engagement, critical reflection, integrative thinking, and self-directed learning, all of which are skills critical to students' future employability. For many students, the process of visualising their future career goals motivated them to work harder and to put more effort into their studies – an indication that they are taking PDP more seriously. For all these reasons, we recommend that those involved in the delivery of modules linked to personal development planning reflect on their pedagogy and how they develop undergraduate students' interest in, and engagement with, the practice of personal development planning.

Diary-in-group method: a constructivist participative group technique

Marie-Louise Österlind PhD

Purpose and focus

This case study describes the Diary-in-Group (DiG) method (personal diary writing combined with group sessions) as used in two research projects, inspired by personal construct theory (Kelly, 1955/1991) and by Schön's (1983) theories on reflective practice, carried out in Swedish public sector organisations. The projects aimed to contribute to new practice-based knowledge on what it means to be a social care manager (project I) or head teacher (project II), and to the learning and development of the participants. The research approach proposed to support a scientific form of knowledge creation, where the process, the personal growth of the participants and the development of praxis were considered as valuable as the generation of new knowledge.

Methodology

The DiG method brings together the individual, subjective perspective with group interaction, adding a time dimension (Lindén, 1996), and was therefore considered especially well suited for these constructivist projects.

The participants, ten social care managers in project I and six head teachers in project II, were regarded as collaborators with the researcher, able to develop ideas and work together in order to understand and change their situation. The participants explored their activities and experiences by keeping a personal diary for two 'ordinary' working days, using their own forms of notation. Each diary writer hosted a subsequent group session, which involved all participants, including readings from the diary interleaved with questions, reflections and explorations of ideas and options for future actions. The nature and length of the group's reflections over the occurring themes varied considerably.

Transcriptions from group sessions provided very rich material, which was analysed using a qualitative, descriptive, phenomenological approach, immersing in the data to identify 'cores of significance' in accordance with the idea of the hermeneutic circle (Gadamer, 1997).

Findings

The results from project I (Österlind, 2013a) show that the social care managers' leadership role ideal was grounded in the construct 'care' which encompassed caring for service delivery, for the caretakers' quality of life and for the staff and their working conditions, by safeguarding their respective interests and by developing quality and staff. The managers' constructions of 'quality' were closely related to a good staff–caretaker relationship, which the managers strove to facilitate. They experienced difficulties in reconciling their caring leadership ideal with senior managers' cost-efficient management service delivery expectations, leading to feelings of inadequacy and frustration. This was particularly evident in the paradoxical situations where unreasonable contradictions in the system made them feel compelled to act in a way which caused negative consequences for both caretakers and staff.

The results from project II (Österlind, 2014) show that the head teachers' leadership role was grounded in the construct 'management'. This construct was also closely related to their constructions of 'quality'. They often felt self-confident and in control, despite their demanding and multifaceted work situation. It seems likely that this personal approach to their professional role, shaped by previous experiences, allowed them to balance the many contrasting demands and to accomplish personal equilibrium. The head teachers put much trust in their teachers' performance and abilities and delegated considerable responsibility for budget, recruiting substitutes and quality of work to the teachers. Most of their perceived difficulties were related to poor service from other municipal units such as the property services and IT department.

The benefits of personal construct psychology

Evaluations of the projects showed that the DiG method can prove a valuable constructivist technique that facilitates reflective processes of shared meaning-making in which the participants can explore important aspects of their daily work and professional roles. The diary writing can encourage individual experience-based reflection, while the group sessions can serve as a forum for feedback and support from colleagues, in which the reflection on, and sometimes resolution of, concerns and problems can strengthen group climate and confidence. However, the process is affected by the group's size and functionality, the regularity or irregularity in the meetings as well as by the participants' initiative and commitment. This suggests that with groups who have a genuine interest in and commitment to the project the DiG method can prove a constructivist technique that contributes to new knowledge as well as to the personal growth of the participants and to the development of praxis.

Snakes and ladders LifeMapping: A process for visual data collection

Nicola Simmons PhD

Introduction

In this example, I outline the use of a data collection method developed from LifeMapping™ based on Kelly's (1955/1991) personal construct theory. I describe two examples of this method: the first to support students' meaning-making and theory creation; the second to collect data on academics' identity development.

LifeMapping and PCP

LifeMapping™ is an application of personal construct theory that 'supports recollection, reflexivity, and reconstruction in making explicit the inner self' (Kompf and Simmons, 2016). Individuals choose significant life events and rate them for impact from –10 to +10, considering the impact when the events occurred, at the present time, and likely future impact. In this way, LifeMapping helps make explicit persons' perceptions about life events towards determining their constructs. Life experiences, meaning-making, and anticipations of future directions can all be examined through this PCP approach.

LifeMapping representations can take many forms and are often portrayed as a timeline graph. Some people have been found to prefer a less linear approach, which led me to develop a snakes and ladders format to portray overlapping positive and negative events. In addition, this approach views such events from the perspective of psychological time rather than chronological time (Kelly, 1955/1991; Kompf and Simmons, 2016).

Teaching application: Students developing personal theories

The snakes and ladders technique was applied in a lifespan development course to help students think about positive and negative factors in their personal and professional lives towards their final project. I provided a blank chart for the activity and the following instructions:

- Pick a location for where you are now.
- Draw in your own snakes and ladders for incidents/times that have affected where you are now, as well as for what will have impact in the future.
- Use snakes as downward paths to represent events/issues/persons that have a negative impact, and ladders as upward paths for events/issues/persons having a positive impact (Simmons, 2009).

Students reported that this activity helped them view life events as supports and challenges to their current (and future) situation and to ponder these events in a new light. They considered how the ways in which they have construed (and reconstrued) past events framed their future anticipations (Kelly, 1955/1991). They built on these insights to create their own lifelong development theory, drawing substantially on Kelly's work.

Research application: Academics' identity development

Recently, I have been exploring how faculty members engaged in the scholarship of teaching and learning (SoTL: academics from all disciplines conducting research on their teaching and learning practices) construct their academic roles in light of this add-on for which they typically have no training and receive no rewards. I interviewed them about what supports and challenges they experience in their role development, and asked them to try the snakes and ladders approach.

I found the distinction in how participants discussed the supports and challenges fascinating. The snakes and ladders seemed to permit them to see the integration of supports and challenges in a more integrated way and (re-)create schemata about their experiences and anticipations. In addition, and perhaps even more noteworthy, the process seemed to engage them in interrogating their own data.

As noted by Kompf and Simmons (2016), situational encounters and events give rise to searches for precedents in construct systems, schemata, or paradigmatic principles in order to reduce anxiety or falling victim to what Kelly (1991a: 10) referred to as being 'caught with his constructs down'.

I found that I did not have to pose additional questions to get at deeper meanings; I simply asked them to do the activity and allow them to see what meaning they could make of the results towards anticipating the future and reducing their anxieties.

Summary

More research remains to be done regarding how the process of creating this visual format unlocks different ways of seeing 'life data', but the initial response from participants has been strongly positive, and it seems to bring to the surface a greater number of the participants' implicit assumptions. Externalising life events and insights according to psychological time helps make them explicit. I continue to explore uses of the snakes and ladders LifeMapping approach; currently, I am using it in a study of graduate students' experiences of their degree path.

In this example, conference attendees at a poster session were asked to create their own snakes (challenges to conducting SoTL work) and ladders (supports to conducting SoTL work), choosing shorter or longer snakes and ladders to indicate impact of each factor.

Using rivers of experience to explore people's relationships with nature

Jamie Sutcliffe, Viv Burr PhD and Nigel King PhD

Purpose and focus

This case study focuses on the use of the rivers of experience (RoE: Iantaffi, 2011) method as part of a larger project aimed at gaining an insight into how people construe their relationship with nature and how this relationship developed over time. The project additionally explored people's relationships with nature through construct elicitation and laddering, but only the findings from the RoE are presented here. The RoE exercise was specifically used to explore how participants understood the development of their relationship with nature over time.

Methodology

Sixteen participants with varying relationships with the natural world were interviewed. The sample was diverse including, for example, a wildlife photographer, an animal rights activist, a fisherman and a farmer.

Participants were interviewed individually using the RoE task. This involved a similar process to that described by Iantaffi (2011) in his adaptation of the 'snake' method (Denicolo and Pope, 1990). Participants were asked to think about any significant people, things and events which they felt had influenced their relationship with nature, starting from as far back as they considered relevant. They were then asked to think of their life as a river, with each of these significant influences being bends in that river, and to draw this as intricately or as simply as they wished, for discussion between the interviewer and participant.

As in past research by Cabaroglu and Denicolo (2008), a content analysis was used which highlighted common features that participants included on their rivers. But how participants responded to the instructions was additionally explored, producing further insights into their experience.

Findings

What participants included in their rivers

Participants were asked to start their river with the first influence on their relationship with nature that they remembered. Although they were not specifically asked to begin at childhood, 13 out of the 16 participants chose to do so. All but one chose to include a significant person or people on their rivers, often a teacher, parent or a well-known figure such as David Attenborough. Many included a trip, holiday or going for walks, often citing travelling, whether home or abroad, as an influence.

How participants used the task

Although all participants were given the same instructions, individuals engaged with the task in different ways. The number of experiences or events participants included varied dramatically, with one participant including only 1 event, while another included 18. The captions written alongside these also varied considerably, from 4 to 471 words, and some added their own drawn images.

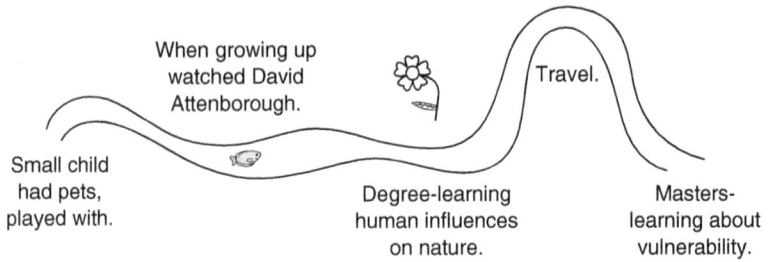

Figure 11.4 Example of river of experience

Of particular interest was the different utilisation of the bends in the river. Some participants did not seem to attach particular significance to the bends, placing them at regular intervals along their rivers, while others used them to represent the chronology of events, and still others used bends of different sizes to emphasise key events and 'high' and 'low' points. An example is Samantha's river (Figure 11.4). Samantha charts a path from playing with pets in early childhood, watching David Attenborough on TV as she grew up, to the huge influence of her travels in Africa, which led to an active engagement with sustainability issues through her master's degree.

Benefits of personal construct psychology

The use of a specific metaphor has advantages in this kind of research. Whereas 'free drawing' tasks may overwhelm some participants, the river metaphor imposes some structure; in adapting this structure to their own needs, participants illustrate important aspects of their experience. The RoE exercise enabled participants to express the development of their relationship with nature in a way that seemed appropriate and meaningful to them. It provided a quick yet rich insight into their construal of their own 'natural' history, populating it with human and animal actors, storying it through encounters with the natural world and capturing events of special significance for them.

Constructivism was seen as an appropriate framework for this research, since it recognises that nature itself, as well as our relationship with the natural and social worlds, are personally and socially constructed. Although the RoE exercise does not explicitly aim to elicit bipolar constructs it nevertheless powerfully illustrates both personal constructions and, like the 'snake' method, how these change over time in response to experience (Denicolo and Pope, 1990). It shares characteristics with other PCP methods; these typically involve active participation and giving research participants 'ownership' of their data. And, as in this case, they often focus on the concrete and particular rather than abstract ideas, which can be surprisingly fruitful. Although their rivers differed considerably in terms of content, the participants all engaged very positively with the task, finding it insightful and enjoyable.

Conclusion

The cases in this chapter have revealed the wider-ranging applications of constructivist research and PCP in particular. The one aspect they have in common is an interest in accessing personal meanings, but the variety of applications across different sectors, functions, activities and interests clearly shows that constructivist research can have particular value whenever we wish to understand people's inner experience. You will have also noticed the variety of techniques across the cases, referring to those we discussed in Chapter Seven. Whilst repertory grid is the most established formal technique, we have selected cases to show this variety and that the technique you use should reflect your particular data collection circumstances. You may have read only those cases that link in some way to your research interest; however, you should never use a technique mechanistically, without knowing how and why it is appropriate, and you should take care when developing novel ways to elicit constructs. You need to carefully consider the theoretical underpinning to any technique you use, and it is for this reason that we included early chapters on philosophy and theory, in addition to discussion on research design and practical issues.

Having illustrated the breadth of applications of constructivism, we now, in the final chapter, consider constructivist research through a different lens, which is through the eyes of one, albeit distinguished, researcher, Maureen Pope. Reading Maureen's story will help you to see not just another perspective on constructivism but how and why constructivism has become such a uniquely established approach to understanding people.

12

Constructive alternatives, psychic mirrors and narrative turns: reflections on a lifetime as a personal construct researcher

Maureen Pope

Introduction

To construe is to hear the whisper of the recurrent themes in the events that reverberate around us. (Kelly, 1991a: 54)

This is only one of the many metaphorical ways in which George Kelly wrote about his theory of personal constructs. What follows is my story of how I first engaged with his ideas and the 45-year journey thereafter. Inevitably the telling of the story is selective, but it does include reference to people, their research and events which have had special meaning and influenced the trajectory of my life as a constructivist researcher. In so doing the reader will get a glimpse of particular socio-historic contexts within which my research, and that of my colleagues, has evolved.

There are recurrent themes or, as Dilthey (in Rickman 1976: 215) called them, 'connecting threads ... which have special dignity ... preserved in memory and lifted out of the endless stream of forgotten events'. The dramatis personae have special meaning so I will include first names. The whispers of my formative years are still strong. This was a time of ...

Considering alternatives

My early exposure to PCP was as an undergraduate student at Brunel University. Don Bannister, in the early 1960s, had toured British university psychology societies as 'Kelly's representative on earth' (Canter, 2007: 1). He campaigned against what he saw as the 'disastrous characteristics' of psychology at the time, with its 'cleavage into loose and tight types of psychology'. By this he meant Freudian and behaviourist psychology, the latter spawning research which was tightly defined and fragmented, 'providing us with the [s]hort term memory for T mazes under electrically induced stress conditions in the decorticate wood louse type of paper' (Bannister, 1970: 59). Of course he presented personal construct psychology as a radical alternative – but always humorously. Brunel became a significant PCP research centre: Neil Warren, who encouraged the development of PCP there, arranged what were known as the 'Kelly seminars'. The first significant PCP symposium outside the USA was held there and Kelly presented his theory in person in 1964.

When I arrived at Brunel in 1970 I was fortunate to find a range of alternative psychological approaches which, unusual for the time, included PCP. I remember fondly and with gratitude three lecturers who introduced me to their specialism, demonstrating enthusiasm and personal commitment to arguing for their ideas about the future of psychology. Parveen Adams highlighted the role of language in thinking and psychoanalytic approaches in psychology. She adopted a feminist perspective (Adams, 1996), and I joined her women's group. Larry Phillips (1973) taught me decision theory and Bayesian statistics. Both recognised the role of a person's beliefs in decision-making and, like PCP, were seen at the time as radical alternatives to generally accepted approaches in psychology and research methods. However, it was Laurie Thomas who introduced me to PCP, and at last I found an approach rooted in a philosophy of knowledge and a view of human development which resonated with my own thinking of myself as learner. A psychology predicated upon coming to an understanding of people, their active choices and personal meanings rather than a focus on their conditioning. Bannister and Fransella's (1971) seminal book *Inquiring Man* provided me with an excellent introduction to George Kelly's personal construct theory – small beginnings to what would become an exciting lifetime journey.

Brunel University operated a system which encouraged the interplay between theory and everyday life through work placements. These afforded me the opportunity to test out the utility of the theories and research methods in real-life practical settings and to anticipate future directions my career in psychology might take. Immediately before enrolling on my degree I had spent several years as a pre-school teacher. I was considering a career as an educational psychologist, so my first placement was as a primary school teaching assistant carrying out classroom observations and considering Piagetian models of child development – the progressive reorganisation and assimilation of knowledge. I experienced the inadequacy of checklist observation scales and questioned the rigidity of Piaget's stages of development. Systematic observation schedules tend to focus on surface aspects of interaction and neglect more meaningful underlying features. I learned by listening to the children rather than merely observing their behaviour. Kelly (1970: 262) recognised the importance of listening to children, seeing learning as personal exploration. For him, the teacher's role entails helping to:

> design and implement each child's own undertakings ... she [*sic*] has to begin, as any apprentice begins, by implementing what others have designed; in this case what her children have initiated.

I welcomed this emphasis on personal exploration (person as scientist) by children themselves. That placement validated my view that teachers' beliefs were fundamental in determining classroom climate. I agreed with Postman and Weingartner (1971: 43):

> There can be no significant innovation in education that does not have at its centre the attitudes of teachers and it is an illusion to think otherwise. The beliefs, feelings and assumptions of teachers are the air of the learning environment; they determine the quality of life within it.

So began my long-term interest in teacher thinking.

My second placement was at Leavesden Mental Hospital. This was housed in grim Victorian buildings, in its heyday presiding over 3,000 patients. Even today I recall the pervading stench of disinfectant. I was attached to the Psychology Department and helped to administer tests such as the Peabody Picture Vocabulary Tests. When I met some patients, such as the elderly lady who had been detained since her early twenties under the Mental Deficiency Act 1913 (repealed in 1959) as a 'moral defective' for having an illegitimate baby, I questioned the relevance of such testing. Having spent so long there, her language was inevitably limited. To me, holding her hand and having a conversation seemed so much more worthwhile, following Kelly's (1991a: 140) dictum: 'If you don't know what's wrong with a client, ask him; he may tell you!' The medical model of care and constant psychometric testing was not for me!

I returned to my interest in psychology in education with my final placement at the National Foundation for Educational Research (NFER). This was a happier experience. Colleagues were generous with their time, and I learned a great deal about the range of educational research being conducted at the time. The NFER remains the largest independent educational research body undertaking contract work for government, schools and charities and providing information services. I might have applied there but my career took a different direction when, on graduation, I won a Social Science Research Council scholarship for a PhD at Brunel with part-time employment to teach field methods to psychology undergraduates. Laurie Thomas offered to be my supervisor. This heralded the dawning of my academic career and my immersion in PCP.

Centre for the Study of Human Learning

Laurie Thomas had become a leading advocate of Kelly's theory and I was keen to explore further the relevance of PCP to educational issues. Laurie was director of the Centre for the Study of Human Learning (CSHL), a self-financing research unit set up in 1967, which was recognised as a major centre conducting PCP research and consultancy in education and training while pioneering interactive programs for the elicitation of repertory grids. I became involved in the field-testing of the programs, the Centre's consultancy work with firms such as Marks and Spencer and ICI, and contributed to a number of its publications.

A fellow student, Mildred Shaw, and I spent many hours discussing the failure of traditional psychology to address the needs of teachers and learners. Mildred had arrived at the CSHL having experience as a teacher in a comprehensive school and as a lecturer in computer science. We shared the journey of coming to know PCP. She developed a suite of computer programs aimed at analysis of individual grids, comparisons between pairs of grids, analysis of a group of grids and an interactive program for self-administration (Shaw, 1980). I was a willing guinea pig, and, in return, was able to use one of her grid analysis programs in my own PhD research.

Examining the prevailing models of psychological development and their underlying theories of knowledge, I argued that much current educational research was based on a cultural transmission of knowledge model and an over-reliance on nomothetic studies. PCP offered an alternative vision and a new mode of enquiry in educational research. The role of teaching practice was then hotly debated in teacher training establishments and within government. I interviewed three groups of student teachers before, during and after teaching practice. Two of the groups also completed three repertory grids; one also received feedback on and discussion of their grids. The research demonstrated that the awareness raising offered by the grid, most evident in the grid with feedback group, helped students gain higher teaching practice grades (Pope, 1978). This convinced me that the repertory grid could be a powerful instrument, providing a firm basis for conversations about teacher education between student and teacher. However, I also realised that it is best seen as a catalyst for a conversation: much valuable information and elaboration came from the process of elicitation itself and the feedback discussions.

Since then I have used repertory grids in research and conducted many training workshops, but I always give health warnings. It is a powerful instrument to be used with care and sensitivity and always with cognisance of its underlying theory. Devoid of its epistemological and philosophical base it becomes a barren instrument. Many people get preoccupied with the grid's numerical aspects, neglecting its flexibility in illuminating others' construing. Martin Fromm noted that researchers can get too focused on issues such as devising the best way of calculating relations between constructs, rather than seeing it as a screen upon which one can project personal meaning. For those without access to an experienced practitioner, Martin's book (Fromm, 2004) provides guidance as he emphasises the active role participants can play in the interpretation of data.

I enjoyed the process of co-authorship (something later valued throughout my academic career) with Mildred (Pope and Shaw, 1981). We agreed with Kelly (1969a: 135) who maintained that 'humanistic psychology needs a technology through which to express its humane intentions' – referring to his repertory grid technique. At the CSHL we explored the grid in conjunction with other techniques that could be used as tools to help in the articulation of personal perspectives. Laurie and his collaborator Sheila Harri-Augstein sought to redefine learning in terms of how the learner develops personal structures of meaning. Their aim was to develop what they referred to as 'psychic mirrors' to elicit learners' personal meaning while raising their awareness of their learning strategies to become self-organised learners (Thomas and Harri-Augstein, 1985).

Regular informal seminars at CSHL included students of Gordon Pask, the cybernetician, from Larry Phillips's Decision Analysis Unit, and visiting students from other institutions. It was a time for loosening our constructs and engaging in several of what Kelly (1991a: 388) called 'creativity cycles'. During this period I recognised the value of making links between George Kelly's theory and other cognate traditions and methods. Gordon Pask, a colourful character often bedecked in a cape, bow tie and carrying a silver topped cane, was a powerful intellect best known for his conversation theory and modelling of cognition as evolutionary and self-organising. Bernard Scott, one of his students, has described him as a radical constructivist, demonstrating the connection between Pask's model and the PCP-based conversational models of Thomas and Harri-Augstein (Scott, 2001). Ranulph Glanville (2006), another of Pask's students, drew attention to the importance of non-verbal construing and has written extensively on design research, cybernetics and constructivism.

We worked hard but had great fun in the process, all accompanying Laurie and Sheila to Oxford for the first international PCP congress in the UK (deemed to be the second international congress – the first being the Nebraska Symposium convened by Landfield in 1975). We all presented our papers, and I remember the hilarious night several of us, now respected academics, created a repertory grid on a room radiator. One of this merry band was Terry Keen, an Open University doctoral student and regular CSHL visitor with whom I shared similar views about the role of PCP in education. Terry had developed a system called TARGET (Teaching Appraisal using Repertory Grid Techniques) for teachers whereby they could elicit their own constructs regarding teaching effectiveness as opposed to normative models of 'good' or 'bad teaching' (Keen, 1979). Our common interests led to the publication of a book (Pope and Keen, 1981) still referenced today by those wishing to explore the relevance of PCP in educational settings. Before this book there had been a paucity of material on educational applications of PCP, the main body of evidence emanating from clinical settings.

After our doctoral studies we all kept in regular contact through the Barbican Research Group convened by Mildred Shaw and Brian Gaines in 1979, joined eventually by our own research students. By 1982 we had all moved on to new ventures, Brian and Mildred emigrating to Canada.

Leaving the fold: new landscapes

I had in 1979 joined the Institute for Educational Technology at Surrey University (later renamed Institute for Educational Development (IED) to better reflect its work). For eight years I had explored PCP within the confines of a psychology department, albeit one that encouraged placement forays into applied settings. When I handed in my notice to the then head of the Psychology Department, he said to me 'you are a good psychologist – are you doing the right thing moving to education?', echoing a prevalent assumption that applied research was somewhat inferior.

The late 1970s had seen a growing critique of the relevance of much psychological research to the realities of the classroom. This was not surprising as much of psychology saw people as reactive rather than constructivist. However, the zeitgeist was changing. As Kelly (1969b: 31) remarked:

> A psychology that pins its anticipations on repetition of events it calls 'stimuli' or on the concatenations of events it calls 'reinforcements', can scarcely hope to survive as man's audacities multiply.

Biggs (1976) referred to the 'end of the honeymoon' between psychology and education. One of my school teacher students, Barrie Jones (1989: 51), remarked:

> Much research related to education had the cutting edge of a sponge ... What I'm trying to say is that their research did not speak the truth to me. These works seemed more concerned with statistics than sensitivities; rats rather than brats; research rather than the researched.

This eloquently sums up teachers' disenchantment. Chris Clark (1995: 21) emphasised the need for a constructivist, collaborative research that could be seen as research in the service of teaching and noted that 'when we look at teaching from the child's point of view, the buzzing confusion of researchers' claims and counter claims falls silent'. My students, colleagues and I have been part of that rapprochement. Researchers as constructivists employ the art of the skilled conversationalist (Pope and Denicolo, 1993): adopting such an approach places an onus on the researcher to strive hard to capture the personal meanings portrayed in the language and stories of participants.

My introductory presentation at the IED advocated a shift from the Newtonian paradigm of the billiard-ball universe often favoured by psychologists to one that embraced the notion of agency as an essential force in human beings. It was clear that my ideas found resonance amongst the group which was predicated on exploring new ways of investigating educational processes in co-operation with secondary and higher education teachers. Lewis Elton, a professor of physics who left his fold to become professor of higher education, established the IED. His commitment to research in higher education and academic staff development is legendary.

Alongside research, the IED provided courses and workshops in staff development and study counselling and supported staff and undergraduate students on an individual basis. That study counselling or staff development work went beyond the usual tips for students' or teachers' approach. The 1980s was a decade of rapid development in knowledge and technology, necessitating learners and teachers to adopt a multiplicity of roles. Staff development strategies that did not invite challenge to a person's implicit theories might have seemed comfortable but seldom led to reappraisal of implicit theories and practice (Pope and Denicolo, 1991a.)

Adopting PCP theory and methods enabled students and teachers to reflect on their personal theories and often deeply held core assumptions about their respective roles. We lent support during the frequently disconcerting process of reconstrual. In most instances participants gained a sense of empowerment leading to transformation of practice as they challenged pre-existing beliefs and considered personally meaningful alternatives to their current practice. It could be emancipatory in fostering a critical response to organisational constraints and perceived social constraints in their own biographies. Pat Diamond (1985: 34), a fellow strong advocate for personal construct approaches to staff development, suggested that 'if teachers can be helped to "open their eyes", they can see how to choose and fashion their own version of reality'.

Leaving the fold of a psychology department had led to new landscapes which fostered my own professional development. It has been a privilege to engage with staff and students in my work in academic staff development and student counselling from which new research collaborations evolved, including invitations to conduct workshops and collaborative action research throughout the UK, Europe, South East Asia and Australia (Pope et al., 1990; Pope and Denicolo, 2003).

Research communities: home and away

Within the IED an ethos of collegiality was encouraged, with staff and students networking outside of the formal research training programme that I helped establish. Many doctoral researchers go on to be colleagues in academic institutions while others hold academic posts in their own countries, so barriers should be minimised. Many years later I found an address given by George Kelly in 1958, only published in 2003 in Fransella's edited book, in which he suggested that universities should cultivate such an interactive community. See Elton and Pope (1992) for more discussion on the value of collegiality within research supervision, the approach we took within the IED. The course adopted principles underpinned by PCP that ensured students were exposed to a wide range of potential research approaches, encouraged to make personal choices and able to justify their decisions. Exploration of personal meaning as researchers and constructive dialogue with supervisors, other staff and students was supported.

Supervision of a large number of doctoral students has been a fulfilling aspect of my life and has led to much research collaboration and friendship. Though they are too numerous to mention individually here, they all know they have a place in my heart. However, one in particular, Pam Denicolo, became both my research collaborator and a dear friend. Together we have travelled the world attending conferences, giving workshops, conducting research and having fun; the personal and professional truly intertwined.

John Gilbert and I co-directed the Personal Construction of Knowledge Group whose endeavours made considerable impact on subsequent research and curriculum development in science education. Members of the group shared an interest in the philosophy of science, commitment to the importance of the personal nature of the construction of formal knowledge and the development of novel techniques for the elicitation of personal models of teaching and learning. The group spanned a range of disciplines, although initially science education was a major focus. PCP provided theoretical coherence to our research on the alternative conceptions of learners and implications for conceptual development and constructivist teaching strategies whereby learners' personal meanings can be elicited and recognised for their importance in the teaching–learning process (Pope, 1982; Pope and Gilbert, 1985; Pope and Watts, 1988; Denicolo, 2003; Gilbert, 2005).

A special feature of the IED was the provision for up to six visiting international staff on sabbatical leave to join the research community. This afforded students and staff opportunities for extensive interchange of ideas. It had long been my contention that PCP is enriched by establishing connections with other constructivist positions such as radical constructivism, phenomenology, social constructionism and interpretative or narrative enquiry. Extending theoretical horizons and moving beyond an overzealous application of the repertory grid by engaging in methodological pluralism is Kellian in spirit and fundamental to constructive alternativism (Pope, 1981; Pope and Denicolo, 2016). I will mention just three international visitors who shared my commitment to devising new approaches to educational research. Ference Marton, of the University of Gothenburg, Sweden, was a frequent visitor whose interest in deep- and surface-level processing has had considerable impact on research about student learning. Ference developed phenomenography as a methodology for educational research (Marton, 2014). A couple of decades later one of my students. Britt Apelgren, also from Gothenburg, drew on both phenomenography and PCP for her thesis on language teachers' personal theories (Apelgren, 2000).

Yvonna Lincoln visited from the USA whilst working on her book *Naturalistic Inquiry* (Lincoln and Guba, 1985). She found PCP to be consistent with her championing of qualitative research methods for social scientists and has since embraced the constructivist paradigm. Lincoln and Guba (2013) set out foundational principles for the conduct of constructivist research, highlighting issues such as the subjective nature of truth and the evolution of research paradigms as the result of shared constructions.

Ortrun Zuber-Skerritt (2011), a prolific writer on professional development in higher education, action learning and action research, first visited in 1984 when I introduced her to PCP as a potential framework for action research. She has used it since and in 1989 invited Pam Denicolo and me to address a symposium on action research she convened in Brisbane (Pope and Denicolo, 1991a).

Over the years I made many reciprocal visits abroad. I particularly valued several study periods based at the Ontario Institute for Studies in Education in Canada. There I was able to work with Alan Brown, a fellow advocate of PCP research into teacher thinking, Michael Connelly and Pat Diamond.

In helping to give voice to teachers' concerns, Kelly's man-the-scientist metaphor has often been replaced with that of person-as-storyteller. Michael, together with Jean Clandinin, was a pioneer of narrative enquiry, the study of 'how humans make meaning of experience by telling and retelling stories about themselves that both refigure the past and create purpose in the future' (Connelly and Clandinin, 1988: 24). Here I saw echoes of Kelly's ideas, especially the anticipatory nature of construing. Of course the language differs, with *images* replacing Kelly's theoretical concept *personal construct*. Kelly's self-characterisation sketch can be seen as a precursor to narrative enquiry methods. Whilst still seeing a place for the repertory grid in PCP research, I took what I call a narrative turn in the direction of my own research. Pat Diamond, whose commitment and research on teacher development I admire, tells his own story of his movement from 'gridder' to embracing arts-based versions of personal enquiries as 'Art proustifies Kelly's PCP' (Diamond, 2006: 196). Pam and I had devised the 'snake' technique, inspired by the Dilthey quotation that started this story, to explore the origins and development (or not) of constructs and that later metamorphosed into 'rivers of experience' in the hands of many of our students (see Chapter Eleven). These are examples, along with Gilbert's (Pope and Gilbert, 1985) 'interview about instances' diagrams, of techniques by which our research groups elaborated construct elicitation beyond the grid.

In 1982, knowing of my research on teacher thinking and advocacy of a paradigm shift in research methodology, Rob Halkes, of the University of Tilburg, solicited my view on the merits of forming a study association on teacher thinking. The seeds of the International Study Association on Teacher Thinking were sown. PCP played a significant role in the birth of the Association (Pope, 1991) which, in 1993, changed its name to International Study Association on Teachers and Teaching (ISATT).

From the outset the prevailing mood of ISATT was one of collaboration, not competition: a collegial safe haven for testing new ideas which opened its doors to graduate students. Rejection of mechanistic metaphors inherent in the then dominant, neo-positivist paradigms of teaching and learning, embracing the teacher-as-constructivist, finding new ways of giving teachers a voice and risking discomfort by challenging their own espoused theories and theories-in-practice are hallmarks of ISATT researchers. Kelly (1969b: 17) commented: 'In order to survive psychology must invent as well as discover.' This also applied to ISATT. I argued it was imperative that we anticipate new horizons, suggesting that to remain progressive more research was needed on, *inter alia*, political constraints on education, interpersonal contexts of teaching, the role of classroom dialogue, and more international comparative research (Pope, 1993). Over the years ISATT has considered these issues and many more besides – a truly progressive programme.

By its 30th anniversary in 2013, ISATT had developed from those early individual conversations into a vibrant research community. The membership spans 45 countries, it has a respected international journal, *Teachers and Teaching: Theory and Practice*, and has published many books of papers selected from presentations at its biennial conferences. See Kompf and Rust (2013) for a complete list, which includes the important work undertaken by Michael Kompf and Pam Denicolo in reprising the books from the 1983–1986 conference period (Kompf and Denicolo, 2003; Denicolo and Kompf, 2005) when print runs were limited. The influence of PCP is manifest. As a 'founder' of ISATT it has been my pleasure to watch generations of new members engage in collegial scholarship and be part of the evolution of this research community.

Turbulence and transitions

Anyone who was an academic back in July 1980 will remember the infamous University Grants Committee letters sent to all universities indicating cuts in funding and, in some instances, closure of departments. On the day it arrived at the University of Surrey the mood was one of sombre foreboding. What followed would eventually have an impact on the IED, and the direction of my own research.

The ensuing decade was one of turbulence. Departments were closed and faculties restructured. Government policies rewarded those institutions which revised their courses and curriculum content in line with needs of business and industry and which responded to the UK government's Enterprise in Higher Education Initiative, sponsored by the Department of Employment. Increased emphasis on vocational aspects meant the careers service and academic departments needed to collaborate. External quality assurance monitoring was imposed for both teaching and research. Well-funded contract research for government bodies or industry became an imperative. The Vice-Chancellor of Surrey, and all other universities, moved from a position of *primus inter pares* to chief executive, heralding the era of managerialism. These pressures for change meant institutional and personal reappraisal and had implications for academic staff development and research as colleagues underwent transition. As a personal construct psychologist I recognised the constructs of threat and hostility amongst many colleagues I worked with on staff development activities, and they were evident in the findings of some of our research. Indeed, at times, this applied to me. As Kelly (1969c: 127) put it, 'one's epistemology does make a difference whether in science or in one's personal life'.

In 1984 the IED was merged with the Department of Adult Education to form the Department of Educational Studies (DES). The Centre for the Advancement Teaching in Higher Education (CATHE) was formed to incorporate the IED's research and staff development work. The Personal Construction of Knowledge Group continued, but the doctoral student base shifted from its initial main focus on science education to include higher, nurse, engineering, sports and dance education. Dance has been a lifelong passion of mine. I was a participant observer at the Annual Gulbenkian International Summer School for Choreographers and Composers, held at Surrey University, producing a confidential report on the creative processes that occurred when dancers, choreographers and composers collaborated (or not) in the making of dance work. With one of my students I explored interconnections inherent in the writings of Laban (a pioneer in dance notation) and Kelly. Both men stressed the importance of personal meaning, valued experiential learning and recognised the potential limits of verbal articulation (Lyons and Pope, 1989).

In contract research it was not always possible to include PCP in the research protocol. It did feature in research on the cross-cultural transferability of computer-based education courseware where teachers' implicit epistemology and theories of learning influenced their readiness to accept US-designed courseware and explore innovative ways of making its use more consistent with their own perspective (Laubli et al., 1985). In research funded by the Department of Education and Science, the PCP approach taken in our staff development activities was extended to include perceptions of leadership roles and the need for development for senior staff (Middlehurst et al., 1992), this being of particular significance following their changing roles due to the shift to managerialism.

The spirit of collegiality we had fostered within the IED became difficult a few years after amalgamation, when staff and students were relocated to different buildings within the University. Creativity did not flourish under an increasingly restrictive climate. Lewis Elton (1988) highlighted change in social systems as one of the unintended consequences of government reforms. This certainly applied to members of IED. In that year he retired, for the first time, and John Gilbert left to take up a professorship at the University of Reading, as did I in 1990, both of us seeking more constructive alternatives in our work.

Transcending professional boundaries: towards a new research community

When I joined the University of Reading, Bulmershe College had just emerged from its own 'sea of troubles' (Rooke, 1992: 145), the teacher training college having merged with the University to form a Faculty of Education and Community Studies consisting of six departments. Professionals in each of these departments had personal identities, departmental loyalties, varying research expertise and differing attitudes to the merger. Individuals had developed professional coping strategies and worldviews that may have served them well in times of relative stability. However, change had been imposed. The creation of a new cohesive faculty would take time, many conversations and sharing of ideas. I relished the challenge and stimulation of working with professionals from such diverse backgrounds.

My initial remit as professor and head of the new Department of Community Studies was to develop the embryonic research culture within the department. Together with John Gilbert, I worked with willing colleagues to establish a research methods programme for doctoral students and some staff across the faculty. The PCP-based staff development approach, well-honed at Surrey, became very relevant in a post-merger situation where new departments were created and some staff did not identify with research, despite the institutional imperative to do so.

Through my teaching and research I introduced PCP and enhanced the range of research methods deployed within the department and faculty. New doctoral students reflected the breadth of professional interests in the department and faculty and included several members of staff. Denicolo and Pope (2001) and Pope and Denicolo (2001) gave examples of the diversity of constructivist research conducted by ourselves and our doctoral students. My commitment to research with teachers in schools remained, but was extended to include professional areas such as nurse education.

Due to UK government policies (for example, Project 2000), extensive curriculum development work was required across nurse education, and nurse educators from the different specialisms had to transcend professional boundaries, engage in their own interprofessional learning and work in teams. These new curriculum initiatives provided research opportunities for students, departmental staff and myself. Despite being in different institutions, Pam Denicolo and I continued working together. We recognised the pressures facing health professionals in adapting to changes, some which may have been construed as potentially threatening, engendering hostility and resistance. We saw dialogue as the starting point for change and engaged in action research in one Health Region. Working with nurses from a range of specialisms and levels, we began with a consideration of how these professionals viewed their current role and work activities. Repertory grids were used to aid reflection and as a vehicle for professional development and team building (Pope and Denicolo, 1991b).

I mentored members of the German Grid group (convened by Joern Sheer, whose PCP portal is now an excellent resource for researchers and practitioners; see www.personal-construct.net), in particular collaborating with Bruce Kirkcaldy in conducting action research in clinical contexts. Effective interprofessional working is critical in ward settings. Professionals with no prior shared learning may have entrenched constructs that inhibit good teamwork. Using repertory grids and reflective feedback, we were able to illuminate the differing constructs regarding patient care held by doctors, nurses and patients and make suggestions on continued professional development (Kirkcaldy and Pope, 1992). This research and that of Pope and Denicolo (above) emphasised the importance of Kelly's sociality corollary which implied the need for participants to come to an understanding of others' points of view in order that they might communicate more effectively. Subsequently, a similar approach was used in research into interprofessional education in nursing (Mazhindu and Pope, 1996; Howkins and Ewens, 1999).

Pam and I set up the PCP Southern Interest Group attended by our respective doctoral students, staff and students from across the South East. This collaborative forum provided critical friendship for members presenting their ideas for discussion. Many students have acknowledged the help given by this extended community of researchers. One member of this group was Nick Reed. He and I worked with Fay Fransella when the Centre for Personal Construct Psychology (CPCP) became a 'virtual organisation' on the closure of its base in London. I arranged for Fay's extensive collection of PCP books and papers to be housed and catalogued within the department at Reading and available to any visiting scholar. The Fransella PCP Collection was a great resource for our staff and students. It was eventually relocated to the University of Hertfordshire when Fay was given a professorship and the CPCP acquired a new home.

Attendance at PCP congresses also provided constructivists with opportunities for critical dialogue. Originally these took place every two years in either North America or the United Kingdom. As finances tightened, and particularly when other locations such as Australia were included, many could not afford to attend. Discussions with leaders of other national regional groups led to the formation in 1990 of the European Personal Construct Association (EPCA) and I was invited to become the first convenor of the Guidance Panel (we rejected notions of chairpersons and committees) and Pam was secretary/treasurer. So I was part of the birth another research community! In 1996 we hosted the third EPCA Conference at the University of Reading and published selected papers (Denicolo and Pope, 1997).

In 1995 I became Dean of Faculty in time to welcome Pam who had gained a readership in the university – the dynamic duo reunited! We co-directed the university Research Centre for Personal Construct Psychology in Education. Pam played a major role in developing the doctoral programmes and working with supervisors; doctoral student numbers continued to increase; the utility of PCP theory and methods was elaborated in diverse contexts (Pope, 2007).

By the time I became professor emerita the sense of collegiality and creativity I had valued so much within the IED had been fully restored: students and staff working together as a research community.

Coda

Kelly's radical ideas, together with those of other constructivists, now permeate education and have helped to transform research and practice in teaching and learning in schools, higher education and the professions. I have played my part in this transformation. I am still in touch with many of my doctoral students, now scattered across the globe, who are introducing PCP and constructivist research methods to the next generation of researchers.

At the ISATT conference in 2013 I was honoured to receive a certificate of appreciation for outstanding service and dedication. Sadly, one of the stalwarts of PCP and ISATT, Michael Kompf, was not able to be present and he died not long after-wards. I still have the pebble plucked from the shores of Niagara on the Lake upon which he drew a smiley face with the date 30-6-85. I had run a summer school on PCP and research methods for him at Brock University, Canada. It will remain a treasured possession.

In the telling of my story I have not been able to acknowledge all of the many people whose conversations I have valued and who have contributed to my life as a constructivist researcher. Nelson Mandela (2002) said: 'It is the difference we have made to the life of others that will determine the significance of the life we live.' Throughout my journey in PCP I hope I have made a difference to at least some of the research participants, colleagues and students I have met along the road. They have certainly had a positive impact on my life for which I am eternally grateful.

The work of many of these friends from this supportive and intellectually stimulating community who have contributed to the move from research on people using neo-positivist methods to work with people using constructivist techniques can be found represented and referenced in this book. Some of those who have remained active in continuing to develop this approach have summarised their work in Chapter Eleven. You can meet others through the networks described in Appendix B. I would like to extend to you a personal invitation to join this world-wide community of scholars.

Postscript

Key Points

- An appraisal of constructivist research
- An invitation

Living and working as a constructivist

We hope that the diverse range of practitioner case studies and the bio-narrative of an experienced constructivist researcher have helped persuade you to try a constructivist approach to your own research. That is, if you, like they, are intent on elucidating others', individual and group, perspectives on topics. Such perspectives may consist of what others call values, beliefs, attributes, and the behaviours that are influenced by those inner workings, but are all subsumed for constructivists by the key word 'constructs'.

All of those contributors and fellow constructivists undertake their research and consultancy with respect for their participants/clients and also for the enormous responsibility they have to do justice to how others view their worlds and why they do so. They recognise too that the tools we have at our disposal, though diverse in nature and constantly being improved (see Chapter Seven and Appendix B), each have their inherent limitations and are subject to our own skills in using them. Therefore when we have emphasised that this kind of research is methodologically powerful and has sharp instruments for accessing people's worldviews, we have also highlighted the need to consider carefully the vulnerabilities of participants. Competent and worthwhile constructivist research requires the researcher to plan assiduously and to devise an ethical approach to the research process. For instance, it is important to:

- Practise your skills and pilot your project design and methods;
- Stay within the agreed remit of the research and the established contract between the researcher and the researched;
- Collect all the data you need without undue or unplanned recursion;
- Collect only the data you need, not simply everything you can think of;
- Remember who is the real owner of the data, so do justice to what they have shared.

You will find that it is possible through constructivist approaches and methods to collect data and leave participants feeling that they have both contributed to and benefited from the process. However, when they share generously they also leave themselves vulnerable; when revelations are afforded to you they may also be new for them, so you must be prepared to support them, or to guide them to support, as well as maintaining research integrity through traditional ethical procedures.

Furthermore, researchers themselves have vulnerabilities. Becoming involved with constructivist work brings with it obligations beyond those of more traditional research approaches. It can be hard to constantly contemplate and try to understand the other's point of view, especially when it is juxtaposed with your own, or your society's, deeply held beliefs. Moreover, the vast amount of data and potential interpretations that result from constructivist techniques, while being a boon, also have the corollary of requiring efficient data management practices. Then, after you have navigated the challenge of managing your data set, there is the challenge of condensing your complex work and results into a short journal article, case study, or book chapter. Fortunately, constructivist methods are more accepted today than ever before, so you are less likely to face a brick wall from stalwart empiricists.

We must remember too that producing a mass of evidence and information does not equate to producing solutions to problems or definitive answers to questions. Each technique only explores a small aspect of a construct system, producing a partial record of events. Triangulation and alternative analyses will unearth alternative explanations, yet the 'answer' should always be situated in context and tentatively offered as a potential, rather than definitive, explanation. We have recognised throughout this book that constructivist methods are best for investigating how people understand and behave in their worlds, but are less useful for generalising results to whole populations. Nevertheless they can give clear indications of pathways to explore at less specific but more general levels for wider populations. Further, they can be complemented by other techniques designed to produce both quantitative and qualitative data that can extend the results of construct exploration, such as observations to see if the way people believe they behave is responded to as they intend.

Let us reiterate that the wealth of techniques available, and those that can be developed by creative researchers with understanding others at the heart of their practice, make possible rich, in-depth explorations. Both the range and flexibility of techniques mean that there is a choice of elicitation and analysis processes to suit a range of purposes, as well as participant ability, preference, age and experience.

Constructivist techniques allow participants to express their constructs, their concerns and how they perceive them, in their own words, avoiding the traditional problem of interviewer bias that pursues the interests of the researcher and 'forced choice' bias when the participant has to choose a response from those provided. Their personal meanings can be explored systematically with a public record made available for conveying to others. This may be in the form of a grid or picture accompanied by text drawn from the conversation that the technique catalyses. The insight that this provides can also be checked, elaborated or extended by either technique or participant triangulation to produce authentic data that is owned by (in both possessive and recognition modes) the participants rather than being an outsider's imposed view which can be readily dismissed. Such ownership is particularly important when we seek to change or develop practice.

However, we must remain alert also to the social, cultural, historic, professional (and so on) processes that help to build our own perspectives as we collect, curate and interpret our data. Reflexivity is an important aspect of constructivist practice so that attention is due to the effect of the researcher on knowledge construction and elicitation to gain the most benefit from the methodology, while a heightened appreciation of the need to interrogate our own constructs/responses demands some self-reflection. For instance, those developing a thesis or dissertation within a constructivist paradigm might consider sharing with their readers the goggles they don when conducting their inevitably situated work. All of us should recognise that our goggles should have self-critical lenses to promote continuous awareness of why we chose the topic, paradigm, approach and techniques and how those choices influence our results and the outcomes of our research. We have provided condensed biographies to help alert you to our prejudices, the colours of our lenses. We have also introduced you to many of our fellow constructivists, many of whom you can debate with further through the networks outlines in Appendix B.

An invitation

By now we hope we have said and shared enough of our constructivist world for you to feel that you might like to try it out for yourself. We invite you to join us as personal scientists in exploring the complex, vulnerable, exciting and awe-inspiring world of trying to understand our own and others' perspectives, understandings, expectations, fears, hopes and meanings.

We also extend a welcome to this community of practice, a community that is very willing to share ideas and resources and eager to have your ideas extend alternatives for our construing.

Glossary

Accumulative fragmentalism: the development of knowledge by the progressive accumulation of independent bits or 'nuggets' of truth.

Audit trail: a step-by-step documentation of the process and outcomes between the raw data and the presented interpretation used as evidence for robust, rigorous research.

Bipolar construct: an interpretation that organises phenomena along a continuum bounded by two poles or descriptors.

Construe: place an interpretation on something by combinations of thinking, feeling and reacting.

Construct: a personal representation which allows an individual to interpret or make discriminations between things.

Construct poles: the description used to define the outer limits of a construct dimension.

Construct system: the network or matrix of all constructs held by a person.

Constructive alternativism: the infinite variety of ways in which an event may be interpreted by different individuals or by the same individual at different times.

Constructivist research: an exploration of the meaning people attribute to aspects of the world as they experience it.

Contrast pole: the pole of a construct opposite to, and giving meaning to, the elicited pole.

Core of the construct system: those central, or maintenance, constructs that define the sense of self or identity (see 'Peripheral constructs').

Corollary: an implication of the central postulate, proposition or theorem.

Deductive research: research which seeks to test existing theory or concepts.

Double hermeneutics: the interaction between the interpretation of others' interpretations (see 'Hermeneutics').

Elements: the events, objects or people that represent the scope or range of a particular identifiable experience.

Elicited pole: the pole of a construct that most readily comes to mind when thinking about elements or events.

Emergent pole (see 'Elicited pole').

Emic perspective: the viewpoint of the participant, or the social group, being studied (see 'Etic perspective').

Empirical research: data elicited from observation or experimentation.

Epistemology: philosophy relating to the nature and scope of knowledge (see 'Ontology').

Etic perspective: the viewpoint of the researcher or observer.

Focus of convenience: the things to which a construct will be of greatest use (see 'Range of convenience').

Full context elicitation (see 'Whole context elicitation').

Fundamental postulate: the basic proposition in an argument.

Grounded theory: theory that is derived from the data directly.

Hermeneutics: the theory and approach of interpretation.

Idiographic: concern for individual experience, behaviours or events (see 'Nomothetic').

Inductive research: research that seeks to build concepts and theory from observations.

Interpretivism: a philosophical position that recognises the individual subjectivity of understanding.

Laddering down: an interview questioning skill that progressively accesses increasingly 'concrete', or 'subordinate', constructs.

Laddering up: an interview questioning skill that progressively accesses increasingly 'value-laden', or 'superordinate', constructs.

Lagniappe: a small gift or something given or obtained gratuitously or by way of good measure.

Life-world: the way in which an individual experiences their own world or reality.

Likert scale: an ordinal scale often used in questionnaires requiring the respondent to select a number that represents their level of feeling about a given concept or item.

Methodology: the overall approach taken in a research project, from underpinning philosophy through to the analysis, and its rationale.

Mores: those social norms that are generally accepted as having greatest moral importance (see 'Norms').

Nomothetic: concern for generalised, group experience, behaviours or events (see 'Idiographic') from which patterns or laws can be derived.

Norms: accepted and expected beliefs and patterns of behaviour (see 'Mores').

Objectivism: the philosophical perspective that meaning exists in things themselves (see 'Subjectivism').

Ontology: philosophy relating to the nature and scope of reality (see 'Epistemology').

Paradigm: an underpinning model, pattern or approach (to research).

Peripheral constructs: those constructs that are not essential to, and, if modified, will not significantly influence, the core system (see 'Core constructs').

Phenomenon: the key subject of the investigation.

Phenomenology: the philosophical study of the internal experience of people (see 'Verstehen').

Pyramiding: (see 'Laddering down').

Range of convenience: all those things to which a construct may be applied (see 'Focus of convenience').

Realism: the philosophical perspective that 'truth' is external, independent of people's consciousness (see 'Relativism').

Relativism: the philosophical perspective that reality is 'relative' to an individual's internal, psychological experience.

Research question: the overarching question that the research seeks to address and on which methodology is designed (see 'Methodology').

Scientific method: a general term referring to systematic observation, measurement, experimentation and analysis.

Subordinate construct: a construct that is subsumed within another (superordinate) construct (see 'Superordinate construct').

Submerged pole: a construct pole of which a person has less awareness, and is therefore less available to apply to events or elements.

Subjectivism: the philosophical perspective that meaning is an internal experience, in the mind (see 'Objectivism').

Superordinate construct: a construct that subsumes other (subordinate) constructs (see 'Subordinate construct').

Theoretical underpinning: the philosophical or theoretical perspective on which the research is based.

Triadic elicitation: a method of gathering data about constructs from people using three elements (see 'Elements').

Universe of discourse: the defined territory which is the focus of a particular constructivist research exploration.

Verstehen: an approach that seeks to understand beliefs and behaviours from the perspective of the actor (see 'Phenomenology').

Whole context elicitation: a method of gathering data about constructs by considering all the elements selected to represent a discourse topic in order to discriminate between them.

Appendix A
The fundamental postulate and the 11 corollaries

The fundamental postulate states that: 'A person's processes are psychologically channellized by the ways in which he anticipates events'.

The construction corollary: 'A person anticipates events by construing their replications'.

The experience corollary: 'A person's construct system varies as he successively construes the replication of events'.

The individuality corollary: 'Persons differ from each other in their constructions of events'.

The choice corollary: 'A person chooses for himself that alternative in a dichotomized construct through which he anticipates the greater possibility for extension and definition of his system'.

The sociality corollary: 'To the extent that one person construes the construction processes of another, he may play a role in a social process involving the other person'.

The commonality corollary: 'To the extent that one person employs a construction of experience which is similar to that employed by another, his psychological processes are similar to those of the other person'.

The organization corollary: 'Each person characteristically evolves, for his convenience in anticipating events, a construction system embracing ordinal relationships between constructs'.

The dichotomy corollary: 'A person's construction system is composed of a finite number of dichotomous constructs'.

The range corollary: 'A construct is convenient for the anticipation of a finite range of events only'.

The modulation corollary: 'The variation in a person's construction system is limited by the permeability of the constructs within whose range of convenience the variants lie'.

The fragmentation corollary: 'A person may successively employ a variety of construction systems which are inferentially incompatible with each other'.

Appendix B
Resources and sources of support

We are hugely grateful to Professor Brian R. Gaines and the PCP internet community for the following contribution to your and our work.

Internet resources for personal construct psychology

There is a wide range of resources supporting researchers and practitioners in personal construct psychology available through the internet. These include mailing lists, calls for contributions to journals and conferences, journal contents, publication archives and conceptual grid elicitation and analysis programs.

The internet and World Wide Web are dynamic resources subject to frequent change. The notes below are not intended to be exhaustive but rather to provide links to reasonably stable starting points from which to explore the support for personal construct psychology available through the internet.

Websites with links to PCP resources

The *PCP-net* site maintained by Jörn Scheer at http://www.personal-construct.net is the only current site that provides a continually updated archive of a wide range of PCP resources on the web. It is a good starting point from which to explore what is available.

The *Internet Encyclopaedia of PCP* at http://www.pcp-net.org/encyclopaedia/ is an ongoing project to provide comprehensive information on PCP.

The George A. Kelly site at http://www.oikos.org/kelen.htm provides a short and readable biography of Kelly, with quotations from his works and links to other relevant commentaries.

The increasing capabilities of sites that index the web in general and provide contextual search facilities, such as Google and Google Scholar, have to a large extent replaced manually maintained sites that attempt to keep track of particular topics but require substantial effort to maintain. The search term 'personal construct psychology', coupled with the specific topics of interest, will usually produce a number of relevant links as starting points for a search.

The abbreviations 'PCP' and 'PCT' are often used in publications but are less useful as general search terms because the same abbreviations are used differently in many other disciplines. They can, however, be useful in searching a relevant journal, as can 'G A Kelly' since his 1955 book, *The Psychology of Personal Constructs*, is frequently cited.

For those interested in his major tool for eliciting construct systems, his conceptual grid, the best search term is 'repertory grid' since a specific form of concept grid, his role repertory grid, has become widely used as a generic name for the technique, even though his general term is more descriptive.

Mailing lists

The PCP mailing list has been operating since 1994 and is fully archived on the web. It was instigated to provide mutual support among researchers and practitioners, and welcomes newcomers with questions about PCP theory, applications, methodology and research design. It is accessible at http://www.jiscmail.ac.uk/lists/pcp.html.

There is an associated list for discussion of computer-based tool usage in personal construct psychology at http://www.jiscmail.ac.uk/lists/pcptools.html.

Each site provides facilities for joining and leaving the associated mailing list, together with access to archives of past mailings.

Journals

Because personal construct psychology and conceptual grid techniques are content neutral and applicable to modelling mental processes in any individual or community, they are widely used in a diversity of otherwise unrelated disciplines, and the application literature is very widely scattered. Journals in many areas, such as psychology, education, anthropology, sensory studies, management and computing, carry articles relating to personal construct psychology and their contents are available on the web through the publisher sites.

The primary journal for PCP is *Personal Construct Theory & Practice* which is open access, well refereed and available at http://www.pcp-net.org/journal/.

The *Journal of Constructivist Psychology* (formerly the *International Journal of Personal Construct Psychology*), also carries relevant material and can be found at http://www.tandf.co.uk/journals/titles/10720537.asp.

Costruttivismi (Associazione Italiana di Psicologia e Psicoterapia Costruttivista, AIPPC) can be found at http://www.aippc.it/costruttivismi/.

The *Rivista Italiana di Costruttivismo* (Italian Journal of Constructivism), has a focus on PCP studies; see http://www.rivistacostruttivismo.it.

Societies and major centres

The first three societies listed each organise regional conferences and jointly coordinate the biennial PCP Congress.

> Australasian Personal Construct Group: http://www.pcp-net.org/aus/
>
> *Constructivist Psychology Network* (CPN, formerly North American Personal Construct Network): http://www.constructivistpsych.org
>
> *European Personal Construct Association* (EPCA): http://www.pcp-net.org/europe/home.html

Other significant societies and centres are the following:

> Italian Constructivist Psychology and Psychotherapy Group: http://www.aippc.it/
>
> Italian Institute of Constructivist Psychology: http://icp-italia.it
>
> UK Personal Construct Psychology Association: http://www.personalconstructuk.org
>
> Società Costruttivista Italiana (Italian Constructivist Society): http://www.costruttivismo.it
>
> The Centre for Personal Construct Psychology: http://centrepcp.co.uk/
>
> Facultat de Psicologia (Universitat de Barcelona): http://www.ub.edu/hipnosiclinica

Software and services

There are a number of generally available repertory grid elicitation and analysis programs. The major ones are listed below in alphabetical order, and others are listed at the PCP-net site cited above. The primary analysis techniques for single grids are variants of Slater's (1976, 1977) *Ingrid* for principal components analysis and Shaw's (1980) *Focus* for hierarchical clustering, and it is noted which packages offer these, together with their specific features. Guides to using such techniques can be found in Fransella et al. (2004), Jankowicz (2004), Caputi et al. (2012) and this book.

> *CLAD* is a web service implementing Korenini's consistent laddering interviews at http://clad.korenini.net.
>
> *GRIDCOR* for Windows provides various analyses including *Focus* and correspondence analysis: http://www.terapiacognitiva.net/record/gridcor.htm.

GridSuite for Macintosh and Windows supports elicitation, *Ingrid* and *Focus* analyses, and comparison of grids based on the same elements: http://www.gridsuite.de/.

Idiogrid for Windows provides *Ingrid*, Procustes analysis and a number of other univariate and bivariate statistics and measures. It is freely downloadable at http://www.idiogrid.com/.

OpenRepGrid offers a set of open source tools for grid analysis in the freeware statistical package R (https://www.r-project.org) at http://openrepgrid.org.

OpenRepGrid on Air offers the analyses as a web service at http://onair.openrepgrid.org.

RECORD (Spanish version of GRIDCOR as web service) is available at http://www.tecnicaderejilla.net.

rep:grid offers web-based elicitation and an interactive 3D presentation of a principal components analysis at freerepgrid.sofistiq.com.

Rep Plus for Macintosh and Windows supports conversational elicitation, *Focus*, *Ingrid*, comparison of grids with common elements or constructs, content analysis and web-based elicitation and analysis, and is user-extensible through scripting. It is freely downloadable through http://webgrid.typed.com.

WebGrid Plus is a web service providing the elicitation and analysis capabilities of *Rep Plus* as a freely available service on the web at a number of sites listed at http://webgrid.typed.com. Grid files may be uploaded to the server in a wide variety of formats, and the online elicitation tools may be used in research studies to elicit and collect grids from remote users.

References

Adams, P. (1996) *Emptiness of the Image: Psychoanalysis and Sexual Differences*. London: Routledge.

Aili, C. and Osterlind, M.-L. (submitted) *Developing a Responsive Research Paradigm: Rejecting Bureaucratic Conformity*. Lund: Lund University.

Algera, P.M. and Lips-Wiersma, M. (2012) Radical authentic leadership: co-creating the conditions under which all members of the organization can be authentic. *Leadership Quarterly*, 23(1), 118–131.

Alvesson, M. and Deetz, S. (2000) *Doing Critical Management Research*. London: SAGE.

Alvesson, M. and Sköldberg, K. (2009) *Reflexive Methodology*. London: SAGE.

Apelgren, B.M. (2000) Foreign language teachers' voices: personal theories and experiences of change in the teaching of English as a foreign language. PhD thesis, University of Reading.

Apelgren, B.M. (2010) Construing learning and assessment in the foreign language classroom – the teacher as the meaning-maker. In D.J. Bourne and M. Fromm (eds), *Construing PCP: New Contexts and Perspectives*. Norderstedt, Germany: Books on Demand.

Bannister, D. (1970) Science through the looking glass. In D. Bannister (ed.), *Perspectives in Personal Construct Theory*. London: Academic Press.

Bannister, D. and Fransella, F. (1971 1st edition, 1986 3rd edition) *Inquiring Man: The Psychology of Personal Constructs*. London: Croom Helm.

Bartone, P.T. and Hystad, S.W. (2010) Increasing mental hardiness for stress resilience in operational settings. In P.T. Bartone, B.H. Johnsen, J. Eid, J.M. Violanti and J.C. Laberg (eds), *Enhancing Human Performance in Security Operations: International and Law Enforcement Perspectives* (pp. 257–272). Springfield, IL: Charles C. Thomas.

Baumgartner, J., Burnett, L., DiCarlo, C.F. and Buchanan, T. (2012) An inquiry of children's social support networks using eco-maps. *Child & Youth Care Forum*, 41(4), 357–369.

Belbin, R.M. (2013) *Management Teams: Why They Succeed or Fail* (3rd edition). London: Routledge.

Benjamin, A. (1981) *The Helping Interview*. Boston: Houghton Mifflin.

Biggs, J.B. (1976) Educology! The theory of educational practice. *Contemporary Educational Psychology*, 1, 274–284.

Blumer, H. (1969) *Symbolic Interactionism: Perspective and Method*. Englewood Cliffs, NJ: Prentice Hall.

Boyatzis, R.E. (1998) *Transforming Qualitative Information: Thematic Analysis and Code Development*. London: SAGE.

Bradley-Cole, K. (2014a) Exploring subordinate leaders' implicit theories of authentic leadership. PhD thesis, University of Reading.

Bradley-Cole, K. (2014b) Utilising the Repertory Grid in Organisational Research: Exploring Managers' Implicit Theories of Authentic Leadership. In *SAGE Research Methods Cases*. London: SAGE. doi: 10.4135/9781446273050135008497.

Braun, V. and Clarke, V. (2006) Using thematic analysis in psychology. *Qualitative Research in Psychology*, 3(2), 77–101.

Braun, V. and Clarke, V. (2013) *Successful Qualitative Research: A Practical Guide for Beginners*. London: SAGE.

Bright, J.C. (1985) A pack of lies. Unpublished dissertation, Centre for Personal Construct Psychology, London.

Bryman, A. (2008) *Social Research Methods*. Oxford: Oxford University Press.

Burnard, P. (2000) Examining experiential differences between improvisation and composition in children's music making. *British Journal of Music Education*, 17(3): 227–245.

Butt, T. (2013). The psychology of personal constructs: Humanism without a self. *Italian Journal of Constructivism*, 1(1), 20–31.

Cabaroglu, N. and Denicolo, P.M. (2008) Exploring student teacher belief development: An alternative constructivist technique, snake interviews, exemplified and evaluated. *Personal Construct Theory & Practice*, 5, 28–40. Retrieved from http://www.pcpnet.org/journal/pctp08/cabaroglu08.pdf

Canter, D.V. (2007) Doing psychology that counts: George Kelly's influence. *Personal Construct Theory and Practice*, 3, 27–38.

Caputi, P., Viney, L.L., Walker, B.M. and Crittenden, N. (eds) (2012) *Personal Construct Methodology*. Malden, MA: Wiley-Blackwell.

Charmaz, K. (1995) Grounded theory. In J.A. Smith, R. Harré and L. van Langenhove (eds), *Rethinking Methods in Psychology* (pp. 27–49). London: SAGE.

Charmaz, K. (2000) Grounded theory: Objectivist and constructivist methods. In N.K. Denzin and Y.S. Lincoln (eds), *Handbook of Qualitative Research* (2nd edition, pp. 509–536). Thousand Oaks, CA: SAGE.

Charmaz, K. (2002) Qualitative interviewing and grounded theory analysis. In J.F. Gubrium and J.A. Holstein (eds), *Handbook of Interview Research: Context & Method* (pp. 675–694). London: SAGE.

Charmaz, K. (2006) *Constructing Grounded Theory: A Practical Guide through Qualitative Analysis*. Thousand Oaks, CA: SAGE.

Clark, C.M. (1995) *Thoughtful Teaching*. New York: Cassell.

Clarke, A.E. (2003) Situational analyses: Grounded theory mapping after the postmodern turn. *Symbolic Interaction*, 26, 553–576.

Connelly, F.M. and Clandinin, D.J. (1988) *Teachers as Curriculum Planners: Narratives of Experience*. New York, NY: Teachers College Press.

Connelly, F.M. and Clandinin, D.J. (1990) Stories of experience and narrative inquiry. *Educational Researcher*, 19(5), 2–14.

Cortazzi, D. and Roote, S. (1975) *Illuminative Incident Analysis*. London: McGraw-Hill.

Crotty, M. (1998). *The Foundations of Social Research: Meaning and Perspective in the Research Process*. London: SAGE.

Dalton, P. and Dunnett, G. (1999) *A Psychology for Living: Personal Construct Theory for Professionals and Clients*. Chichester: Wiley.

deMarrais, K. and Lapan, S.D (2004). *Foundations for Research*. Mahwah, NJ: Lawrence Erlbaum Associates.

Denicolo, P.M. (1996) Explorations of constructivist approaches in continuing professional education: Staff development for changing contexts. In D. Kalekin-Fishman and B. Walker (eds), *The Construction of Group Realities: Culture, Society, and Personal Construct Theory* (pp. 267–282). Malabar, FL: Krieger.

Denicolo, P.M. (1999) Exploring metaphors in the making of meaning: Art, science and PCP. In J. Fisher and D. Savage (eds), *Beyond Experiment into Meaning* (pp. 3–14). Preston: EPCA Publications.

Denicolo, P.M. (2003) Elicitation methods to fit different purposes. In F. Fransella (ed.), *The International Handbook of Personal Construct Psychology* (pp. 123–132). Chichester: Wiley.

Denicolo, P.M. (2005) A range of elicitation methods to suit client and purpose. In F. Fransella (ed.), *The Essential Handbook of Personal Construct Psychology* (pp. 57–66). Chichester: Wiley.

Denicolo, P.M. (2013) Understanding the doctoral student experience: Constructivist action research with a reflexive twist. In *SAGE Research Methods*. London: SAGE. doi: 10.4135/9781446273050135077677.

Denicolo, P.M. and Becker, L. (2012) *Success in Research: Developing Research Proposals.* London: SAGE.

Denicolo, P.M. and Kompf, M. (2005) *Teacher Thinking and Professional Action.* Hoboken, NJ: Taylor and Francis.

Denicolo, P.M. and Pope, M.L. (1990) Adults learning – teacher thinking. In C. Day, M.L. Pope and P.M. Denicolo (eds) *Insights into Teachers' Thinking and Practice.* (pp. 155–169). London: Falmer Press.

Denicolo, P.M. and Pope, M. (eds) (1997) *Sharing Understanding and Practice.* Farnborough: EPCA Publications.

Denicolo, P.M. and Pope, M.L. (2001) *Transformative Professional Practice: Personal Construct Approaches to Education and Research.* London: Whurr.

Dentry-Travis, S.J. (2013) Canadian soldiers' construction of their role-sets. *Personal Construct Theory & Practice*, 10, 28–39.

Dentry-Travis, S.J. (2014) Survey Research and focus groups using personal construct psychology. In *SAGE Research Methods Cases*. London: SAGE. doi: 10.4135/97814462730 5014527685.

Denzin, N.K. and Lincoln, Y.S. (2005) *The Handbook of Qualitative Research.* London: SAGE.

Diamond, C.T.P. (1985) Becoming a teacher: An altering eye. In D. Bannister (ed.), *Issues and Approaches to Personal Construct Theory* (pp. 15–35). London: Academic Press.

Diamond, C.T.P. (2006) Art proustifies Kelly's PCP: Personal searchings and revisiting. In J.W. Scheer and K.W. Sewell (eds), *Creative Construing: Personal Constructions in the Arts* (pp. 196–207). Giessen: Psychosozial-Verlag.

Dunn, M.D. (2007) British Army leadership – is it gendered? *Women in Management Review*, 22(6), 468–481.

Dunn, M.D. (2015) All at sea. Leadership and gender in the Royal Navy. *Gender in Management Review*, 30(6), 434–456.

Easterby-Smith, M., Thorpe, R. and Lowe, A. (2002) *Management Research.* London: SAGE.

Edmondson, A.C. and McManus, S.E. (2007) Methodological fit in management field research. *Academy of Management Review*, 32(4), 1155–1179.

Ekman, P. (1964) Body position, facial expression, and verbal behavior during interviews. *Journal of Abnormal and Social Psychology*, 68, 295–301.

Elton, L. (1988) Accountability in higher education: The danger of unintended consequences. *Higher Education*, 17(4), 377–390.

Elton, L. and Pope, M. (1992) Research supervision – the value of collegiality. In O. Zuber-Skerritt (ed.), *Starting Research: Supervision and Training* (pp. 69–85). Brisbane: University of Queensland.

Festinger, L. (1957) *A Theory of Cognitive Dissonance.* California: Stanford University Press

Flanagan, J.C. (1954) The Critical Incident technique. *Psychological Bulletin*, 51(4), 327–358.

Ford, J. and Harding, N. (2011) The impossibility of the 'true self' of authentic leadership. *Leadership*, 7(4), 463–479.

Fransella, F. (1995) *George Kelly.* London: SAGE.

Fransella, F. (ed) (2003) *International Handbook of Personal Construct Psychology*. Chichester: John Wiley & Sons.

Fransella, F. (2005) *The Essential Practitioner's Handbook of Personal Construct Psychology*. Chichester: John Wiley & Sons.

Fransella, F. and Bannister, D. (1977) *A Manual for Repertory Grid Technique*. London: Academic Press.

Fransella, F., Bell, R. and Bannister, D. (2004) *A Manual for Repertory Grid Technique* (2nd edition). Chichester: Wiley.

Friborg, O., Hjemdal, O., Martinussen, M. and Rosenvinge, J. (2009) Empirical support for resilience as more than the counterpart and absence of vulnerability and symptoms of mental disorder. *Journal of Individual Differences*, 30, 138–151.

Fromm, M. (2004) *Introduction to the Repertory Grid Interview*. Münster: Waxmann Verlag.

Gadamer, H. (1997) *Sanning och metod: i urval*. Göteborg: Daidalos.

Gardner, W.L., Avolio, B.J., Luthans, F.O., May, D.R. and Walumbwa, F. (2005) 'Can you see the real me?' A self-based model of authentic leader and follower development. *Leadership Quarterly*, 16(3), 343–372.

Gergen, K.J. (1999) *An Invitation to Social Construction*. Cambridge, MA: Harvard University Press.

Gilbert, J.K. (2005) *Constructing Worlds through Science Education*. London: Routledge.

Gill, J. and Johnson, P. (2010) *Research Methods for Managers*. London: SAGE.

Glanville, R. (2006) Construction and design. *Constructivist Foundations*, 1(3), 61–68.

Glaser, B.G. and Strauss, A. (1967) *The Discovery of Grounded Theory: Strategies for Qualitative Research*. Chicago: Aldine.

Golsorkhi, D., Rouleau, L., Seidl, D. and Vaara, E. (2010) *Cambridge Handbook of Strategy as Practice*. Cambridge: Cambridge University Press.

Hackman, J.R. and Oldham, G.R. (1980) *Work Redesign*. Reading, MA: Addison-Wesley.

Harrison, R. and Leitch, C. (1996) Discipline emergence in entrepreneurship: Accumulative fragmentalism or paradigmatic science. *Entrepreneurship, Innovation and Change*, 5(2), 65–83.

Hartman, A. (1995) Diagrammatic assessment of family relationships. *Families in Society*, 76, 111–122.

Higgins, E.T. (1987) Self-discrepancy: A theory relating self and affect. *Psychological Bulletin*, 94(3), 319–340.

Howkins, E. and Ewens, A. (1999) Inter-professional work: Is effective communication possible between professionals who speak different languages? In J.M. Fisher and D. J. Savage (eds), *Beyond Experimentation into Meaning* (pp. 72–80). Farnborough: EPCA Publications.

Iantaffi, A. (2011) Travelling along 'rivers of experience': personal construct psychology and visual metaphors in research. In P. Reavey (ed.), *Visual Methods in Psychology: Using and Interpreting Images in Qualitative Research* (pp. 271–283). New York: Routledge.

Jankowicz, D. (2004) *The Easy Guide to Repertory Grids*. Chichester: Wiley.

Joffe, H. (2011) Thematic analysis. In D. Harper and A.R. Thompson (eds), *Qualitative Methods in Mental Health and Psychotherapy: A Guide for Students and Practitioners* (pp. 209–223). Chichester: Wiley.

Jones, B. (1989) In conversations with myself: becoming an action researcher. In P. Lomax (ed.), *The Management of Change: Increasing School Effectiveness and Facilitating Staff Development through Action Research* (pp. 47–62). Cleveden: Multilingual Matters.

Keen, T.R. (1979) Pedagogic styles in physics education: An attitude scaling and repertory grid study. PhD thesis, Open University, Milton Keynes.

Kelly, G.A. (1955a) *The Psychology of Personal Constructs. Volume 1: A Theory of Personality*. New York: Norton.

Kelly, G.A. (1955b) *The Psychology of Personal Constructs. Volume 2: Clinical Diagnosis and Psychotherapy*. New York: Norton.

Kelly, G.A. (1963) *A Theory of Personality. The Psychology of Personal Constructs*. New York: Norton.

Kelly, G.A. (1969a) Humanistic methodology in psychological research. In B. Maher (ed.), *Clinical Psychology and Personality: The Collected Papers of George Kelly* (pp. 133–146). New York: Wiley.

Kelly, G.A. (1969b) Ontological acceleration. In B. Maher (ed.), *Clinical Psychology and Personality: The Collected Papers of George Kelly* (pp. 7–45). New York: Wiley.

Kelly, G.A. (1969c) The strategy of psychological research. In M.B. Maher (ed.), *The Collected Papers of George Kelly: Clinical Psychology and Personality: The Collected Papers of George Kelly*. New York: John Wiley.

Kelly, G.A. (1970) Behaviour as an experiment. In D. Bannister (ed.), *Perspectives in Personal Construct Theory*. London: Academic Press.

Kelly, G.A. (1991a) *The Psychology of Personal Constructs. Volume 1: A Theory of Personality*. London: Routledge.

Kelly, G.A. (1991b) *The Psychology of Personal Constructs. Volume 2: Clinical Diagnosis and Psychotherapy*. London: Routledge.

King, N. (2004) Using templates in the thematic analysis of texts. In C. Cassell and G. Symon (eds), *Essential Guide to Qualitative Methods in Organizational Research* (pp. 256–270). London: SAGE.

Kirkcaldy, B. and Pope, M. (1992) A structural analysis of a psycho-oncology unit. *European Work and Organisational Psychologist*, 2(1), 33–51.

Kompf, M. and Denicolo, P. (2003) *Teacher Thinking Twenty Years On: Revisiting Persisting Problems and Advances in Education*. Lisse: Swets and Zeitlinger.

Kompf, M. and Rust, F.O'C. (2013) The International Study Association on Teachers and Teaching: Seeing tracks and making more. In C.J. Craig, P.C. Meijer and J. Broeckmans (eds), *From Teacher Thinking to Teachers and Teaching: The Evolution of a Research Community* (pp. 3–38). Bingley: Emerald Group Publishing.

Kompf, M. and Simmons, N. (2016) Reconstructing lifelong learning. In D.A. Winter and N. Reed (eds), *The Wiley Handbook of Personal Construct Psychology*. Chichester: Wiley.

Lakatos, I. (1970) Falsification and the methodology of scientific research programmes. In I. Lakatos and A. Musgrave (eds), *Criticism and the Growth of Knowledge*. Cambridge: Cambridge University Press.

Lakoff, G. and Johnson, M. (1980) *Metaphors We Live By*. Chicago: University of Chicago Press.

Lakoff, G. and Johnson, M. (1999) *Philosophy in the Flesh: The Embodied Mind and its Challenge to Western Thought*. New York: Basic Books.

Laubli, L., Pope, M. and Hinton, T. (1985) Implications of the cross-cultural transfer of computer based education courseware. *Journal of the Association of Educational & Training Technology*, 22(3), 224–229.

Lawler, J. and Ashman, I. (2012) Theorizing leadership authenticity: A Sartrean perspective. *Leadership*, 8(4), 327–344.

Lewins, A. and Silver, C. (2014) *Using Software for Qualitative Data Analysis: A Step-By-Step Guide* (2nd edition). London: SAGE.

Lincoln, Y.S. and Guba, E.G. (1985) *Naturalist Inquiry*. Thousand Oaks, CA: SAGE.

Lincoln, Y.S. and Guba, E.G. (2013) *The Constructivist Credo*. Walnut Creek, CA: Left Coast Press.

Lindén, J. (1996) Theoretical and methodological questions concerning a contextual approach to psychosocial issues of working life development of a diary-in-group method. *Science Communication*, 18(1), 59–79.

Long, T. (2013) Work engagement, disengagement and meaningfulness: Achieving the simultaneous benefits of high work performance and individual well-being. PhD thesis, University of Reading.

Long, T. (2014) Work engagement and meaningfulness: The application of personal construct theory in iterative, exploratory research. In *SAGE Research Methods Cases*. London: SAGE. doi: 10.4135/978144627305013505057.

Lyons, S. and Pope, M.L. (1989) Constructs in motion: Some reflections on the potential interplay between the notions of Laban and Kelly in the context of therapy. In B. Kirkcaldy (ed.) *Normalities and Abnormalities in Human Movement* (pp. 147–165). Basel: Karger.

Mahoney, M.J. (1991) *Human Change Processes*. New York: Basic Books.

Mandela, N. (2002) Address given on the occasion of the 90th Birthday of Walter Sisulu. Johannesburg, 18 May.

Marton, F. (2014) *Necessary Conditions of Learning*. New York: Routledge.

Mazhindu, G. and Pope, M. (1996) Inter-professional education in nursing. In J. Scheer and A. Catina (eds), *Empirical Constructivism in Europe: The Personal Construct Approach* (pp. 260–267). Giessen: Psychosozial-Verlag.

Mead, G.H. (1934) *Mind, Self, and Society: From the Standpoint of a Social Behaviorist*. Chicago: University of Chicago Press.

Morgan, G. (1997) *Images in Organizations* (2nd edition). London: SAGE.

Middlehurst, R, Pope, M and Wray, M. (1992) The changing roles of university managers and leaders: Implications for preparation and development. *CORE*, 16(1), Fiche 5E11.

Naidoo, J. and Wills, J. (2000) *Health Promotion: Foundations for Practice* (2nd edition). Edinburgh: Baillière Tindall.

Neimeyer, R. A. (2009) *Constructivist Psychotherapy*. London: Routledge.

Novak, J. and Gowin, B. (1984) *Learning How to Learn*. Cambridge: Cambridge University Press.

Osborne, R.J. and Gilbert, J.K. (1980) A technique for exploring students' views of the world. *Physics Education*, 15, 376–379.

Oscarson, M. and Apelgren, B.M. (2011) Mapping language teachers' conceptions of student assessment procedures in relation to grading: A two-stage empirical inquiry. *System*, 39(1), 2–16.

Österlind, M.-L. (2013a) Is it possible to be a caring and efficient manager? Problems, dilemmas and paradoxes handled by Swedish social care managers.

Österlind, M.-L. (2013b) Diary-in-Group Method: Contributions to New Practice-Based Knowledge and to the Learning and Development of the Participants. In *SAGE Research Methods*. London: SAGE. doi: 10.4135/978144627305014531367.

Österlind, M.-L. (2014). 'What have you been up to today?' Construing and re-construing head teachers' work and role. Paper presented to the European Personal Construct Association. XII Biennial Conference. Brno–Praha, Czech Republic. 20–23 June 2014.

Parlett, M. and Hamilton, D. (1976) Evaluation as illumination. In D. Tawney (ed.), *Curriculum Evaluation Today: Trends and Implications* (pp. 84–101). London: Macmillan.

Phillips, L. (1973) *Bayesian Statistics for Social Scientists*. London: Thomas Nelson.

Pidgeon, N. (1996) Grounded theory: theoretical background. In J.T.E. Richardson (ed.), *Handbook of Qualitative Research Methods for Psychology and the Social Sciences* (pp. 75–85). Oxford: BPS Blackwell.

Pink, D.H. (2011) *Drive: The Surprising Truth about What Motivates Us*. London: Canongate.

Pope, M. (1978) Monitoring and reflecting in teacher training. In F. Fransella (ed.), *Personal Construct Psychology 1977* (pp. 75–86). London: Academic Press.

Pope, M. (1981) In true spirit: constructive alternativism in educational research. Paper presented at the 4th International Congress on Personal Construct Psychology, Brock University, St Catharines, ON, Canada.

Pope, M. (1982) Personal construction of formal knowledge. *Interchange*, 13(4), 3–14.

Pope, M. (1991) Researching teacher thinking: A personal construction. In M. Carretero, M. Pope, R.-J. Simons and J. I. Pozo (eds), *Learning & Instruction: European Research in an International Context* (pp. 499–525). Oxford: Pergamon Press.

Pope, M. (1993) Anticipating teacher thinking. In C. Day, J. Calderhead and P. Denicolo (eds), *Research on Teacher Thinking: Understanding Professional Development* (pp. 19–33). London: Falmer Press.

Pope, M. (2007) A personal account of my relationship with PCP. *Personal Construct Theory and Practice*, 4, 46–49.

Pope, M. and Denicolo, P. (1991a) Developing constructive action: Personal construct psychology, research and professional development. In O. Zuber-Skerritt (ed.), *Action Research for Change and Development* (pp. 93–112). Aldershot: Avebury.

Pope, M. and Denicolo, P. (1991b) Quality care: A constructivist perspective. Paper presented at the 9th International Congress on Personal Construct Psychology, University of Albany, NY.

Pope, M. and Denicolo, P. (1993) The art and science of constructivist research in teacher thinking. *Teaching and Teacher Education*, 9(5–6), 529–544.

Pope, M. and Denicolo, P. (2001) *Transformative Education. Personal Construct Approaches to Practice and Research*. London: Wiley-Blackwell.

Pope, M.L. and Denicolo, P.M. (2003) Images of teaching: Reflections from student teachers, experienced teachers and teacher educators. In G. Chiari and M.L. Nuzzo (eds), *Psychological Constructivism and the Social World* (pp. 123–31). Pequod: Ancona/EPCA Publications.

Pope, M. and Denicolo, P. (2016) From periphery to core: Personal construct psychology's permeation of education. In D.A. Winter and N. Reed (eds), *The Wiley Handbook of Personal Construct Psychology* (pp. 333–351). Chichester: Wiley.

Pope, M., Denicolo, P. and Bernardi, B. (1990) Professionalism and Teacher Education. *International Journal of Personal Construct Psychology*, 3(3): 313–326.

Pope, M. and Gilbert, J.K. (1985) Constructive science education. In F. Epting and A. Landfield (eds), *Anticipating Personal Construct Psychology* (pp. 111–127). Lincoln: University of Nebraska Press.

Pope, M. and Keen, T.R. (1981) *Personal Construct Psychology and Education*. London: Academic Press.

Pope, M. and Shaw, M.L.G. (1981) Negotiation in learning. In H. Bonarius, R. Holland and S. Rosenberg (eds), *Personal Construct Psychology: Recent Advances in Theory and Practice* (pp. 157–165). London: Macmillan.

Pope, M. and Watts, M. (1988) Constructivist goggles: Implications for process in teaching and learning physics. *European Journal of Physics*, 9(2), 101–109.

Postman, N. and Weingartner, L. (1971) *Teaching as a Subversive Activity*. London: Penguin.

Potter, J. and Edwards, D. (1992) *Discursive Psychology*. London: SAGE.

Procter, H.G. (1987) Change in the family construct system. In R.A. Neimeyer and G.J. Neimeyer (eds), *Personal Construct Therapy Casebook* (pp. 153–171). New York: Springer.

Raskin, J.D. (2002) Constructivism in psychology: Personal construct psychology, radical constructivism, and social constructionism. In J.D. Raskin and S.K. Bridges (eds.), *Studies in Meaning: Exploring Constructivist Psychology* (pp. 1–25). New York: Pace University Press.

Raskin, J.D. (2011) On essences in constructivist psychology. *Journal of Theoretical and Philosophical Psychology*, 31(4), 223–239.

Raskin, J.D. (2012) Evolutionary constructivism and humanistic psychology. *Journal of Theoretical and Philosophical Psychology*, 32(2), 119–133.

Ravenette, A.T. (1998) *Tom Ravenette: Selected Papers, Personal Construct Psychology and the Practice of an Educational Psychologist*. Farnborough: EPCA Publications.

Richards, B. (2011) Working with suicidal people: An exploration of the meaning to front-line, non-mental-health professionals. PhD thesis, University of Reading.

Rickman, H.P. (1976) *Dilthey Selected Writings*. Cambridge: Cambridge University Press.

Rooke, P. (1992) *Bulmershe: The Life of a College 1964–89*. Reading: University of Reading.

Saúl, L.A., López-González, M.A., Moreno-Pulido, A., Corbella, S., Compañ, V. and Feixas, G. (2012) Bibliometric review of the repertory grid technique: 1998-2007. *Journal of Constructivist Psychology*, 25, 112–131.

Schmitt, R. (2005) Systematic metaphor analysis as a method of qualitative research. *Qualitative Report*, 10(2), 358–394.

Schön, D. (1983) *The Reflective Practitioner. How Professionals Think in Action*. Aldershot: Avebury.

Schwandt, T.A. (1994) Constructivist, interpretivist approaches to human inquiry. In N.K. Denzin and Y.S. Lincoln (eds), *Handbook of Qualitative Research* (pp. 118–137). London: SAGE.

Scott, B. (2001) Gordon Pask's conversation theory: A domain independent model of human knowing. *Foundations of Science*, 6(4), 343–360.

Seale, C., Gobo, G., Gubrium, J.F. and Silverman, D. (2004) *Qualitative Research Practice*. London: SAGE.

Shaw, M.L.G. (1980) *On Becoming A Personal Scientist: Interactive Computer Elicitation of Personal Models of the World*. London: Academic Press.

Simmons, N. (2009) Global views, personal perspectives: Connecting to self as scholar. In A. Wright, M. Wilson and D. MacIsaac (eds), *Collected Essays on Learning and Teaching, Vol. II.* (pp. 140–144). Windsor, ON: Centre for Teaching and Learning, University of Windor. Online at https://www.researchgate.net/publication/277256154_24_Global_Views_Personal_Perspectives_Connecting_to_Self_as_Scholar#full-text

Slater, P. (ed.) (1976) *Dimensions of Intrapersonal Space: Volume 1*. London: Wiley.

Slater, P. (ed.) (1977) *Dimensions of Intrapersonal Space: Volume 2*. London: Wiley.

Smith, J.A. (1995) Semi-structured interviewing and qualitative analysis. In J.A. Smith, R. Harré and L. Van Langenhove (eds), *Rethinking Methods in Psychology*. London: SAGE.

Smith, J.A., Flowers, P. and Larkin, M. (2009) *Interpretative Phenomenological Analysis: Theory, Method and Research*. London: SAGE.

Strauss, A. and Corbin, J. (1990) *Basics of Qualitative Research: Grounded Theory Procedures and Techniques*. Newbury Park, CA: SAGE.

Strauss, A. and Corbin, J. (eds) (1997) *Grounded Theory in Practice*. London: SAGE.

Swanborn, P. (2010) *Case Study Research*. London: SAGE.

Thomas, L.F. and Harri-Augstein, E.S. (1985) *Self-Organised Learning: Foundations of a Conversational Science for Psychology*. London: Routledge.

Tjok a Tam, S. and Denicolo, P.M. (1997) Snapshots of strategic management. In P. Denicolo and M. Pope, *Sharing Understanding and Practice* (pp. 112–122). Farnborough: EPCA Publications.

Walker, B.M. and Winter, D.A. (2007) The elaboration of personal construction psychology. *Annual Review of Psychology*, 58, 453–477.

Winter, D.A. and Reed, N. (eds) (2016) *The Wiley Handbook of Personal Construct Psychology*. Chichester: Wiley.

Zuber-Skerritt, O. (2011) *Action Leadership: Towards a Participatory Paradigm*. Dordrect: Springer.

Index

'This book is a welcome guide to an empirically grounded understanding of the constructivist approach. With its focus on research practice in a multitude of fields, it is of great value both for the budding researcher and the seasoned professional.'

Jörn Scheer, Emeritus Professor of Medical Psychology, University of Giessen

'An excellent overview of the issues facing the constructivist researcher. Graduate students will value its helpful handling of the paradigm debate, while the newcomer to constructivist research will receive a solid grounding in constructivist methods that goes beyond the basic grid interview technique.'

Devi Jankowicz, Professor of Constructivist Managerial Psychology, Heriot Watt University

This book provides a comprehensive overview of personal construct psychology that will help researchers understand the whys, whats and hows of conducting a rigorous constructivist research project.

Mixing theoretical underpinnings with practical values, these expert authors explain how to conduct interpretative, constructivist research from inception to completion. Key topics include:

- Understanding research philosophies and paradigms
- Constructing and exploring personal realities
- Establishing effective research procedures
- Evaluating grids, mapping, narrative and other methods
- Managing fieldwork practicalities
- Analysing and presenting data.

Featuring activities and procedural examples from a range of disciplines and two special chapters with in-depth case studies from constructivist researchers, this book helps readers grasp the tools, designs, and opportunities of constructivist approaches.

An essential companion for both researchers and practitioners looking to understand people's values, attitudes, beliefs, perceptions, or motivations.

Pam Denicolo is Professor Emerita, University of Reading, and HE consultant.

Trevor Long is an independent educator and consultant.

Kim Bradley-Cole is a Chartered Psychologist and an Associate Fellow of the British Psychological Society.

ISBN 978-1-4739-3030-8

SAGE www.sagepublishing.com
Los Angeles | London | New Delhi | Singapore | Washington DC | Melbourne

Cover design • Shaun Mercier
Cover image © dinodentist/Shutterstock

9 781473 930308